# TRACKING AMERICA*S ECONOMY

# TRACKING AMERICA'S ECONOMY

## by Norman Frumkin

M. E. SHARPE, INC.
ARMONK, NEW YORK
LONDON, ENGLAND

**Library of Congress Cataloging-in-Publication Data**

Frumkin, Norman.
    Tracking America's economy.

    Includes bibliographies and index.
    1. Economic forecasting—United States.
2. United States—Economic policy—1981–
3. Economic indicators—United States. I. Title.

HC106.8.F78   1987    338.5'44'0973   87-9694
ISBN 0-87332-437-4
ISBN 0-87332-438-2 (pbk.)

Printed in the United States of America

*To Sarah, Jacob, and Samuel*

# CONTENTS

# TRACKING
# AMERICA*S
# ECONOMY

# • Introduction

Data on the state of the U.S. economy abound. With what some may call information overload, federal agencies publish statistics for the most recent month or quarter on economic growth, finance, employment and inflation. Trade associations and other private organizations add to this data base with their own surveys on particular sectors of the economy.

These indicators are typically historical and descriptive, although they also include forecasts such as business plans for investment in plant and equipment, Federal Reserve Board target ranges for the money supply, and projections of the federal budget by Congress and the president. They are reported in the newspapers and on radio and television, with economists and politicans offering interpretations of the most recent trends and their implications for future economic activity.

Yet after all these assessments, the question remains: what do these economic indicators mean?

## OBJECTIVES OF THE BOOK

This book is aimed at giving beginning students in economics, and persons with no special background in the field, a basis for monitoring economic trends and assessing what the experts and politicians are saying about the current and future state of the economy. It is directed at better understanding the past and current strengths and weaknesses in the economy and at analyzing these factors in projecting future trends. In this sense, it is a book on economic forecasting, although it doesn't give mathematical formulas for plugging in the relevant data and deriving specific forecasts of the economy. That there is no consensus on the economy is clear, as experts as well as politicians continually differ in interpreting the significance of the same data. The book deals with this in everyday language by highlighting the main characteristics of the indicators and how to use them, thus opening the baffling subject and arcane jargon to a wider audience.

Macroeconomics is the branch of economics that focuses on the performance of the overall economy in terms of economic growth, business cycles, unemployment and inflation, and on methods for improving the performance.[1] Macroeconomic indicators trace the ups and downs of overall economic activity in the expansion and recession stages of business cycles. They also portray longer-term trends in the growth rate over several business cycles. While the book emphasizes cyclical movements of the macro indicators, it puts them in the context of longer-run trends. For example, in considering goals for an acceptable level of unemployment, the book examines how and why the definitions of full or high employment have changed since the end of World War II. The focus is on the assessment of current and future trends in unemployment and inflation because these are the main public policy concerns of macroeconomics. In economic theory, when unemployment falls below certain levels, unemployment and inflation develop an inverse relationship—as unemployment decreases, inflation increases and vice versa. This relationship in turn leads to a tradeoff between the two, which is central to much of the political debate on appropriate economic policies. The disagreement occurs on the timing and extent of the tradeoff—when and to what degree a reduction in unemployment should be balanced against an increase in inflation, or a reduction in inflation against an increase in unemployment. The book concentrates on the empirical evidence of business expansions and recessions since World War II and their effects on unemployment and inflation, and relates these business cycle trends to theoretical and analytic concepts. Examination of these relationships in turn points up how well economic theories conform to experience.

The reader should gain a framework for assimilating the vast array of economic data, or at least a basis for asking relevant questions and evaluating the answers. Depending on interest and background, he or she will become more self-sufficient in conducting independent economic analyses, deciding which experts give the most credible explanations, and recognizing when another opinion is needed.

Why would the nonexpert want a better understanding of economic indicators? At a pragmatic level, some household and businesses activities, such as buying a house or investing funds, are influenced by the overall economy, and more understanding of the economy will help the reader to anticipate some of the fluctuations that could affect these decisions. Knowledge of economic trends may also be helpful in assessing the statements made by candidates for public office. And, more generally, the economy is so much in the news that some people simply have an intellectual interest in learning more about it.

## MACRO VS. MICRO ANALYSIS

The indicators in the book are at the *macro* level. The macro level summarizes into broad totals the activities of all households, businesses, state and local governments, and the federal government. For example, spending by households for food, housing and other items is encompassed into a single figure for all households in all income groups. By contrast, the *micro* level focuses on individual decisions; micro analysis of consumer spending distinguishes differential spending and saving rates for low-, middle- and high-income households.

However, the distinction is more than one of separate and consolidated units. At the micro level, the decisions to spend, save and invest by individual households, businesses and governments result from buyers and sellers in the marketplace agreeing or disagreeing on the price and quantity of the item to be sold. At the macro level, these marketplace transactions are reflected in and affected by overall trends in economic aggregates such as employment, income, and inflation. There also is an interaction between the two, as micro decisions to buy and sell are made partly in the context of how buyers and sellers think the macro environment will affect them.

Figure 1 highlights the micro-macro factors influencing the purchase of a house. Basic questions asked by prospective homeowners are: Can the monthly payments be made without being strapped? Is this a good time to buy in terms of the overall economy? Analysts resort to macro indicators to summarize the activities of individual decision units at the micro level because economic methodology is not sufficiently advanced to quantitatively bridge the effect of micro decisions on overall macro trends.

## ECONOMIC INTERPRETATION
## IS NOT A SCIENCE

Despite the fund of available information, the continuing expert analyses of trends in the private and public sectors, and advances in economic theory and analytic techniques, the beginning student and others with limited exposure to the field should realize that analysis and forecasting of economic activity is not a science. Although fairly refined measures of economic activity have been available since the 1940s, the major economic events of recent years—the slow economic growth and high inflation (stagflation) of the 1970s and the deep recession and subsequent moderation of inflation in the first half of the 1980s— were not anticipated by economic and political experts.

Interpreting economic data remains an art for several reasons. First, in order to be available quickly, the indicators are based on preliminary data; subsequent revisions, based on more complete and accurate information, may give a different picture of current trends. Moreover, because the relationships between the factors affecting the economy are complex, interpretations are heavily colored by the most recent movement in the indicators. Experts frequently revise their forecasts as the latest wiggles in the gross national product, unemployment rate or consumer price index diverge from their expectations of where the economy is heading. The speed with which forecasts of economic growth, employment and inflation are outdated indicates the complexity of the subject.

Second, the signals of current and future economic activity given by the

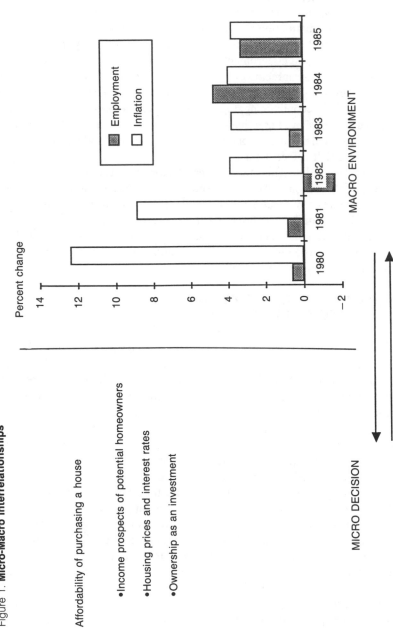

Figure 1. **Micro-Macro Interrelationships**

indicators will not always seem consistent—for example, rising federal deficits and falling interest rates. This may be due to relationships that are not fully understood, such as those between the money markets, unemployment, and inflation; or to technical problems with the data, which will result in revisions; or to inherent shortcomings in the data, such as changes in an industry that make unrepresentative a sample of firms in a survey.

Third, interpretation is complicated by the historical instability of certain relationships used in developing the forecasts (for example, the impact of the federal deficit and the money supply on trends in the gross national product). The tentativeness of interpretation has a positive side, since it moderates any tendencies toward doctrinaire rigidity. But it also indicates weakness in the understanding and quantification of the mechanisms and dynamic changes, both at home and abroad that drive the economy, such as the volatility in the foreign exchange value of the dollar.

Finally, interpretation is clouded because political and psychological factors that may have a significant bearing on economic trends are difficult to quantify. Examples are the emergence of the Organization of Petroleum Exporting Countries as an effective cartel, our relations with the Soviet Union, political philosophies affecting the federal budget deficit, and inflationary or deflationary expectations affecting household spending and business investment. Factors such as these have major effects on the economy, but do not show up explicitly in the indicators.

## ORIGIN AND OUTLINE OF THE BOOK

The idea for the book came from a course I give at the Graduate School of the U.S. Department of Agriculture on interpreting economic trends. In preparing for the course, I found there is no suitable single volume on the topic and decided to write one. My work has benefited considerably from the thoughtful and perceptive questions and discussions by class members. They come from a variety of professional fields in both the private and public sectors, including some from foreign countries, and range from individuals in the early stages of their careers to retired persons.

The first two chapters provide background material for the subsequent discussion of the specific economic indicators. Chapter 1 addresses the implications of monthly and quarterly wiggles in the indicators, the uses of index numbers, and the macroeconomic effect of the underground economy. Chapter 2 focuses on the determination of expansions and recessions in business cycles, the role of fiscal and monetary policies and attempts to moderate the extremes of expansions and recessions, and the use of economic forecasts for developing these policies.

Chapters 3 to 8 cover the economic indicators that represent the main forces associated with trends in economic growth, employment, inflation and financial markets. These are the gross national product; industrial production and capacity utilization indexes; unemployment, employment and productivity; the consumer price index; money supply; and leading, coincident and lagging indexes. These chapters highlight the key factors driving the indicators and suggest which items to consider when interpreting trends in the data; advice to the analyst is highlighted in italics. Each chapter has two parts: a methodological section with the definitions, estimation, and limitations of the indicators (Part A); and an analytic section on their relationships and significance over the post-World War II business cycles (Part B). Readers with some background in the methodological aspects may wish to move directly to Part B.

## NOTE ON DATA SOURCES

All tables and figures in the book are based on information available as of December 1986, with annual data for the year 1985 and quarterly data for the third quarter of 1986. These include the historical benchmark revisions to data on industrial production, capacity utilization and the gross national product that became available in 1985 and 1986. Reference in the text is made to the 1987 benchmark revision of the consumer price index, and to revisions in 1987 and expected in 1988 for the leading, coincident and lagging indexes.

The statistics are from four primary data sources, published monthly: the *Survey of Current Business* and the *Business Conditions Digest* of the Bureau of Economic Analysis in the U.S. Department of Commerce; the *Monthly Labor Review* of the Bureau of Labor Statistics in the U.S. Department of Labor; and the *Federal Reserve Bulletin* of the Federal Reserve Board. Most of the data from these sources relevant to the book are compiled monthly in a handy form in *Economic Indicators*, which is prepared by the U.S. Council of Economic Advisers for the Joint Economic Committee of Congress. The annual *Economic Report of the President* provides excellent appendix tables of historical data. All of these publications are sold by the U.S. Government Printing Office. Single copies of the *Economic Report of the President* are available free from the Executive Office of the President.

## ACKNOWLEDGMENTS

Several people were helpful in reviewing sections of drafts, and I want to thank them. They are: Gopal Ahluwalia, Jack Bame, Alvin Bauman, Richard Belous, James Boughton, John Bregger, Frank de Leeuw, Gary Gillium, Daniel Ginsburg, John Gorman, George Green, Albert Hirsch, Zoltan Kenessey, Jerome Mark, Grace Milgram, Richard Raddock, Markley Roberts, Harry Rosenberg, Dennis Roth, Henry Schechter, Milo Sunderhauf, Feliks Tamm, Vito Tanzi, Henry Townsend, Joseph Wakefield, John Williamson and Donald Wood. Computer assistance for the graphics was given by Henry Hertzfeld, Audri Lanford and Terence Monks. I also benefited from discussions with Barry Beckman,

Jerry Donahoe, Paul Flaim, Thomas Holloway, Malcolm Knight, and Theodore Torda.

Jody Foster was the style editor, and I am especially grateful for her work.

Above all, I am indebted to my wife, Sarah, who made the writing of the book possible.

While these individuals gave important assistance, this doesn't imply that they agree with my views. I am solely responsible for everything in the book.

## NOTES

1. Sherman J. Maisel, *Macroeconomics: Theories and Policies* (W. W. Norton & Company, Inc.: 1982), pp. 3–4.

# 1 • Common Problems
## Affecting the Indicators

At the outset, beginning students and others with a limited background should familiarize themselves with several technical problems, inherent in economic indicators generally, which may affect their interpretation at particular times. While the nonexpert typically does not get into the details, it is important to be aware of these factors and how they can distort the picture of the economy given by the indicators. The most problematic factors are revisions to the data, index numbers, and the underground economy. This chapter provides a generic topical discussion of these factors; they will also be referred to in chapters on the individual indicators.

## REVISIONS

The statistics on production, unemployment, prices, money supply, etc., published month after month, sometimes have up-and-down movements with no discernible trend over several months. While this may reflect actual events in the marketplace for which no explanations have yet become evident, it may also result from problems with the accuracy of the data. In some of these cases, the preliminary information will be revised. These revisions sometimes change the pattern of the earlier information—e.g., an indicator that had portrayed a robust economy could turn out to indicate a sagging one and vice versa.

There are several reasons why the preliminary data may be inadequate. The most common is erroneous survey information. Many indicators are based on information collected from households, businesses or governments responding to surveys. Often, early erroneous reports from some respondents must be corrected, or reports not received in time for the publishing deadline must be included later. Errors in survey data can be particularly troublesome when the problem respondents, such as large companies, account for an important share of the survey.

Another kind of revision is due to seasonal adjustment factors. These allow for the tendency of economic activity to be substantially higher or lower than average during particular periods of the year. Examples of seasonality are the increase in retail sales before Christmas, the increased labor force during the summer due to students looking for work, high tax collections in April, and reduced construction work in the winter. To make sure that these expected movements are not interpreted as real changes in the economy, the raw data are seasonally adjusted to smooth out the normal ups and downs. Figure 2 shows how the monthly patterns of actual retail sales in 1985 differed from the seasonally adjusted monthly movements.

However, there are considerable methodological problems in developing seasonal factors that can at times cause seasonally adjusted data to be misleading for a few months. Also, seasonal adjustment factors at any point in time are based on data from previous periods (e.g., adjustment factors used for 1986 data typically are based on experience through 1985 or earlier). Therefore, first statistics are often revised as new adjustment factors are developed for previously published preliminary information. In addition, revisions in the seasonal factor typically occur as part of more comprehensive "benchmark" revisions, made at scheduled annual and multi-year periods to reflect the most complete and accurate information available. They are based on the economic censuses of industries taken every five years (those years ending in 2 and 7) as well as more frequently obtained information, all of which are considered definitive. Benchmarks represent the "final" figure, which undergoes no further revisions.

Benchmarks incorporate a variety of data which it is not feasible to use on an ongoing basis, including the most representative samples of survey respondents and the development of improved methodologies for statistical estimating. However, because they are so late in coming, they are used for revising analytic relationships of one indicator to another rather than in policymaking or interpreting the current movement of the indicators.

Because of wiggles in marketplace activity and revisions (other than the benchmarks) that become available shortly after the preliminary data are released, it is important not to be swayed by the most recent blip in the indicators. A trend of at least two quarters should be identified before it is determined that a significant change is occurring. In addition, some indicators are published with numerical ranges of error due to sampling or revision problems (e.g., there may be an expected error in the data in 19 out of 20 cases of plus or minus 3 percent). In such cases, one should allow for a lower and upper range of the figure in assessing trends over time. When the error range is larger than the movement in the current indicator (say, the error is plus or minus 3 percent and the monthly movement in the indicator is only 1 percent), the single-period movement is highly tentative. If such small movements cumulate in one direction over several periods, that trend is more significant. For example, a change in the unemploy-

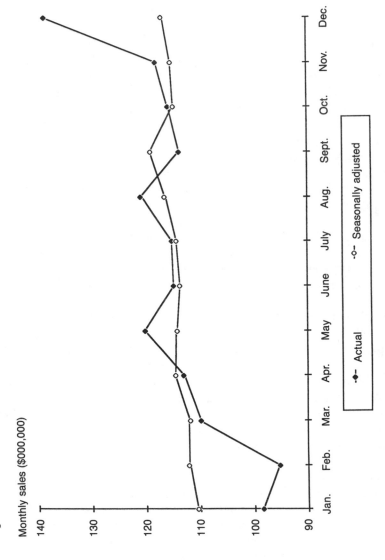

Figure 2. **Seasonal Patterns of Retail Sales: 1985**

Monthly sales ($000,000)

-•- Actual     -○-- Seasonally adjusted

*Note:* Based on Bureau of the Census data.

ment rate of 0.1 percent in one month is not statistically significant because it is within the range of likely error. But if the unemployment rate rises or falls by 0.1 percent in the same direction for two or more months, the cumulative change is significant.

## INDEX NUMBERS

Some economic indicators are shown as index numbers, which state the figure for the current period as a percent of a base period that is established as 100. For example, if the base period is 1977 (1977 = 100) and the figure for the current month is 142, then the indicator shows a 42 percent increase since 1977; if the current figure is 88, the series has decreased by 12 percent since 1977. Index indicators discussed in later chapters are the industrial production index, the capacity utilization index, and price indexes.

Index numbers are a convenient way to combine a wide range of items into a single figure to show their overall relative change. Indexes are calculated by multiplying each item's importance in the base period by the percent change in the item's value since the base period; the sum of the products of all the items is the index for the current period. The combination of several items in an overall index also causes a problem, however, because the relative importance of the various items in the index will have changed some since the base period. (For example, see the discussion of production indexes in Chapter 4 and of price indexes in Chapter 6.)

Some index number indicators are based on the same fixed proportions of items that add up to 100 in the base period. Other index numbers allow these proportions to change with actual production or consumption: some items increase in use and others become less important because of changes in buyer preferences, competition from substitute products, etc. Because individual items in the index change at different rates over time (e.g., housing costs may rise faster than food prices in the consumer price index), the overall index will show different rates of change depending on whether the base-period or current-period proportions are used. This "product mix" problem has been a long-standing issue in the construction of index numbers.

There is no right or wrong way to construct index numbers. Usually the choice of which period proportions to use is based on a judgment concerning the use of the index. In most cases the government develops only one index, typically using base-period proportions, and the user has no estimate of the rate of change using alternative proportions. When there are alternative period calculations, such as are provided in the price measures developed from estimates of the gross national product (GNP), the user has an upper and lower range to consider as part of the analysis. This is a way of handling the dilemma of shifting proportions, as distinguished from an expected error range associated with the sampling and revision problems discussed above.

## THE UNDERGROUND ECONOMY

The "underground economy" refers to income, derived from both legal and illegal activities, that is not reported on tax returns and surveys. Legal sources of income include employment, investments, and income-support programs that are consistent with national and state laws. Illegal income is typically associated with street drugs and unauthorized gambling and prostitution. In addition to hampering tax collection and law enforcement, the underground economy creates a problem in assessing macroeconomic trends.

Economic indicators typically do not reflect criminal activity, either because it is excluded from the definitions used or because, as a matter of reality, it is unlikely to be reported on tax returns and surveys. However, the income generated from illegal activity affects the "regular" economy as the money is spent for legitimate purposes. (This exclusion of illegal activity should be remembered when making economic comparisions with countries in which certain activities are not banned.)

Clearly, the level of activity in the underground economy will affect the analytic relationships used in economic forecasts, such as the economic growth required to maintain a steady unemployment rate or to reduce unemployment by specified amounts. However, since underground activities are not reflected in surveys, tax returns, applications for income maintenance payments, and other documents used to develop economic indicators, official statistics understate the actual of economic activity and overstate unemployment.

In recent years, estimates of the underground economy from private and government sources range from 5 to 33 percent of the GNP.[1] Some observers have also concluded that the underground economy has been growing faster than the "regular" economy, which suggests that the official indicators are giving increasingly misleading information.[2] If the economy is in fact substantially stronger than the indicators suggest, fiscal and monetary policies (discussed in Chapter 2) that are based on the indicators will tend to be more expansionary than they would be otherwise, and possibly inflationary, because they assume a larger pool of unemployed workers.

Government estimates of the underground economy are relatively recent, so there are limited official figures on which to base an assessment of impact over time. In 1985, the Bureau of Economic Analysis in the U. S. Department of Commerce published the 1977 benchmark revisions of GNP data that incorporate adjustments for misreporting of income on income tax returns (in addition to previously incorporated adjustments). These revisions increased the GNP for 1984 by $44 billion, or 1 percent.[3] Monitoring such trends will help determine the extent to which the underground economy modifies the growth rates on which fiscal and monetary policies are based.

Two different methodologies are used to estimate the underground economy. One uses "direct" measurements—for example, studies of compliance with the income tax laws in reporting business incomes. The "indirect" approach uses information that suggests attempts to hide income, such as the tendency to use cash rather than checks in business transactions. Generally, government estimates are based on the direct approach and tend to be lower than private estimates, which are more likely to be based on the indirect technique.[4] In either case, statistics on the underground economy should be regarded as rough estimates.

## NOTES

1. Carol S. Carson, "The Underground Economy: An Introduction," *Survey of Current Business*, May 1984, Table 3, p. 33.
2. *Ibid.*, Table 4, p. 34.
3. For a discussion of the methodology used in estimating the misreported income, see Robert P. Parker, "Improved Adjustments for Misreporting of Tax Return Information Used to Estimate the National Income and Product Accounts," *Survey of Current Business*, June 1984.
4. A government study using the indirect approach also showed a higher figure for the underground economy than did estimates based on the direct technique, although with qualifications regarding movements over time and possible errors in statistical estimation. See Frank de Lecuw, "An Indirect Technique for Measuring the Underground Economy," *Survey of Current Business*, April 1985, p. 71. In an update of that study based on the subsequent benchmark revisions to the GNP, which incorporated explicit additions to the GNP to correct for understatement due to measured underground activity, the indirect estimate still indicates some understatement. Statistically, however, it cannot be ruled out that the understatement may result from errors in the data used in the estimation rather than from an understatement in the GNP growth rates. See Frank de Leeuw, "An Indirect Technique for Measuring the Underground Economy: A Note on Revised Data," *Survey of Current Business*, September 1986, p. 22.

# 2 • Business Cycles, Economic Indicators and Management of the Economy

Business cycles are the recurring rises and falls in the overall economy as reflected in production, employment, profits, and prices. They are associated with capitalistic societies in which production, employment, prices, wages, etc. are largely determined in the private sector marketplace. Business cycles reflect the inability of this marketplace to accommodate smoothly such factors as new technologies, changing needs for occupational skills, shifting markets for new and substitute products, uncertainties and risks in business investments, and shortages and high prices created by wars and bad harvests.

Theoretically, business cycles do not occur in socialist countries with centrally planned economies, as the information underlying the plan and the plan's implementation are assumed to anticipate and smoothly accommodate the main dynamic changes. In practice, the rapid changes characteristic of business cycles seem to be less of a problem for centrally planned economies. However, such economies apparently do not encourage basic changes in production technologies, cater to shifting consumer preferences for substitute and new products, or avoid bad harvests. These rigidities in the socialist system have not resulted in lower long-term economic growth rates (i.e., trends in production that span the shorter-term business cycles) in these countries as compared with the more fluid capitalistic economies, according to worldwide estimates of real GNP compiled by U.S. and international organizations.[1] But the economic cost of centralized planning in socialist countries may be reflected in worse everyday living conditions of the average person. Anecdotal reports by visitors to those countries indicate lower levels of ownership and less quality, variety, and availability of consumer goods.

The overall thrust of the American economy fits the capitalistic model even though the U.S. government provides public services and intervenes in the economy in other ways, and though there are monopolistic aspects in the private sector that are insulated from fully competitive markets. While the American economy has changed considerably over the past two centuries because of new technologies and the growing population, business cycles are not new. They have occurred repeatedly in the 19th and 20th centuries.

The rising phase of a business cycle is typically referred to as expansion, and the falling phase as recession. Although business cycle analysis focuses on the overall economy, it recognizes that particular sectors may be moving against the overall trend—a smokestack industry may not participate in the prosperity of a general expansion, for example, or a growth industry may be insulated from a general recession.

## DESIGNATION OF RECESSIONS AND EXPANSIONS

What is a recession? Generally speaking, we know a recession when we see one because of slack business activity and high unemployment (sometimes aggravated by anomalously high inflation). But there also exists an observable measure of a recession period. By common agreement in the economics profession, the National Bureau of Economic Research, Inc. (a private, nonprofit organization) officially designates such periods.

Under the auspices of the NBER, a committee of economists with diverse views on economic policies determines the beginning and ending points of recessions and expansions by assessing the preponderant direction of a wide range of indicators. The NBER has established a reputation for objectivity, and its designations are accepted by a wide range of liberal and conservative economists and politicians.

The advantage of having a nongovernmental body such as the NBER designate recessions and expansions is clear. It reduces the possibility that the administration in office will politicize the designations to put its own policies in the most favorable light, or even revise designations for previous periods to make the opposition party look worse.

The NBER designates a recession as beginning in the month in which the overall direction of several economic indicators is downward; the beginning of an expansion is designated as the month in which the overall direction is upward.[2] While various numerical tests are applied to the indicators to assess their direction, ultimately the decision is based on the judgment of the NBER committee. For example, a recession is generally defined as occurring when the quarterly real gross national product (i.e., the GNP in constant dollars) declines for two quarters in a row. However, this is not a fixed rule, and the NBER considers a variety of monthly and quarterly data before making a designation, including GNP in current and constant dollars, business sales, bank debits outside New York City, the industrial production index, the unemployment rate, nonfarm employment and hours worked, and personal income.

A notable exception to the typical designations occurred after World War II. In 1946 the real GNP declined by 19 percent, which was larger than any annual decline in the depression years of the 1930s. The sharp drop was due entirely to the demobilization and concomitant plunge in defense outlays. As the private sector and civilian government components of the GNP were rising during the demobilization, 1946 was not considered a recession year because business in general was rising.

A few terms relating to designation of recessions and expansions should be noted. A "growth recession" occurs when overall production and unemployment rates are both rising. Production in such cases is not keeping pace with the growing ranks of young people just out of school as well as unemployed persons with job experience.

While expansion is the general term for the upward phase of the cycle, the upturn immediately following the recession is often referred to as "recovery." When overall activity in the recovery exceeds the highest levels attained before the recession, this higher-growth period is called expansion. A comparable designation in the downward phase is the transition from recession to contraction. The immediate downturn is called recession; if overall activity falls below the lowest level of the previous recession, the depresed period may be called "contraction." However, economic literature gives little attention to contraction. It has not occurred since the depression of the early 1930s except for the decline in 1981–82, which by the "coincident" measure in the system of leading, coincident and lagging indexes (see Chapter 8) fell below the low point of the 1980 recession. Expansion is typical of the United States' long-term growing economy. Figure 3 depicts these phases of the business cycle from 1973 to mid–1986.

The high point of the expansion before it turns downward to recession is called the "peak," and the low point of the recession before it turns upward to recovery is the "trough." A complete cycle is composed of both the expansion and recession phases, and is typically viewed from the peak of one expansion to the peak of the following expansion. This way of looking at the cycle emphasizes the long-term growth of the economy independent of short-term cyclical movements, although for some analyses it may be useful to measure the cycle from the trough of one recession to the trough of the next recession.

All told, as indicated in Table 1, in the eight business cycles since World War II (excluding the expansion that began in late 1982 and was in progress in mid–1986 when this book was written), the average expansion was 45 months and the average recession was 11 months. For the six peacetime cycles (excluding the Korean and Vietnam Wars), the average expansion was 34 months and the average recession 11 months. Thus, since World War II, the average expansion has lasted about three to four times longer than the average recession. These durations are an improvement over the experience of the previous century, when the length of expansions was closer to the length of recessions.

Figure 3. **Stages of the Business Cycle: Composite Coincident Index of Economic Activity (Production, Sales, Income, Employment)**

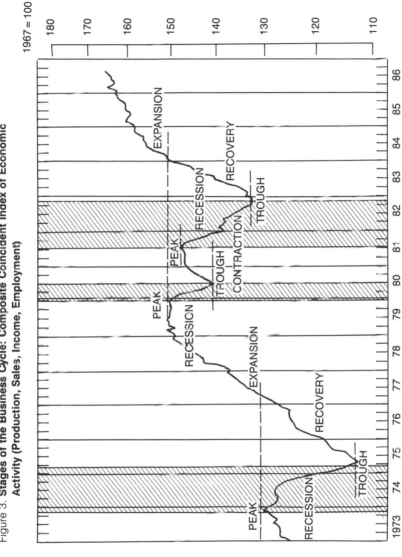

*Note:* Based on data from the Bureau of Economic Analysis, U.S. Department of Commerce. Lined bars are recession periods. The recovery, expansion, recession, and contraction stages were designated by the author.

Table 1

**Average Duration of U.S. Business Cycles
(in months)**

|  | Expansion | Recession |
|---|---|---|
| *All Cycles* | | |
| 1854–1919 (16 cycles) | 27 | 22 |
| 1919–1945 ( 6 cycles) | 35 | 18 |
| 1945–1982 ( 8 cycles) | 45 | 11 |
| *Peacetime Cycles* | | |
| 1854–1919 (14 cycles) | 24 | 24 |
| 1919–1945 ( 5 cycles) | 26 | 20 |
| 1945–1982 ( 6 cycles) | 34 | 11 |

*Source*: Bureau of Economic Analysis, U.S. Department of Commerce, *Handbook of Cyclical Indicators: A supplement to the Business Conditions Digest*, 1984, p. 178.

## ECONOMIC POLICIES

The federal government and the banking system attempt through fiscal and monetary policies to moderate cyclical fluctuations and maintain steady long-term economic growth. Fiscal policy refers to management of federal spending and tax rates by the President and Congress, while monetary policy is management of the money supply, bank reserves, and interest rates by the Federal Reserve Board.

This section centers on fiscal and monetary policies because they are the main instruments used in managing the economy. From time to time they are supplemented with incomes policies, which are either voluntary wage-price guidelines or mandatory wage-price controls. Incomes policies diverge from the complete market determination of prices and wages, and they are instituted only when it is thought that fiscal and monetary policies are too blunt to have the desired effect in curbing inflationary behavior at the micro level by business and labor unions. They are resorted to as a temporary device to break the inflationary psychology engendered when wages and prices spiral upward with no end in sight, and when it is believed that a recession and high unemployment caused by restrictive fiscal and monetary policies are too high a price to pay for breaking the inflationary behavior. Mandatory price and wage controls were used in World War II, part of the Korean War (1950–51), and part of the Vietnam War (1971–73); voluntary price-wage guidelines were used in 1962–65 and 1978–79. Economists debate their effectiveness; some say they distort price and profit relationships among products and result in higher inflation after they are removed, while others say they hold inflation below what it would have been, without undue interference with market determined wages and prices, so long as they are temporary. Incomes policies are not analyzed in this book because of their sporadic use. But if they are used in the future, the analyst will have to take them into account in assessing economic trends.

Although there is considerable sophistication in analyzing the effect of fiscal and monetary policies, the causes of and remedies for business cycles are complex, and the application of such policies is an art rather than a science. Fiscal and monetary policies must take many factors into account: purely economic considerations such as balancing sales, production, employment, investment, prices and interest rates; and political and other influences such as wars, harvests, consumer and business optimism and pessimism, international tensions, cartels and protectionism.

Interpreting economic indicators requires an understanding of the way fiscal and monetary policies react with each other. It should be kept in mind that fiscal policy is enacted through federal spending and taxes, which do not exist solely to manage the economy. Government spending is first aimed at meeting needs that society feels are best satisfied by the public sector, and taxation aims to finance that spending consistent with concepts of ability to pay, equity and efficient collection. By contrast, monetary policies, which are adopted and modified throughout the year by the Federal Reserve Board, are aimed solely at managing the economy's level of activity through manipulation of the money supply and the availability of credit. Hence, fiscal policy is derived as a secondary agenda while monetary policy's primary purpose is to manage the economy. In addition, fiscal policy is not as flexible as monetary policy, because spending and tax changes require a lengthier legislative process than do changes in monetary policy, which can be made on a relatively current basis. Thus, while fiscal and monetary policies are both important, monetary policies are easier to implement.

Perhaps the major achievement of these policy tools is that no recession since World War II has degenerated into a cataclysm such as the depression of the 1930s.[3] In addition, the Kennedy-Johnson period during the 1960s went eight years without a recession, a very long time by historical standards. Although part of the stimulus came from the increased military spending for the Vietnam War and inflation was in fact rising toward the end of the period, that general success created the hope that fiscal and monetary policies combined with incomes policies (voluntary wage-price guidelines) could maintain steady growth without recessions. In the next two decades, however, hopes for a recession-free economy evaporated. The challenge remains: maintaining steady, recession-free growth, low unemployment, and little or no inflation in peacetime.

## ECONOMIC FORECASTING

Managing the economy to produce maximum growth and employment while minimizing inflation depends on forecasts of what will happen under alternative combinations of fiscal and monetary policies. Although in retrospect forecasts have been disturbingly inaccurate, they remain the best tool available for judging proposed policies. In addition, it should be kept in mind that it is impossible to completely offset shocks caused by offshore events such as wars and the formation of successful cartels. Nor can we ignore the preferences of other countries with regard to economic growth, inflation, and exchange rates.

Historical and current trends in the economic indicators covered in this book are the foundation of economic forecasting. Varied techniques are used to develop forecasts—e.g., econometric models based on mathematical and statistical equations that relate all sectors of the economy, in-depth analysis of key sectors, and analysis of money-supply movements as a key determinant of future economic activity. However, the basic methodology in all of them is similar. It consists of analyzing the factors contributing to the current conditions, the past relationships of these factors, and the ways these relationships may change in the future.

Despite the mathematical methodology, one cannot expect economic forecasts to be precisely on target. While a single forecast number is the most frequently used and the easiest to comprehend (such as, "The unemployment rate will be 7.5 percent a year from now"), such pinpointed figures give a false impression of certainty. Because the economy is subject to complex domestic and international forces, it is more realistic and useful to give an expected range of the forecasts along with the reasons why the figures are expected to be toward the upper or lower end of the range.

A good forecast will account for current trends in the various indicators which may be giving conflicting signals on the state of the economy (e.g., employment may be up and manufacturers' orders down). Insightful analysis of such apparently ambiguous trends is an important component of forecasting, both for assessing the credibility of the forecast and for adapting it to the user's particular needs. The forecast should also include milestones, intermediate points before the target date, to enable the analyst to monitor how well the forecast assumptions and trends are in fact working out, and to warn of significant departures. These would provide the basis for modifying the forecast based on the new developments.

Certain concepts important in determining future patterns of economic activity will be discussed in detail in later chapters. These include the stimulating or restraining effects of the federal budget on the economy based on the "cyclically adjusted" or "high-employment" budgets; the relationship between trends in the gross national product and the unemployment rate, as developed in current versions of "Okuns' Law"; the trade-off between unemployment and inflation from analyses using the "Phillips curve"; and the idea that the current phase of the business cycle contains the seeds of the following phase, which is the basis of the system of "leading and lagging indexes."

## NOTES

1. *Economic Report of the President*, February 1985, Table B-109, p. 356.

2. For a discussion of the methodology, see Geoffrey H. Moore, *Business Cycles, Inflation and Forecasting*, Second Edition, National Bureau of Economic Research Studies in Business Cycles, No. 24 (Ballinger Publishing Company, a Subsidiary of Harper & Row, Publishers, Inc.: 1983), pp. 3–9.

3. In addition, automatic government programs, such as unemployment compensation and various income maintenance programs, provide an income floor during recessions.

# 3 • Gross National Product

As a system of accounts recording income and spending in both the domestic and international economies, the gross national product (GNP) is the most important and comprehensive macroeconomic indicator for assessing the overall state of the American economy. The GNP accounts function as an integrated construct for tracking trends in economic growth and inflation and for analyzing the effects past fiscal, monetary and incomes policies have had on the economy. As such, the GNP also provides the best basis for developing economic projections based on assumed fiscal, monetary and incomes policies and for anticipating the likely impact of potential changes in those policies. The GNP estimates are developed quarterly by the Bureau of Economic Analysis in the U.S. Department of Commerce.

## PART A: ESTIMATING METHODOLOGY

### DEMAND (MARKETS) AND
### SUPPLY (COSTS)

The GNP summarizes in a single number the total economic output of the nation valued in dollars. It is derived by organizing the various sectors of the economy— the household, business, government and international sectors—into a system of spending and income accounts. These are referred to as the "national income and product accounts," "national economic accounts," or simply the "national accounts."

The summary GNP figure consolidates spending and its counterpart income flows to represent the nation's output from two perspectives, the differing components of demand and supply. The *demand* concept (known as the "product side") refers to the end-use markets for goods and services produced in the U.S. It appears in the national accounts as sales of these items (plus inventory accumulation or depletion) to households, businesses, governments and foreigners. The *supply* concept (known as the "income side") refers to the costs involved in producing these goods and services. It is shown in the accounts as the wages of workers, profits of business, depreciation allowances for business plant and equipment, and sales and property taxes.[1]

Table 2 below shows the product and income sides of the GNP in 1985 and their major components. The figures indicate the dominance of consumer expenditures on the product side (65 percent of the GNP) and employee compensation on the income side (59 percent of GNP). However, as will become apparent, these and the other components move at different rates over the business cycle, and it is this volatility that affects overall GNP growth rates.

## MEANING OF PRODUCTION

The GNP is constructed on a "value added" basis. This means that as goods pass through the various stages of production—from raw materials to semi-finished goods to final products—only the value that is added in each stage is counted for GNP purposes. If goods and services purchased from other businesses for use in production were included, their value would be endlessly recounted. The value-added method counts only the total resources used in producing the final item, as represented in the wage, profit, and other income side components and the final markets of the product side. This prevents double counting of items on either the product or income side of the GNP accounts.

Another key point in the definition of production is that the GNP excludes capital gains and losses in the sale of securities, land and used goods. These are considered valuation changes in the transfer of assets, and while they may have effects on future production, they do not change output at the time of the transfer. However, brokerage charges associated with these transactions are in the GNP because the broker's service is current production.

GNP measures production without making any value judgments on the worth to society of the activities measured. Equal weight is given to purchases of goods and services for everyday living, investment for future production, and public services—food, housing, machinery, inventories, education, defense, etc. are all valued strictly in dollar terms. Similarly, the labor and capital resources necessary to product this output are measured strictly in dollar amounts as workers' wages and business profits. This objective measure of the nation's output may be contrasted to measures that could account for the nation's "welfare" or "well-being" by assigning a positive or negative value to activities based not only on their marketplace value but also on their intrinsic worth.

A GNP that accounted for welfare would measure the nonmaterial effects of activities by deducting from production for "bad" items and adding for "good" items. Such a computation would assign new values for industrial activity that generates pollution; crime that leads to the need for police protection; international tensions that result in the production of weapons to be used only for

Table 2

## GNP and Major Components, 1985

| | Product side | | | Income side | |
| | $ billions | percent | | $ billions | percent |
| --- | --- | --- | --- | --- | --- |
| Gross national product | 3,998.1 | 100.0 | Gross national product | 3,998.1 | 100.0 |
| Personal consumption expenditures | 2,600.5 | 65.0 | Compensation of employees | 2,368.2 | 59.2 |
| Durable goods | 359.3 | 9.0 | Wages and salaries | 1,965.8 | 49.2 |
| Nondurable goods | 905.1 | 22.6 | Supplements | 402.4 | 10.1 |
| Services | 1,336.1 | 33.4 | Proprietors' income[c] | 254.4 | 6.4 |
| Gross private domestic investment | 661.1 | 16.5 | Farm | 29.2 | 0.7 |
| | | | Nonfarm | 225.2 | 5.6 |
| Nonresidential[a] | 458.2 | 11.5 | Rental income | 7.6 | 0.2 |
| Residential[b] | 191.8 | 4.8 | Corporate profits | 280.7 | 7.0 |
| Inventory change | 11.1 | .3 | Net Interest | 311.4 | 7.8 |
| Net exports | −78.9 | −2.0 | Indirect business taxes[d] | 331.4 | 8.3 |
| Exports | 369.8 | 9.2 | | | |
| Imports | 448.6 | −11.2 | Capital consumption allowances[e] | 437.2 | 10.9 |
| Government purchases | 815.4 | 20.4 | Business transfers, Government subsidies and government enterprises | 12.7 | 0.3 |
| Federal | 354.1 | 8.9 | | | |
| State and local | 461.3 | 11.5 | Statistical discrepancy | −5.5 | −0.1 |

*Source*: Bureau of Economic Analysis, U. S. Department of Commerce, *Survey of Current Business*, July 1986.

[a]Business plant and equipment.
[b]Mainly new housing construction.
[c]Profits of unincorporated business.
[d]Mainly sales and property taxes.
[e]Mainly depreciation allowances.

*Note*: Detail may not add to totals due to rounding.

destruction; a shorter workweek that provides more leisure time; do-it-yourself, unpaid labor such as homemaking and child-rearing performed by parents; and the services of consumer durables over their useful life such as automobiles, furniture, and household appliances. In the 1970s, the Bureau of Economic Analysis began to develop estimates of such items that economists could use to modify the conventional GNP measures, but the project was discontinued for lack of funding. (By contrast, some nonmarket activities are included as "imputed" estimates in the GNP, the main one being the rental value of owner-occupied housing. These imputed items currently account for 9 percent of the GNP.)

# REAL GNP AND INFLATION

GNP in constant dollars, also referred to as "real GNP," gives the growth in the *quantity* of economic activity. Real GNP measures total output abstracted from price increases or decreases, which are included in GNP in current dollars (also known as "nominal GNP").[2] The absolute real GNP figures, expressed in constant 1982 dollars are difficult to relate to in their own right because of price changes since the 1982 base year. The main interest in the real GNP is in the *rate of change* in the quarterly or yearly movements. The absolute real GNP figures are used for analytic relationships such as those comparing GNP to employment for estimating labor productivity (see Chapter 5), and those comparing income to population for assessing trends in living conditions.

The real GNP figures also yield measures of price change. There are three variants of these indexes of inflation (rising prices) and deflation (falling prices). The first is the "implicit price deflator," which is derived by dividing current-dollar GNP by constant-dollar GNP. The deflator reflects continuing shifts in tastes and spending patterns because it accounts for actual spending as new or substitute products replace old ones and as consumers choose between higher- and lower-priced products. Thus, the deflator's measure of price change includes "pure" price movements as well as the effect of the changing mix of items bought.

The "fixed-weighted price index" is one that keeps spending patterns constant between the GNP benchmark estimates which are calculated every five years (but with lags of three to thirteen years from the introduction of the new benchmarks— e.g., the 1972 benchmark was completed in 1980 and the 1977 benchmark was completed using 1982 prices in 1985). It assumes no shifts in spending toward new products or between higher- or lower-priced lines until the new benchmark is completed. To illustrate, the spending patterns used for the fixed-weighted price index from 1972 through 1985 were based on the 1972 experience; in 1985 the index was updated to reflect the 1982 patterns. This time lag in the fixed-weighted index can be limiting. For example, despite the sharp increases in oil prices instituted by the Organization of Petroleum Exporting Countries in 1973 and 1979 with the Arab oil embargo and the Iranian revolution, the structure of this index did not reflect the product substitution due to the 1973 price increases until 1985. It was in that year that the new benchmark revised the fixed-weighted price index average annual increase in the fixed-weighted price index from 1972 to 1984 downward from 7.3 to 6.6 percent. Similarly, the substitution effects of the 1979 price increase will not be reflected in the index until the 1982 benchmark is done in 1990, and those of the 1985–86 price decline will first appear with the 1987 benchmark in 1995. The advantage of the fixed-weighted index, however, is that it allows the user to see clearly what inflation changes occurred due simply to price changes and not product substitution.

A third kind of index is the "chain price index," which maintains constant expenditure patterns between each quarter or year—e.g., the first- to the second-quarter price change refers to expenditure patterns in the first quarter, and the second to third quarter price change refers to expenditure patterns in the second quarter. Thus, this index represents expenditure patterns somewhere between the continually moving ones in the implicit price deflator and the relatively constant ones in the fixed-price index, but it is closest in nature to the deflator.

These alternative price indexes highlight the classic index number problem of a shifting product mix (in this case, expenditure patterns). As noted in Chapter 2, it is difficult to choose one index as superior. The most useful approach is to treat them as providing a range of lower and upper bounds for the actual inflation occurring in the everyday world.

In addition to the problem of shifting base period proportions, price indexes are beleaguered by the problem of accounting adequately for changes in the goods and services being priced that affect their value. These indexes purport to measure only changes which are in fact a "pure" price increase or decrease, not one caused by changes in the quality or specifications of the item. For example, if a loaf of bread increases in price without a change in quality or size, that is a price increase for purposes of GNP measurement. But if the loaf increases in size equivalent to the price increase, there is no price change for GNP measurement. Or if the price of the bread is unchanged but the loaf is now larger or contains a nutritious new ingredient, a price decrease will be registered.

Price measurement issues are discussed more fully in Chapter 6, which treats the consumer price index. They are noted here simply to indicate that price measurement is an imprecise concept.

## GOVERNMENT BUDGETS

The GNP measurement of government *purchases* of goods and services is less inclusive than that of *expenditures* in federal, state, and local budgets. Government purchases include outlays for goods, services, and construction bought from the private sector and wages paid to government workers. They exclude transfer payments to individuals for Social Security and other income maintenance programs; federal grants to state and local governments and state grants to local governments; interest on government debt; foreign economic aid; and government loans less repayments—all of which are included as spending in official government budgets.

The spending generated by the items not included in government purchases is included in the GNP markets that use the money to buy goods and services. For example, spending of Social Security and other income maintenance payments shows up in consumer expenditures; state and local government spending of federal grants appears in state and local purchases; foreign spending of economic aid appears in net exports; and interest payments on government debt and government loans and subsidies appear in the spending by the recipients of these funds in the domestic and foreign components of the GNP. Thus, while these transfer-type items are excluded from government purchases in the GNP, they are accounted for in the other sectors.

Nevertheless, the exclusion of these items from GNP's accounting of the government sector limits one's view of the economic impact of government. For example, in fiscal year 1985, federal purchases in the GNP of $342 billion represented only 44 percent of all the outlays in the official federal budget. One way to more fully analyze the economic impact of government in the GNP framework is to use supplementary data in the national accounts on government budgets which include total expenditures and receipts. These are similar to the official budgets, but are modified to make them more useful for estimating the effects of expenditures, receipts, and the budget surplus or deficit on economic activity.

Besides definitional differences such as distinctions in coverage of government loans, purchases of land, contributions to government-employee retirement funds, and spending and receipts in U.S. possessions outside the 50 states and the District of Columbia, the two budgets—the GNP measurement and the official budget—differ in terms of timing. The official budget shows expenditures when the checks are paid and receipts when tax payments are received, while the budget in the GNP framework is on an accrual basis in which expenditures are recorded when the item is delivered and receipts are recorded when the tax liability is incurred. This accounting method is more useful for economic purposes because, in general, production is geared to deliveries and investment decisions are shaped by advance indication of profits after taxes. Budgets in the GNP framework are used in fiscal and monetary policymaking, where the overall impact of expenditures, receipts and the surplus or deficit are of major concern. By contrast, official budgets generally are linked to planning expenditures for individual programs and agencies in the appropriation process and in changing tax rates through legislation.

Because of the two methods of accounting, the national accounts deficit is less (or the surplus is more) than the official budget deficit (or surplus), but the overall magnitudes are not substantially different. Table 3 shows that for 1980–85, the national accounts deficit ranged from $8 to $30 billion less than the official budget deficit. On a relative basis, this difference declined from 31 percent in 1980 to 7 percent in 1982, and subsequently rose to 14 percent in 1985. For practical purposes, most economic analyses and projections are based on the national accounts budget, and if necessary for the analysis they are then modified for known or expected special transactions to assess their impact on particular programs such as defense or agriculture.

Table 3

**Federal Budget Deficit (in billions of dollars)**

| 1<br>Fiscal year | 2<br>Official<br>budget | 3<br>National-<br>accounts<br>budget (GNP) | 4<br>Difference<br>(national accounts<br>minus official) | 5<br>Difference as<br>a percent of<br>official figure<br>(4)/(2) |
|---|---|---|---|---|
| 1980 | −$72.3 | −$50.4 | −$22.3 | 31% |
| 1981 | −73.9 | −58.5 | −15.4 | 21 |
| 1982 | −120.0 | −112.6 | −8.3 | 7 |
| 1983 | −208.0 | −184.4 | −23.6 | 11 |
| 1984 | −185.6 | −164.8 | −20.8 | 11 |
| 1985 | −221.6 | −191.2 | −30.4 | 14 |

*Sources*: *Economic Report of the President*, February 1986, pp. 339 and 345, and Joint Economic Committee of Congress, *Economic Indicators*, July 1986, pp. 32 and 34.

## Selected Technical Topics

This section addresses several technical aspects of the GNP relevant to interpreting trends: alternative summary measures, seasonally adjusted annual rates, error ranges, the statistical discrepancy, net exports, and valuation adjustments.

### Alternative Summary Measures

In addition to the GNP, other summary measures of the national accounts are available to better reflect special circumstances in the domestic or international economies. These measures are final sales, final sales to domestic purchasers, gross domestic product (GDP),and command GNP. Another alternative GNP measure, GNP on the income side, is discussed in the Statistical Discrepancy section below.

*Final sales* are the GNP excluding inventory change. In the GNP, an inventory increase is added to final sales and an inventory decrease is deducted from final sales. Inventory movements arise from differences between production and sales—inventories increase when production is larger than sales, and they decrease when sales are greater than production. Businesses augment or cut back on their stocks of goods based on their perceptions of future sales and prices, or because of unexpected market developments such as substantially greater-than-anticipated rises or falls in sales, in which case the subsequent inventory depletion or accumulation is referred to as "unplanned." The unplanned changes may in turn generate deliberate actions to bring inventories into a desired balance with sales. Short-term inventory movements can be important signals that production may increase because inventories are low in relation to sales, or that production may decrease because inventories are relatively high.

It is also informative to assess how the economy is performing independent of inventory movements, by focusing on the strength of demand in all GNP markets as evidenced in sales. For example, if sales are level or falling but production is adding to inventories, the overall GNP growth rate may be deceptively high. Or if sales are increasing and inventories are being depleted because of production bottlenecks, the GNP growth rate may understate the underlying strength in the economy. The purpose of the final sales measure is to capture this underlying strength in demand.

*Final sales to domestic purchasers* are final sales minus exports and plus imports. This gives a measure of underlying demand (excluding inventory movements) in the domestic economy. By excluding exports, it abstracts from foreign demand for American production, and by including imports, it recognizes an American domestic demand that is not being met by American industry.

*Gross domestic product (GDP)* is the GNP modified to subtract the effect of profits arising from foreign investments. It focuses on economic activity within the geographic boundaries of the 50 states and the District of Columbia, in contrast to the GNP which treats profits of multinational companies according to the nationality of the company's ownership. In the GNP, profits from foreign operations of U.S.-owned companies are included as business income and treated as exports on the product side, while profits from operations in the U.S. of foreign-owned companies are excluded from business income and treated as imports. However, for some analyses of the American economy there is a greater interest in the economic activity occurring only in the geographic United States. While financial flows of profits of international companies across national borders affect business decisions on investment and operations, the direct impact of these profits occurs in the region where they are generated. Thus, to focus on the geographic aspect of these activities, GDP excludes profits of U.S.-owned companies earned from foreign operations and includes profits of foreign-owned companies from their U.S. operations. This reverses the treatment in the GNP.

*Command GNP* is a shortened version of "Command over Goods and Services, GNP Basis." It expresses the notion that as prices for exported and imported items diverge and substantially change the terms of trade (the ratio of export prices to import prices), the conventional deflation of exports and imports by their respective price trends affects real GNP growth rates by giving foreigners a higher or lower claim on U.S. production.

This impact results from the accounting need to subtract imports from exports for the net export component of the GNP (see later section on net exports). This is done to offset the inclusion of imports in the other product side GNP components of consumer expenditures, investment and government purchases. If imports were not subracted from exports, the product and income sides of the GNP would not balance, because there are no income side wages and profits associated with the production of imports.

The impact occurs when there are relatively large price changes in important internationally traded items such as petroleum. For example, for some years in the 1970s and in 1980, when the price of imported oil rose very sharply, constant-dollar imports were much lower than current-dollar imports. This in turn raised constant-dollar net exports (because net exports are gross exports minus gross imports) and therefore real GNP. This suggested that Americans had a greater supply from which to "command" goods and services because of the higher import prices. This is an anomaly of the accounting need to deduct imports, because higher import prices *lower* the availability of goods and services for consumption. Analogously, the decline in oil prices from 1981 to 1986 falsely suggests a lower command of goods and services over that period in the conventional GNP.

The concept of command GNP handles such problems by changing the deflation procedure of net exports. The conventional GNP method deflates exports and imports separately by export and import prices, and then subtracts constant-dollar imports from constant-dollar exports. Command GNP deflates net exports in a single step, using import prices as the only deflator (export prices as the single deflator would yield similar results). This device tends to moderate anomalies produced by the accounting need to subtract imports in the net export component.

## Seasonally Adjusted Annual Rate

The GNP is estimated quarterly, but the figure for each quarter is published as if the activity in the quarter were at an annual rate. This facilitates comparison of the current volume of the economy with past and projected annual levels. There are two measures involved in this concept: the first is the GNP absolute level for the quarter at an annual rate, and the second is the percent change in this level from the previous quarter at an annual rate.

The GNP level is the sum of the seasonally adjusted data for the three months of the quarter, multiplied by four to raise it to an annual level. For example, for the first quarter of the year, the seasonally adjusted data for January, February and March are summed, and the total is multiplied by four. The resulting figure is the quarterly GNP at a seasonally adjusted annual rate.

To derive an annual percent rate of change in the current-quarter GNP from the preceding quarter, the relative change for the present quarter is *compounded* to represent an annual rate. The procedure is to raise the rate of growth or decline in the current quarter to the fourth power, subtract 1.0, and multiply by 100, as shown here.

$$\left( \frac{\text{Seasonally adjusted annual GNP (current quarter)}}{\text{Seasonally adjusted annual GNP (previous quarter)}} \right)^{4} - 1.0 \times 100$$

## Error Range

The preliminary GNP estimates published shortly after each quarter are tentative, as is evident from the size of the revisions made as more complete and accurate information becomes available. Experience with these revisions has shown that, in nine cases out of 10, their likely effect on seasonally adjusted annual growth rates for quarterly real GNP is in the ranges indicated in Table 4. The annual revisions—the GNP estimates developed in the successive annual and benchmark revisions in the years following the actual quarter—are regarded as the "correct" figures, and usually appear in the July issue of the *Survey of Current Business*.

Clearly, GNP estimates in any particular quarter are subject to quite sizable revision. For example, in the case of the preliminary estimate of real GNP that comes out 15 days *after* the end of the quarter and is based on actual data for only the first month of the quarter, the revision typically ranges from minus 2.4 to plus 3.5 percentage points. This means that a preliminary GNP showing a seasonally adjusted annual growth rate of 3 percent is likely to be revised within a range of 0.6 to 6.5 percent. This is a highly significant span, as it makes considerable difference in projections for unemployment, inflation and the federal deficit. If the growth rate is less than 1 percent, unemployment will be rising significantly; if it exceeds 6 percent, unemployment will be falling significantly.

---

Table 4

## Potential Revisions to Constant Dollar GNP Estimates

| Publication schedule of preliminary and revised current GNP estimates for the same quarter | Range of revisions in quarterly real GNP annual growth rates seasonally adjusted (9 of 10 revisions) |
|---|---|
| Preliminary GNP (15 days after the quarter) | −2.4 to 3.5 percentage points |
| First revised GNP (45 days after the quarter) | −2.1 to 2.8 percentage points |
| Second Revised GNP (75 days after the quarter) | −2.4. to 2.7 percentage points |

*Source*: Bureau of Economic Analysis, U.S. Department of Commerce, GNP press release of July 22, 1986.
*Note*: Revision range is based on experience from 1974 to 1983 using GNP data before the 1986 benchmark revision.

---

As subsequent refined estimates become available, upward revisions for a particular quarter tend to become smaller—although for downward revisions, surprisingly, the estimate released 45 days after the quarter is typically revised a little less than the one that comes out the following month. *No single GNP figure should be interpreted to indicate a trend, but rather should be viewed in the context of trends for previous quarters to suggest whether something different may be occurring.* In general, one should also wait for the second revision of 75 days after the most recent quarter before concluding that the numbers reflect the actual circumstances of the quarter.

## Statistical Discrepancy

Conceptually, the product and income sides of the GNP measure in grand total the same output. In practise, limitations in the underlying data mean that the totals are rarely equal. The data are obtained from a variety of surveys, tax records, and other sources that have varying comparability with the pure GNP concepts. They also have varying degrees of accuracy, because the survey samples are not necessarily representative and the respondents may provide erroneous information.

The difference between the totals on the product and income sides is the *net* effect of these inconsistencies and inaccuracies, and is referred to as the "statistical discrepancy." There is nothing systematic in the discrepancy from quarter to quarter, as different data problems are always occurring. By convention, the discrepancy is calculated as the product side minus the income side, and it appears on the income side. In some cases the deficiencies are offsetting, which results in the statistical discrepancy's being smaller than if the *gross* deficiencies were added without regard to their upward or downward direction.

From the user's perspective, the discrepancy allows alternative GNP growth rates to be calculated from the product- and income-side information. These upper and lower bounds recognize that, due to data shortcomings, neither the product nor income side is inherently more accurate and that "reality" is more a range than a precise number. (This is similar to the approach suggested previously for the alternative price indexes.)

For analytic purposes, the user should be aware that a noticeable change in the discrepancy could affect the growth rate. For example, in a $4 trillion GNP, a $10 billion discrepancy is 0.25 percent and a $20 billion descrepancy is 0.5 percent of the GNP. If the GNP on the product side is growing at a rate of 3 percent for two quarters in a row, and the discrepancy increases from $10 billion to $20 billion in the two quarters, the alternative growth rate for the second quarter will become 2.75 percent, which—while not startling, as will be seen later—suggests a greater possibility for higher unemployment.

## Net Exports

Net exports of goods and services is the GNP component that represents U.S. transactions with other countries. It is derived by subtracting imports from exports. The net concept is necessary to keep the product and income sides of the GNP accounts in balance, due to the special situation of imports.

Because imports are produced abroad, their production does not generate wages and profits in the United States, and thus there are no income-side payments associated with their production. However, imported items do appear on the product side as households, businesses and governments buy the imported goods and services. If nothing was done to offset purchases in the consumption, investment, and government components on the product side, that side would be higher than the income side. Therefore, imports are deducted from exports in the net export component to neutralize their inclusion in the other product-side components.

The deduction of imports, however, causes the net export component to appear as a deceptively small share of the GNP. In 1985, for example, net exports were − $79 billion ($370 billion of exports minus $449 billion of imports), or a deficit of 2 percent of the GNP. This relatively small net figure masks the much higher actual economic impact of exports and imports separately, as exports were 9 percent and imports were 11 percent of the GNP in 1985.

While net exports give an overall view of the differential effect of exports and imports and of money flows between the United States and other countries (and can be important for foreign-exchange values and U.S. monetary policies), exports and imports taken separately are more relevant for assessing the impact of international trade on American production and prices. Exports and imports impact and are affected by employment and inflation in the United States, American competitiveness in international markets, the value of the dollar, and the pace of the American and world economies.

## Valuation Adjustments for Inventories and Depreciation

Special adjustments are made for the effect of price movements on the change in business inventories and on depreciation allowances for equipment and structures as conventionally reported by companies. These adjustments are particularly important during periods of high inflation and when depreciation allowances in the tax laws differ substantially from the lifetime use of capital facilities in business practice.

In both cases, the purpose of the adjustments is to reflect the *replacement cost* of inventories and capital facilities based on prices when they are used up, as distinct from prices at the time the inventories and capital facilities were acquired (their historical cost). Doing so eliminates the effect of valuation gains and losses on inventories due to price increases or decreases of goods since they were acquired.

And for capital facilities, the adjustment provides a truer picture of the actual costs of replacing outmoded or inefficient plant and equipment as compared with the depreciation deductions allowed in income tax laws.

The *inventory valuation adjustment* (IVA) appears in the change in business inventories on the product side and in business profits on the income side of the GNP. During periods of rising prices, the IVA is a negative to offset valuation profits when goods are sold; when prices are falling the IVA is positive to offset the valuation losses. Since prices generally are rising, the IVA is typically negative, although the amounts vary considerably depending on the rate of inflation. For example, the IVA was -$51 billion in 1979 and -$50 billion in 1980, but only − $1 billion in 1985. Thus, inventory change on the product side as derived from conventionally reported business inventories, and business profits on the income side, were reduced by these amounts in the corresponding years. Because inventories are continually replenished and sold at current prices, the IVA provides a more realistic assessment of actual inventory build-ups and depletions and of business profits.

The *capital consumption adjustment* (CCAdj) mainly affects the income side of the GNP accounts and appears as offsetting items to business profits and capital consumption allowances (mainly depreciation). The CCAdj is affected by tax laws and the rate of inflation. When depreciation allowances applied to the life of equipment or structure permit tax deductions to recoup the original cost of capital facilities faster than businesses actually use them up, the CCAdj is a positive item in business profits and a negative item in capital consumption allowances. When prices of capital goods are rising and thus raising the cost of new capital facilities, the CCAdj is deducted from profits and added to capital consumption allowances. The opposite occurs when the tax laws allow slower depreciation rates than those at which business tends to use up capital facilities and when capital goods prices are falling. Thus, the CCAdj affects the distribution between profits and depreciation, but it does not affect the total GNP.

The CCAdj has changed considerably in recent years as a result both of the Economic Recovery Tax Act of 1981 (which greatly accelerated depreciation tax deductions by shortening the ''tax life'' of capital facilities) and of the recent slowdown of inflation. Thus, for corporations and nonfarm unincorporated businesses, the CCAdj shifted from − $65 billion in 1980 to $30 billion in 1985. This shift increased profits and decreased capital consumption allowances by the same amounts. Because profits are an important element driving future investment in capital facilities, shifts of these magnitudes can have a significant effect on plant and equipment investment. (The CCAdj for unincorporated farm businesses and rental income of persons reflects changes in the capital goods inflation rate, but does not reflect differentials between tax law depreciation and actual business practice in accounting for capital costs. This occurs because: (a) data problems in the case of unincorporated farm businesses and income from rental property limit the use of tax return information; and (b) rental income is mainly composed of "rent" for owner-occupied dwellings that is imputed as if it were a cash payment to a landlord, but for which no depreciation is taken on the individual income tax return.)

## PART B: ANALYSIS OF TRENDS

This portion of the chapter covers the main patterns taken by American business cycles since the 1945–48 expansion and highlights the major factors driving these trends. This period represents a major change from the depression of the 1930s and World War II both in the nature of the economy and the tools available for moderating business cycles. These postwar cycles are assessed from two perspectives: (a) a "top-down" view based on the total GNP and alternative summary GNP measures; and (b) a "building-block" approach focusing on the household, business, government and international components.

According to the National Bureau of Economic Research, there have been nine expansions and eight recessions since World War II, as measured from the 1945–48 expansion to the expansion that began at the end of 1982 and was in progress in mid-1986. There was a recession from February to October 1945, but because it was so closely linked to the war and the demobilization, it is not included in this analysis. The subsequent expansion from 1945 to 1948 was affected by the pent-up demand from the steadily growing incomes and deferred purchases of wartime, and thus the war had an important, although indirect, effect. Therefore, the 1948–49 recession was the first postwar cyclical movement that was sufficiently removed from the war not to have been affected by the war's aftermath.

The turning point used here to mark the peak of expansions and the trough of recessions is the change in direction of the real GNP. The real GNP turning point is used as a standard to allow a consistent analysis of the movement among the GNP components. These may fall in the same quarter or the quarter immediately before or after the turning point designated by the National Bureau of Economic Research, which is specified as a particular month (see Chapter 2 under "Designation of Recessions and Expansions").

Table 5 shows the beginning and ending quarters of the postwar business cycles used in this analysis. For expansions, the first date is the quarter the economy turned up from the previous recession and the second date in the last quarter (peak) of the expansion before the economy turned down into the next recession. For recessions, the first date is the quarter when the economy turned down and the second date is the last quarter (trough) of the recession. For example, the 1950–53 expansion lasted from the first quarter of 1950 to the second quarter of 1953, and the subsequent recession lasted from the third quarter

Table 5

**Duration of Expansions and Recessions Based on Real GNP Beginning and Ending Quarters**

| Expansions | Duration (quarters) | Recessions | Duration (quarters) |
|---|---|---|---|
| 1945:4–48:4[a] | 13 | 1949:1–49:4 | 4 |
| 1950:1–53:2 | 14 | 1953:3–54:2 | 4 |
| 1954:3–57:3 | 13 | 1957:4–58:1 | 2 |
| 1958:2–60:1 | 8 | 1960:2–60:4 | 3 |
| 1961:1–69:3 | 35 | 1969:4–70:4 | 5 |
| 1971:1–73:4 | 12 | 1974:1–75:1 | 5 |
| 1975:2–80:1 | 20 | 1980:2–80:2 | 1 |
| 1980:3–81:3 | 5 | 1981:4–82:3 | 4 |
| 1982:4–86:3[b] | 16 | | |

*Note*: The beginning and ending quarters are shown after the colon of each year.

[a]Quarterly real GNP data are not available before 1947. Use of 1945:4 as the starting point of the 1945–48 expansion follows the designation by the National Bureau of Economic Research of November 1945 as the beginning of the expansion (see text).
[b]The expansion starting in 1982:4 was in progress in the summer of 1986, when this was written.

of 1953 to the second quarter of 1954.

As noted in Chapter 2, in the postwar period expansions averaged three years in peacetime and four years in wartime, and recessions averaged one year in both cases. However, the duration of individual cycles varies widely around these averages. The expansion of the 1960s lasted nine years, but business cycles occurred with greater frequency in the 1950s and 1970–86. Still, the duration of the expansions was far more varied during 1970–86 than in the 1950s; this change in part probably reflects the growing internationalization of the economy, which makes it more vulnerable to economic events around the world and thus subject to greater variability.

## COMPARISON OF REAL GNP
## AND OTHER SUMMARY MEASURES

This section concentrates on the postwar cyclical movements of the GNP and other summary GNP measures. To put these cyclical movements in a longer-run context, it first briefly highlights postwar trends in economic growth. Economic growth in relation to unemployment is discussed in Chapter 5.

## Long-term Trends

Long-term trends in real GNP that span several business cycles show distinct shifts in the annual rate of growth from 1948 to 1985. The average for the entire period is 3.2 percent. As indicated below, the 1950s and 1960s were increasingly above the long-term average, while the 1970s and the first half of the 1980s had progressively slower rates of growth below the average.[3]

The slowdown in the growth rate during 1970–85 was accompanied by the greater variability (previously noted) in the duration of expansions, while the rapid growth of the 1960s occurred during an exceptionally long expansion. A theoretical case could be made that fewer or possibly more uniform cyclical fluctuations result in faster economic growth or vice versa, although such relationships are difficult to quantify. Nonetheless, in assessing future trends it is worthwhile to consider the possible effects that domestic and international industrial and financial changes may have on the cyclical and growth aspects of the economy.

---

### Annual Average Growth in Real GNP

| | |
|---|---|
| 1948–59 | 3.6% |
| 1959–69 | 4.1 |
| 1969–79 | 2.8 |
| 1979–85 | 2.0 |
| 1948–85 | 3.2 |

---

## Cyclical Movements

Figures 4a, 4b, 4c and 4d summarize the movements of real GNP and the other summary GNP measures over the postwar business cycles. Final sales (GNP excluding inventory change) and final sales to domestic purchasers (final sales including imports and excluding exports) are the only alternative summary GNP measures that diverged substantially from the real GNP. Figures 4a and 4c show that real GNP is more volatile than final sales; GNP rose in expansions and declined in recessions more sharply than final sales. During expansions, the GNP typically increased by 1 to 3 percentage points more than final sales and final sales to domestic purchasers; in recessions, GNP typically fell by 1 to 2 percentage points more than both final sales categories. (In the recessions of 1949, 1960, and 1969–70, both final sales categories actually increased.) When compared with the average increase in real GNP in expansions of 19 percent and the average GNP decrease in recessions of 2.5 percent, the final sales movements indicate the much

Figure 4a. **Business Cycle Movements of Real GNP and Other Summary GNP Measures: Expansions**

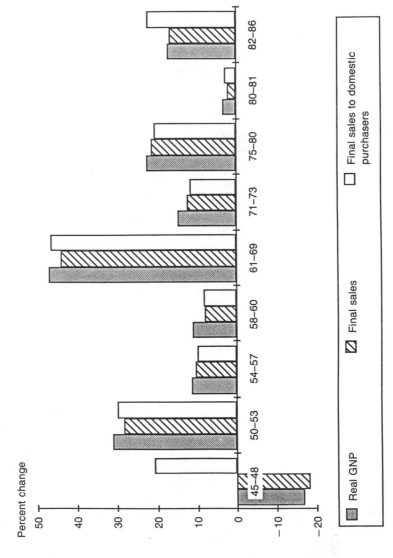

Percent change

*Note:* Based on Bureau of Economic Analysis data. All figures are in 1982 dollars.

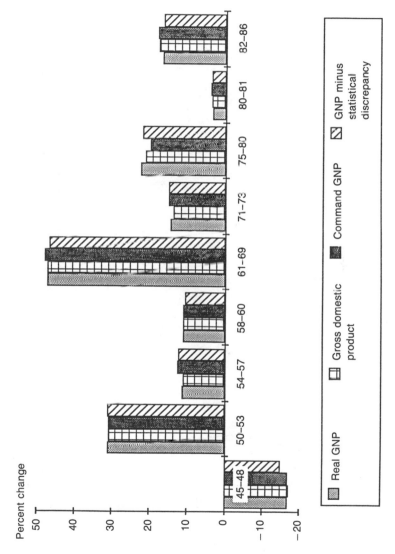

Figure 4b. **Business Cycle Movements of Real GNP and Other Summary GNP Measures: Expansions**

Percent change

Real GNP  Gross domestic product  Command GNP  GNP minus statistical discrepancy

*Note:* Based on Bureau of Economic Analaysis data. All figures are in 1982 dollars.

42

Figure 4c. **Business Cycle Movements of Real GNP and Other Summary GNP Measures: Recessions**

Percent change

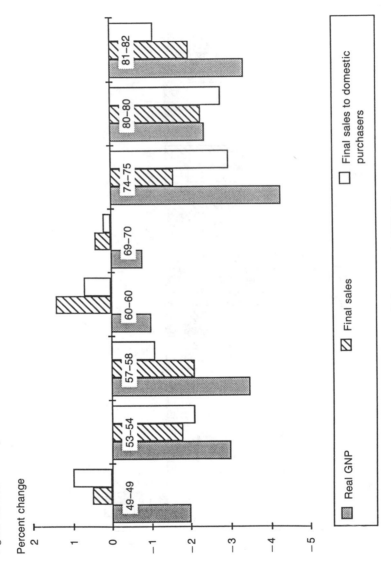

*Note:* Based on Bureau of Economic Analysis data. All figures are in 1982 dollars.

Figure 4d. **Business Cycle Movements of Real GNP and Other Summary GNP Measures: Recessions**

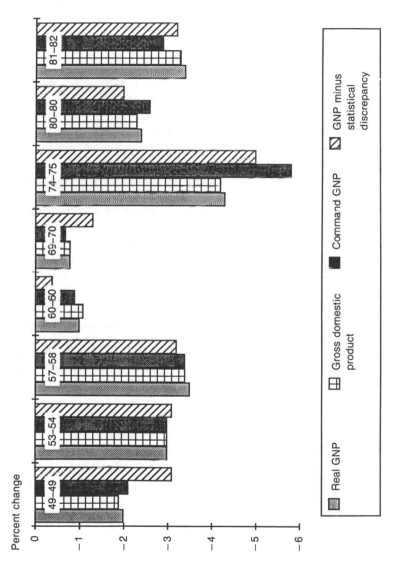

*Note:* Based on Bureau of Economic Analysis data. All figures are in 1982 dollars.

greater proportionate weight that inventories have in recessions.

Figures 4b and 4d show that other GNP measures—gross domestic product (GNP adjusted for foreign earnings of multinational companies), command GNP (GNP modified by the import deflator to deflate the net export component), and GNP less the statistical discrepancy—are not significantly different from those of real GNP. They indicate that the differences are typically less than 0.5 of a percentage point. There were only a few instances when they differed by 1 to 1.5 percentage points. In expansions, these were GNP minus the statistical discrepancy in 1945–48, command GNP in 1954–57, and gross domestic product and command GNP in 1975–80. In recessions, they were GNP minus the statistical discrepancy in 1949 and command GNP in 1974–75.

These differences reflect the working off of "unplanned" inventory accumulations in recessions due to the unexpected decline in sales from the previous expansion. During expansions inventories are replenished, although usually at a slower rate than sales; but as the expansion matures and sales begin to slow down, inventories are likely to become higher than businesses wish to maintain for normal sales and production levels.

This pattern points up the importance of watching final sales during an expansion. When final sales slow down, businesses are likely to retrench from ordering new goods. Even though the greatest impact of excessive inventories occurs mainly in recessions, the problem emerges in the latter part of expansions when sales become sluggish and retailers and manufacturers cut back on orders. Thus, the challenge is recognizing the emerging inventory excess.

Inventory shortages may also affect the rate of growth. Sometimes during expansions when businesses can use more goods than their suppliers can furnish because the demand exceeds the suppliers' productive capacity, inventory shortages may temporarily reduce the rate of growth; however, unless the shortages are severe enough to cause much higher prices (as in the case of some raw materials in 1973), they do not have the significant cyclical impact that excessive inventories do.

Although inventories are only one element of business cycles, better inventory planning probably could moderate the steepness and duration of recessions. Recent reports in the press have indicated that businesses are deliberately working with smaller inventories. But statistical evidence of a tendency to hold lower inventories only appears in 1983 to 1985, and it is unclear whether this modest reduction is a trend. As seen in Figure 5, ratios of nonfarm inventories to final sales in constant dollars (the number of months inventories would last at current sales rates) since the 1950s indicate that inventories in relation to sales have often been lower than in recent years. Observation of future patterns is needed to assess the magnitude of the reported tendency of business to work with leaner inventories.

In addition to the long-standing volatility of inventories, an important factor affecting GNP movements in recent years has been the greater inroads made by

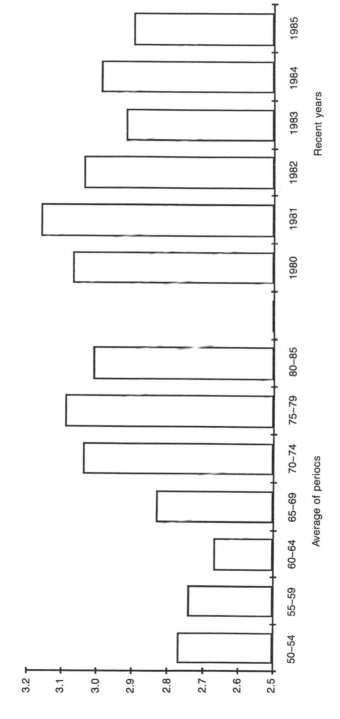

Figure 5. **Turnover of Nonfarm Inventories: Inventory/Final Sales Ratio**

Months of inventories at current sales rates

Average of periods

Recent years

*Note:* Based on Bureau of Economic Analysis data. All figures are for the fourth quarter of the year in 1982 dollars.

foreign goods in U.S. markets. This is apparent in the domestic demand concept of final sales to domestic purchasers. In the 1981–82 recession, this measure declined by 1.1 percent, noticeably less than the declines of 2.0 percent in final sales and 3.4 percent in GNP. In the subsequent expansion starting in 1982:4 and continuing as of 1986:3, final sales to domestic purchasers increased by 5.6 percentage points more than final sales and 4.9 percentage points more than GNP. Thus, underlying *domestic* demand in the 1980s gives a somewhat stronger picture of the U.S. economy than does the conventional GNP treatment of the foreign sector. This is discussed further in the section on exports and imports.

These similarities between real GNP and the alternative summary measures (other than final sales and final sales to domestic purchasers) tend to confirm the GNP movements over the complete business cycle, although for shorter periods the other measures sometimes give a slightly different picture, which bears watching. The typical pattern prevailed in the slowdown from 1984:3 to 1986:3, when real GNP increased at an annual rate of 2.5 percent, compared with an annual 5.9 percent increase in the first part of the expansion from 1982:4 to 1984:2. Except for final sales and final sales to domestic purchasers, which rose at annual rates of 3.3 and 4.1 percent respectively during the slowdown, the other summary GNP measures were practically the same as real GNP. *Thus, the foreign sector accounted for 0.8 of a percentage point (4.1–3.3) of the slowdown in the economic growth rate, a significant amount although perhaps less than would be expected from the publicity given to the adverse effect of the high value of the dollar on exports and imports.*

A footnote on the gross domestic product is that it is most relevant for countries in which foreign investments (by the home country abroad and by foreigners in the home country) are a major factor in the nation's economy. While foreign investments are important in certain industries in the United States, overall they don't have a dominating role. However, two factors—a belief by American and foreign business that the dollar remains substantially overvalued compared to other nations' currencies, and/or the continuance of worldwide tariffs and other import barriers—will encourage both American investments abroad, in order to be more competitive in export markets, and foreign investments in the United States. In this scenario, the cumulative effect of these foreign investments could raise the importance of the gross domestic product as an alternative indicator to the GNP.

## CONSUMER EXPENDITURES

In simple terms, the ultimate purpose of economic activity is to provide for the needs of the population at as high a level as possible, and consumer purchases of goods and services are the most direct measure of living conditions. Among the main GNP components, consumer spending is the largest. This spending by households for necessities and luxuries typically ranges from 62 to 65 percent of the GNP; in 1985, such expenditures accounted for 65 percent of the GNP. In addition to this prominent share of the overall economy, consumer spending has an important indirect effect on the demand for investment in plant and equipment. Because consumers are the ultimate users of most of the goods and services provided by business, the growth in consumer spending leads to outlays for modernizing and expanding plant and equipment.

The cycles of consumer spending are not as extreme as those of the GNP as a whole, particularly during recessions. For example, as indicated in Figures 6a and 6b, in five of the eight recessions since World War II, consumer spending rose while real GNP declined. Consumer spending declined by smaller amounts than the GNP in the other three recessions; in two of them (1957–58 and 1974–75) the consumer spending decline was under 1 percent and the differential with GNP was substantial. During the nine postwar expansions, consumer spending increased less rapidly than the real GNP in seven cases. In these instances the differentials were at most 2 percentage points, except for the 1949–53 expansion, which had a large increase in government spending for the Korean War. In only two postwar expansions did consumer spending increase faster than the GNP: in 1945–48, government spending dropped precipitously because of the military retrenchment following the war resulting in a decline in the GNP, and in 1954–57 the differential was 2 percentage points. Generally, the differential movements between consumer spending and GNP are more noticeable during recessions than in expansions. *In view of these less extreme cyclical movments and the overall importance of consumer spending, the analyst when monitoring economic trends should closely observe consumer spending as a major item both for maintaining growth during expansions and for moderating the decline in recessions.*

## *Consumer Spending Components— Volatility of Durable Goods*

Consumer expenditures comprise three broad categories: durable goods, nondurable goods, and services. Durable goods are items intended to last three or more years, such as cars, furniture and household appliances. Nondurable goods last less than three years, such as food, clothing and gasoline. Services are noncommodity items such as housing rent (including both tenant rentals and nonmarket imputed rent for owner-occupied housing,)[4] utilities, public transportation, private education and medical care, and recreation.

These main categories of consumer spending have noticeably different cyclical and longer-term movements. Durable goods account for the smallest share of consumer outlays, ranging from 12 to 15 percent of the total. But because of the longer life of these items, it is easier for households to defer purchasing them when economic conditions, such as unemployment or inflation, are adverse. Thus, while spending for durable goods is much smaller than that for nondurables and services, durable goods outlays are far more volatile over the business cycle.

Figure 6a. **Business Cycle Movements of Real GNP and Consumer Expenditures: Expansions**

Percent change

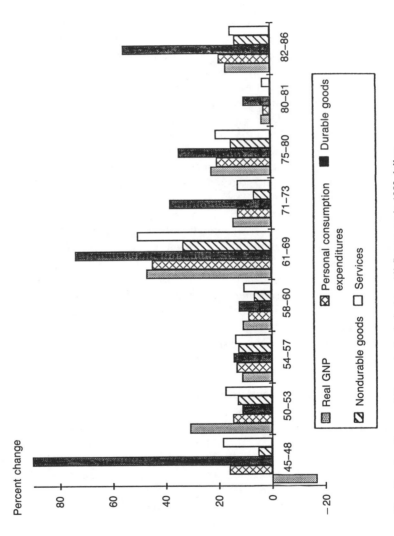

*Note*: Based on Bureau of Economic Analysis data. All figures are in 1982 dollars.

Figure 6b. **Business Cycle Movements of Real GNP and Consumer Expenditures: Recessions**

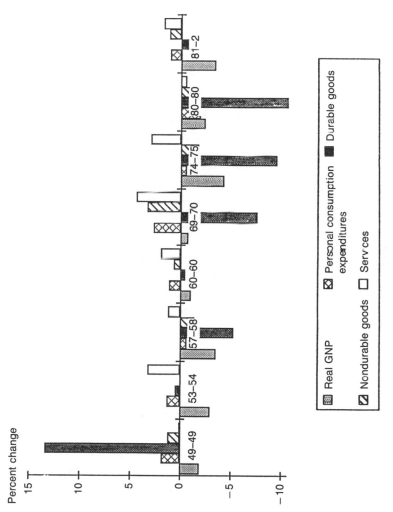

*Note:* Based on Bureau of Economic Analysis data. All figures are in 1982 dollars.

Figures 6a and 6b indicate this volatility in both the expansion and recession phases of the business cycle. In eight of the nine expansions, durable goods spending increased more than did spending for nondurables and services. The differentials between durables and the other categories are also substantially larger starting in the 1960s, with durables increasing two to four times faster than nondurables and services during these more recent expansions. As for recessions, durable goods spending declined in every postwar downturn except 1949, nondurable goods purchases declined in four of the eight recessions, and purchases of services increased in all recessions except 1980. In cases when both durable and nondurable goods spending declined, the durable goods decline was much steeper. For example, in the 1974–75 recession, durable goods declined by 9.5 percent compared with 2 percent for nondurables, and in the 1980 recession, the durable and nondurable declines were 11 and 1 percent respectively.

The tendency for consumer spending to be consistently less cyclical than the rest of the GNP results from two offsetting patterns: (a) the long-term shift from nondurables to the more cyclically insulated services (from 1948 to 1985, nondurable goods dropped from 55 to 35 percent of all consumer spending, while services increased from 32 to 51 percent), and (b) the increasing volatility in durable goods spending since the 1960s. *However, although these patterns were offsetting in the past, they may ot be so in the future, particularly if there is a slowdown or end to the shift to services. Thus, the analyst should monitor these components to determine if a change is occurring in the less cyclical nature of consumer spending.*

## Key Factors Affecting Consumer Spending

Consumer decisions to spend are affected by two broad considerations. One is the macroeconomic environment of employment and inflation; the other is the individual consumer's purchasing power as reflected in household income, loans, and existing savings and other wealth.

### Macroeconomic Environment

Employment and price trends weigh heavily in the timing and types of consumer spending. Households in which the primary worker or workers are currently employed with little likelihood of being unemployed are among the best candidates to spend in the near future, both for necessities and deferrable items. By contrast, households in which workers are employed but expect to be unemployed, or in which they are unemployed with low expectations of finding a job, are likely to curtail spending sharply for deferrable items such as a new car, clothing or recreation while maintaining or reducing somewhat outlays for necessities. These households are far more constrained, both by a currently limited income and by the need to save money for future spending, than are households with more secure job situations.

Consumer spending decisions are also affected by current and anticipated inflation. Ideally, consumers time their purchases to buy at the lowest price. For deferrable items, if prices are rising rapidly and inflation is expected to continue at a high rate, consumers are likely to feel it is better to buy immediately. If prices are rising now but are expected to decline within a certain period, consumers may defer some purchases. In addition to affecting timing, prices can also affect the overall amount of spending depending on relative prices between necessities and deferrable items. For example, a sharp rise in gasoline prices may curtail spending for other items. Or if deferrable items (say, television sets) drop sharply in price, spending for these items may increase.

Two private organizations conduct surveys to track the combined effects of these employment and inflation factors on consumer attitudes toward spending: the University of Michigan's Survey Research Center publishes an "index of consumer sentiment," and The Conference Board publishes a "consumer confidence index." These indexes have been advance indicators of the turning points of business cycles, turning down before a general recession sets in and turning up before a general recovery begins. However, as in the case of all such indexes giving advance signals, they should be viewed as giving general notions of future trends rather than specific forecasts, since their timing varies from cycle to cycle and they sometimes give false signals (see Chapter 8 on leading and lagging indexes) *These indexes provide the basic information on the macro environmental influences on consumers' spending decisions, but in using them for specific situations, the analyst should examine how well they performed in predicting consumer spending in the most recent six to twelve months.*

### Consumer Purchasing Power

Consumer purchasing power refers to consumers' capability to finance spending. It encompasses personal income from wages and all other sources, consumer installment credit loans, existing household savings in bank deposits, financial assets (money market accounts, stocks and bonds, etc.), and less liquid assets (such as real estate). All of these sources may be used to finance current consumer spending and repay consumer debt, by liquidating savings and other assets or by using these assets as collateral for further loans. Because the end result of using all these financing sources is reflected in personal income, spending, and saving, this discussion and the following section on personal saving integrate them in the framework of personal income and saving.

*Personal income* is primarily income received by households, before the payment of income taxes, from wages and fringe benefits, profits from self-employment, rent, interest, dividends, Social Security benefits, unemployment insurance, food stamps, and other income maintenance programs. (Social security taxes paid by employees and employers are excluded from personal income.) It also includes investment income of life insurance companies, noninsured pension funds, private nonprofit organizations, and trust funds, which in recent years have accounted for 3 percent of personal income.

Personal income is dominated by wages and fringe benefits (these represented 65 percent of personal income in 1985). It thus increases steadily during expansions and times of rising employment, but increases more slowly or declines in recessions. Figures 7a and 7b show that the less extreme cyclical movement of personal income compared with the GNP is most apparent in recessions. This stabilizing effect of unemployment insurance occurs even though the benefit payments to unemployed workers account for a relatively small share of personal income. For example, in the 1981–82 recession, unemployment insurance rose from $15 billion in the third quarter of 1981 to $26 billion in the third quarter of 1982, or from 0.6 to 1 percent of personal income in those periods (in the fourth quarter of 1982, when the real GNP turned up, unemployment insurance rose to its peak of $32 billion or 1.2 percent of personal income). Yet these relatively small shares were enough to soften the decline in the real GNP during the recession of 3.4 percent to a decline in real personal income of 0.9 percent.

An important factor influencing the availability of personal income for spending is taxation. The measure of after-tax income is *disposable* personal income, which is income after the payment of income, estate and gift taxes, and miscellaneous fines and penalty taxes (as noted, Social Security taxes paid by the employee and employer are excluded from personal income). It thus represents the actual purchasing power available to consumers from current income. These taxes (which exclude sales and property taxes) are dominated by income taxes; for example, federal, state, and local income taxes in 1985 were 84 percent of all personal taxes collected by all three levels of government, while federal income taxes accounted for 70 percent of all personal taxes. All told, the personal taxes of $487 billion in 1985 were 15 percent of the $3.3 trillion personal income. Theoretically, disposable personal income is more stable than income before taxes because of the progressive income tax (a main attribute of federal income taxes). Under the progressive income tax, higher proportions of income are paid as taxes as income increases; conversely, as income declines, relatively lower proportions are paid in taxes. This progressivity should result in less income after taxes being available during expansions and more being available during recessions, thus tending to restrain income and spending growth during expansions so as to moderate economic growth and inflation, and to shore up income and spending during recessions so as to stimulate growth and employment.

The conceptual greater cyclical stability of disposable personal income compared with personal income is borne out in practice. Figure 7a indicates that in seven of the nine postwar expansions, real disposable personal income increased relatively less than personal income. The two exceptions are the 1945–48 and the 1982–86 expansions. In 1945–48, the sharp drop in defense spending caused a decline in personal income, but the concomitant reduction in

Figures 7a. **Business Cycle Movements of Real GNP, Personal Income, and Disposable Personal Income: Expansions**

Percent change

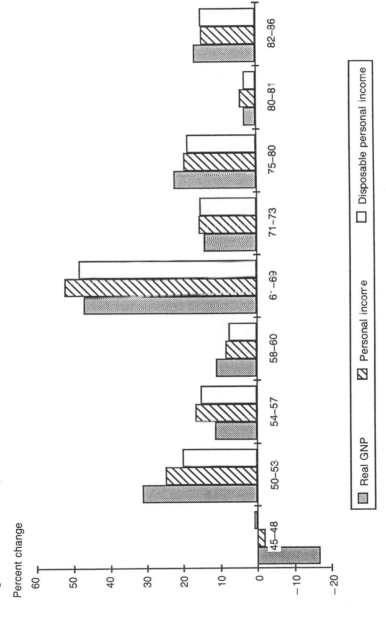

*Note:* Based on Bureau of Economic Analysis data. All figures are in 1982 dollars.

Figure 7b. **Business Cycle Movements of Real GNP, Personal Income, and Disposable Pesonal Income: Recessions**

Percent change

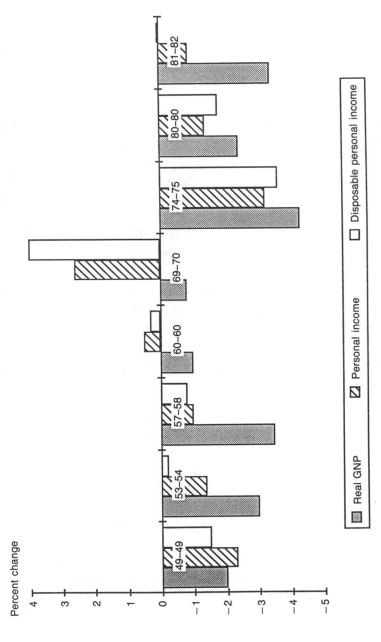

*Note:* Based on Bureau of Economic Analysis data. All figures are in 1982 dollars.

tax rates led to an increase in disposable income. In 1982–86, the slightly greater increase in disposable income is attributable to the reduction in income tax rates and the slowdown in inflation (which reduced income tax "bracket creep").

During recessions, income showed less extreme cyclical movements than personal income in six of the eight cases (Figure 7b). Disposable income declined less than personal income in four of the eight downturns; in one recession, disposable income increased more than personal income, and in another, disposable income was unchanged while personal income declined. In two cases when disposable income fell more than personal income, the recessions of 1973–75 and 1980, the greater fall in disposable income probably was due to the high inflation of those periods; by pushing individual incomes into higher tax brackets, inflation more than offset the falling incomes from higher unemployment.

The Economic Recovery Tax Act of 1981 contains a provision to index personal income taxes for inflation. This provision first went into effect for 1985 incomes, and is likely to have further effects on the cyclical behavior of after-tax income. The indexing provision limits the extent to which wage increases lift individuals into higher tax brackets. The higher tax bracket will only apply when, after deducting wage increases equivalent to the percent increase in inflation according to the consumer price index, the remaining increase in income is sufficient to put the individual in the higher bracket. For recessions accompanied by high inflation, the indexing probably will prevent disposable income from declining more than personal income, such as occurred in the 1974–75 and 1980 downturns; this will increase the likelihood that disposable income will cushion the decline in consumer purchasing power in recessions. On the other hand, during expansions the indexing is likely to lessen the differential growth rates between personal and disposable income, thus decreasing the inflation-related stabilizing effect of progressive income taxes on consumer purchasing power during upturns.

To recapitulate, the major factor in stabilizing personal income during business cycles is the increase in unemployment benefits during recessions. The federal income tax system also gives some stability to disposable income, particularly during recessions. The indexing of income taxes for inflation starting with 1985 incomes probably will have different effects on this stabilizing property of income taxes, enhancing it during recessions and lessening it during expansions, thus modifying effects of the tax laws that existed before indexing began. Any subsequent major changes in federal tax laws, such as tax reform or actions to reduce the budget deficit, could have still different stabilizing or destabilizing features for macroeconomic policy. *In assessing future trends in disposable personal income, the analyst should allow for the effect of inflation indexing on after tax income as well as any new tax legislation that could affect trends in disposable income over the business cycle.*

### Personal Saving

Personal saving is what is left of disposable income after all personal outlays. Personal outlays are mainly composed of consumer spending for goods and services (96.9 percent in 1985), but also include interest on loans paid by consumers to business (3.1 percent) and net personal payments by U.S. households to foreigners (less than 0.1 percent). Because personal outlays are financed by personal income plus other sources of consumer purchasing power available from installment credit, existing savings, and loans obtained on real estate and other financial assets, personal saving is affected by the use of credit, existing savings, and sale of existing assets as well as by current personal income. For items bought on credit, their total value is included as spending when the purchase is made; and in later periods, repayments of the principal of the loan are included as saving. In addition, while personal outlays exclude household purchases of homes and investments such as stocks, bonds, money market instruments, and real estate, personal saving includes the equity in these housing and investment transactions if they are financed from current income. However, these items are not included in saving to the extent that they are financed by selling homes or other assets to other households or by interpersonal gifts (e.g., from parents to children).

The saving rate measures actual saving as a percent of disposable personal income. Figure 8 shows that the saving rate fluctuated considerably over the postwar business cycles. The typical range was 5 to 8 percent, but it occasionally had more extreme lows of 3 to 4 percent and highs of 10 to 11 percent. The typical saving rate range of 5 to 8 percent results in substantially different rates of spending, depending on whether saving is at the lower or upper end of the range.[5] For example, in 1985 the saving rate was 5.1 percent and real consumer expenditures (consumer spending in constant dollars) increased by 3.5 percent. Assuming the same level of income and inflation, if the saving rate were 8 percent, real consumer spending would have increased by only 0.5 percent, thus resulting in a much lower rate of economic growth.

Intuitively, a low saving rate is associated with high spending, and high saving with with low spending. Thus, low saving would be expected during expansions and high saving during recessions, except for very deep recessions in which a precipitous drop in income results in small saving or even dissaving (by requiring the use of existing assets to maintain minimum living needs).

In practice, however, there is little difference in the average saving rate during expansions and recessions—6.8 percent in expansions and 7.0 percent in recessions. In addition, the movements have been quite volatile *within* the expansion and recession phases. *Thus, in projecting saving rates to anticipate consumer spending, the analyst should develop saving rates that appear appropriate for that phase of the cycle. These saving rates may be based on historical experience as*

Figure 8. **Personal Saving Rate**

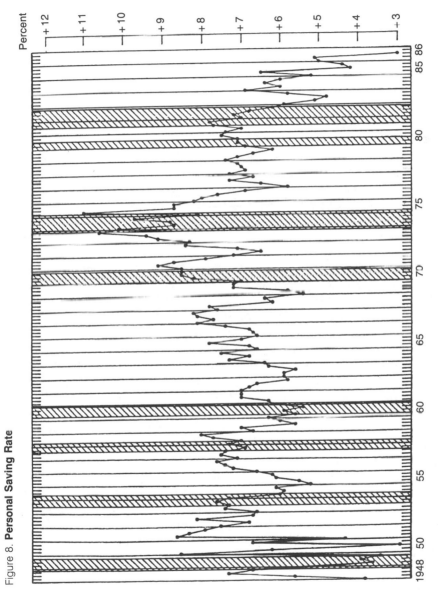

*Note:* Based on Bureau of Economic Analysis data. Lined bars are recession periods.

*well as current factors such as the tendency to use consumer installment credit or household assets to finance spending.*

### Consumer Installment Credit

Because of interest in the effect that the debt burden from existing consumer credit can have on consumer spending, this section focuses explicitly on consumer installment credit. Data on consumer installment credit provided by the Federal Reserve Board encompass loans to households by banks, credit companies and retail stores in which there is the option to repay in two or more monthly payments. Consumer installment credit includes credit for purchases of automobiles, the range of items available on credit cards, home improvements, mobile homes, and personal cash loans. It excludes home mortgages, but because of classification problems in the reporting from lending organizations, in practice the data include some consumer loans backed by housing equity as well as consumer loans used for business purposes. The extent of this inclusion is not known, but it is considered relatively small according to a 1985 Federal Reserve Board study.[6]

An overall measure of consumer debt burden is the proportion of consumer installment credit to personal income. As the proportion increases, it may be surmised that at some point, consumers will retrench in spending because of an unwillingness to take on additional debt and/or because lenders, noting the higher debt burdens and associated increase in loan defaults, will become stricter in extending credit to consumers. However, from postwar experience it is difficult to quantify at what point or range this takes place.

Figure 9 shows that consumer installment credit outstanding as a percent of personal income rose substantially over the postwar period, from 4 percent in 1948 to over 16 percent in mid–1986, with varying rates of growth and factors affecting the debt load over those 38 years.[7] Most of the rise occurred by the mid–1960s. The increase from 1948–65 resulted variously from the pent-up demands from World War II, growth of household formation, greater willingness of consumers and lenders to finance spending with credit, and a tendency to lengthen the period for repaying consumer loans.

Since the mid–1960s, there has been a slower and less consistent upward movement. For example, in the last half of the 1960s, which was associated with the substantial buildup of the Vietnam War, continuation of the expansion of the early 1960s, and the onset of more rapid inflation, the ratio declined; consumers may have felt it was desirable to build up their liquid assets of savings deposits and savings bonds (i.e., those assets that are readily transferrable into money without the loss of capital value). The opposite behavior occurrred in the expansion of the late 1970s when inflation was very high (the consumer price index rose 9 percent in 1978 and over 13 percent in 1979): consumers increased their debt burden to 14 percent in 1979 (the pre-1986 peak). This increase reflected the

59

Figure 9. **Consumer Installment Credit as a Percent of Personal Income**

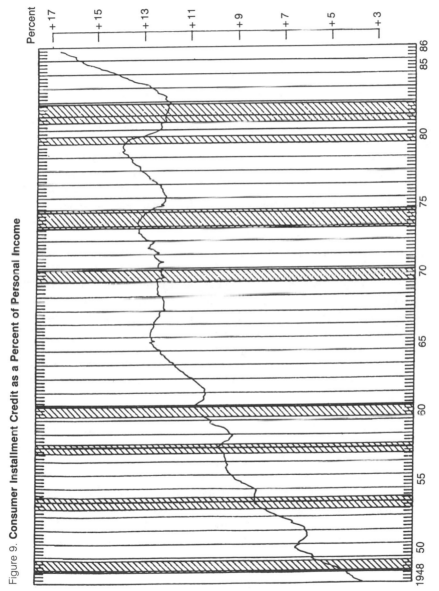

*Note*: Based on Bureau of Economic Analysis data. Lined bars are recession periods.

inflationary expectations of the time, as concern that prices would continue to rise rapidly caused consumers to increase their current purchases to avoid buying at much higher future prices. The data in this period even understated the credit expansion, as the sharp rise in housing prices led to the additional use of mortgage credit to finance consumer purchases, but as noted previously, mortgages are not included in the consumer credit data.[8]

Subsequently, the debt burden ratio declined from 1980–82, which included two recessions and one very limited expansion. As of mid–1986, the ratio had been rising rapidly since the recovery from the previous recession began in late 1982.

The ratio of consumer credit to personal income is classified as one of the major lagging indicators, turning down after a general recession sets in and up after a general recovery begins (see Chapter 8). Yet a review of the postwar trends makes it difficult to establish if there is some point where the debt burden becomes excessive. The problem is partly the nature of the consumer credit data, which are limited to the total amount of credit for all persons but do not distinguish the amount of credit for persons in different income categories where differential debt burdens could be significant.

From the lender's viewpoint, of course, a main factor in determining whether to make a consumer loan is the creditworthiness of the borrower. Information on the overall risk of nonpayment of existing consumer loans is available in the data on delinquency rates for consumer loans. The delinquency rate is the percent of consumer loans, held by banks, that have delinquent payments of 30 days or more. The delinquency rate is a leading indicator in that it turns down before a general recession begins and turns up before the subsequent recovery, and is charted monthly in *Business Conditions Digest*. However, the delinquency rate is quite volatile, and thus it is often difficult to establish the directional trend of a current period.

*Determining when debt burden (consumer installment credit as a percent of personal income) appears excessive, and thus is likely to lead to a slowdown or retrenchment of loans and consumer spending, is very difficult. In making these assessments, the analyst should focus on the debt burden ratio in expansions as it approaches or exceeds previous high rates. This is a frame of reference for analyzing underlying demand factors for loans such as household formation, inflation, and the availability of new credit instruments. In turn, these demand factors should be compared with trends in the delinquency rate in the repayment of existing loans which determines the overall risk of extending new loans from the viewpoint of the lender.*

## PRIVATE INVESTMENT

Of all GNP components, private investment expenditures for business plant and equipment, residential construction, and inventory change have the most extreme cyclical movements. Private investment increases more in expansions and decreases more in recessions than other GNP components. This volatility is the main factor causing cyclical fluctuations in overall economic activity.

This section focuses on plant and equipment investment and residential construction; inventory change was discussed in the comparison of real GNP and final sales movements.

## *Plant and Equipment*

Business investment in plant and equipment provides the industrial capacity to produce goods and services for household, business, government and export markets. It covers all construction (building and nonbuilding), machinery, and other capital equipment used to expand, replace, and modernize capital facilities, as well as first-time investments in new businesses. It encompasses capital spending in all private profit and nonprofit organizations, nonfarm and farm. Plant investment includes factory, office, retail, and warehouse buildings, electric-power and telephone-transmission structures, and oil- and gas-well drilling; machine tools, trucks, computers, and office furniture are examples of equipment. Investment expenditures are depreciated over the life span of each item and thus become an annual cost of production, which appears as depreciation allowances in business income tax returns. Plant and equipment investment is referred to as "nonresidential fixed investment" in the GNP, with separate catagories for plant (structures) and equipment.

The long-term share of plant and equipment investment in the GNP during 1950–85 rose gradually from an average of 9.6 percent in the 1950s to 11.4 percent in the first half of the 1980s. This increase was most pronounced in the 1970s and 1980s, when as previously noted, the overall GNP growth rate slowed from its pace in the 1960s. Thus, at the economy-wide level, slower economic growth did not disproportionately affect plant and equipment investment; in fact, the rate of mechanization continued to increase.

Figures 10a and 10b show the postwar cyclical movements of real GNP and plant and equipment investment. These indicate that plant and equipment spending increased more than the GNP in seven of the nine expansions, and declined more than the GNP in seven of the eight recessions. The differential movements between plant and equipment and GNP were substantial. In expansions, plant and equipment outlays typically increase 60 to 75 percent faster than GNP, an exception being the 1980–81 expansion, when the differential was 135 percent. In recessions, plant and equipment investment most commonly fell by two to three times the rate of decline in the GNP, the notable exceptions being the still greater decline of plant and equipment investment in the 1949 and 1969–70 recessions. Clearly, while the long-term average trend of plant and equipment investment relative to GNP has been rising, plant and equipment has shown considerable cyclical fluctuation.

Figure 10a. **Business Cycle Movements of Real GNP and Private Nonresidential Fixed Investment: Expansions**

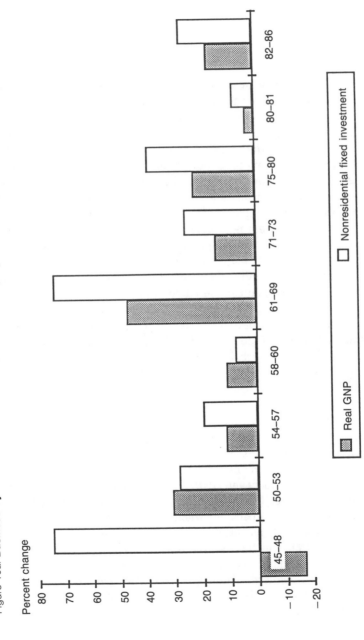

*Note:* Based on Bureau of Economic Analysis data. All figures are in 1982 dollars.

Figure 10b. **Business Cycle Movements of Real GNP and Private Nonresidential Fixed Investment: Recessions**

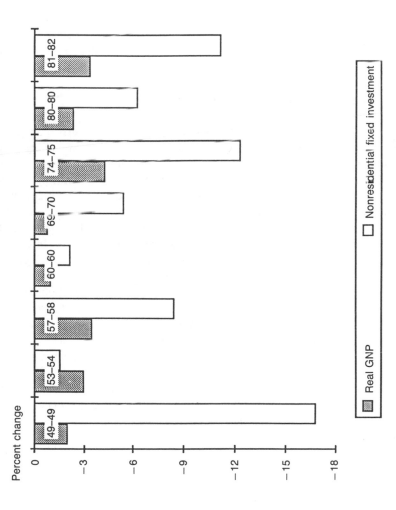

*Note*: Based on Bureau of Economic Analysis data. All figures are in 1982 dollars.

The sharp cyclical patterns arise from the fact that such investment is deferrable, and from the difficulty of anticipating demand for the goods and services produced with these capital facilities. Investment is deferrable because businesses often can "make do" with existing facilities, although doing so may result in profits below their potential: the facilities are less efficient than more modern technology would allow and are unable to meet sudden surges in demand. The difficulty of anticipating demand results in waves of optimism and pessimism, which in turn lead to substantial additions of capital facilities during expansions, only to be followed by overcapacity in recessions and accompanying deep cutbacks in investment outlays.

In addition to these cyclical movements, plant and equipment investment is a major factor affecting long-term productivity improvements, which in turn affect living conditions and inflation over time. (Productivity is discussed in Chapter 5.)

### Profits and Plant and Equipment Investment

Because the basic purpose of business is to make a profit, current and anticipated profits are the main factors determining the pace of plant and equipment investment. Anticipated profits are the incentive to invest in capital facilities, while past and current profits are an important source of funds for the investment.

Profits are sales less costs. They reflect both the demand for a company's products and its ability to meet the demand at efficient costs. If profits are rising, business tends to be optimistic that markets for its products will be growing; it is thus encouraged to invest in new facilities to meet those markets. In contrast, during periods of declining profits and shrinking markets there is little urgency to expand productive capacity, and more of the new investment is limited to replacing and modernizing existing facilities in order to lower production costs.

Profits provide financing for plant and equipment investment in two ways. First, as internally generated funds from company operations, profits provide money to buy the capital facilities. Second, a business' profits are a key factor for lenders' and investors' decisions to provide external funds through bank loans, debt instruments (e.g., bonds), and equity capital (e.g. stock).

Like spending for plant and equipment, business profits show more extreme cyclical movements than the overall economy. The similar although not identical cyclical patterns of investment and profits are consistent with their strong theoretical relationship.

Business profits as reported in the national accounts are the combined income of corporations and unincorporated business (proprietors' income) before the payment of income taxes and including the adjustments for inventory valuation and capital consumption. Figures 11a and 11b show the patterns of business profits and national income (employee compensation, rental income, proprietors' income, corporate profits and net interest) over the postwar business cycles in

Figure 11a. **Business Cycle Movements of National Income and Business Profits: Expansions**

Percent change

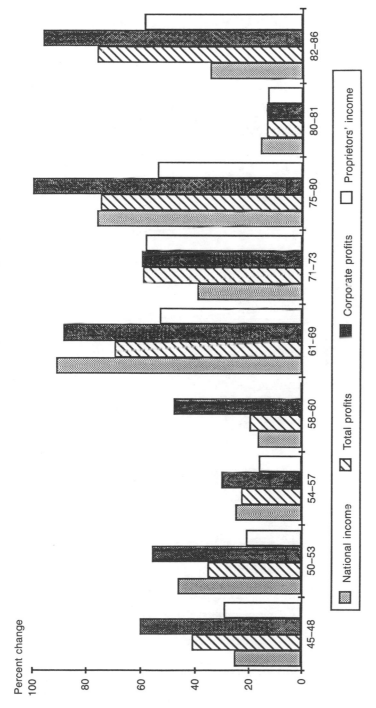

*Note:* Based on Bureau of Economic Analysis data. All figures are in current dollars.

66

Figure 11b. **Business Cycle Movements of National Income and Business Profits: Recessions**

Percent change

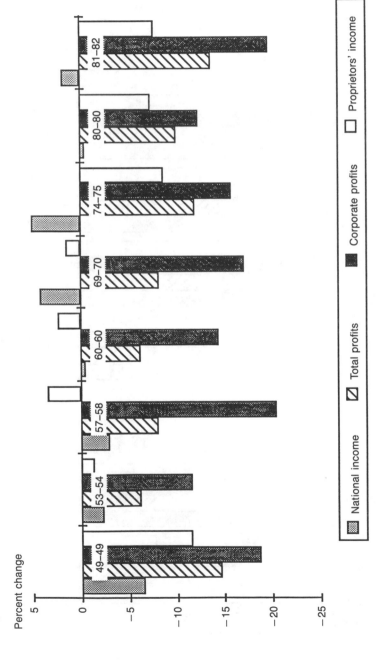

*Note:* Based on Bureau of Economic Analysis data. All figures are in current dollars.

current dollars (see footnote 23 for use of national income rather than GNP). Business profits increased more than national income in only four of the nine expansions. Profits decreased more than national income in all eight of the postwar downturns (national income increased in three recessions). The differential movements between profits and national income were much larger in recessions than in expansions—profits fell by several multiples more than national income in recessions, while profits increased more than national income by less than one multiple in expansions (except for 1982–86, when profits rose at more than twice the rate of national income).

These differential patterns are associated with the long-term decline in profits as a proportion of national income, from 31 percent in 1950 to 17 percent in 1985; in the 1980s, this share fluctuated in a range of 13 to 17 percent. In relation to other components of the national income, most of the decline in profits is related to increasing shares of employee compensation (primarily from the rapidly growing fringe benefits, as distinct from money wages) through the 1960s, and of interest in the 1970s and 1980s. The long-term relative decline in profits is difficult to explain, other than to state that business as a whole did not pass along costs into higher prices sufficiently to maintain profit margins, apparently because demand for its goods and services was not considered strong enough to sustain the higher prices. Explanations such as that profits in the earlier years were too high or that business feared government antitrust actions or price controls if prices were increased to maintain the earlier profit margins, are difficult to substantiate.

However, as discussed in the following section on depreciation, the long-term relative decline in profits is not apparent when depreciation allowances on existing plant and equipment investment are added to profits. Because of the close relationship between profits and depreciation allowances, it is more useful to consider the effects of both in assessing long-run incentives for plant and equipment investment.

### Impact of Taxes and Depreciation on Investment

Funding for plant and equipment investment is available from profits and depreciation allowances generated by company sales and investments (internal sources), and from outside lenders and investors (external sources). Because internally generated funds are the basis of a company's economic well-being, as well as the underlying incentive for lenders and investors to provide external funds, this discussion concentrates on internal funding.

Profits after business income taxes and depreciation allowances on existing plant and equipment make up the funds available from internal sources for distribution to owners of the company and for further spending on plant and equipment investment, inventories and other operational needs. This internal funding is called cash flow; a refined version referring to corporations is "current production cash flow," which is undistributed profits (profits after the payment of income taxes and distributions of dividends to owners) plus depreciation allowances, including inventory valuation and capital consumption adjustments.

Depreciation allowances for the wear and tear and obsolescence of plant and equipment are deducted as a cost in figuring how much is due in business income taxes.[9] Depreciation increases steadily over the years, even in recessions, because it reflects the *cumulative* investments of previous periods—a gradually increasing total, regardless of whether all of the facilities are used in a particular period. Since depreciation also accounts for the preponderant share of cash flow (71 percent of corporate current production cash flow in 1985), the cyclical movements of cash flow are less extreme than those for profits. For example, during the 1981–82 recession, undistributed corporate profits declined by 46 percent while current production cash flow *increased* by 1 percent; and in the expansion during 1982–86, undistributed profits increased by 367 percent compared with a cash flow increase of 50 percent. Thus, in addition to providing funds for the long-term replacement of older capital facilities, depreciation allowances are a particularly important source of financing for plant and equipment investment in recessions.

Since World War II, corporate current production cash flow as a share of GNP has fluctuated in a narrow range of 7 to 9 percent. This stability resulted from offsetting effects of the rising importance of depreciation allowances and the declining share of profits. The relative increase in depreciation is due to the increasingly faster write-offs of capital facilities allowed over the postwar period (until the slower write-offs adopted in the Tax Reform Act of 1986), and to the tendency for an increasing share of investment to be in shorter-lived equipment, which has faster write-offs than structures.

As noted in Part A of this chapter under "Valuation Adjustments for Inventories and Depreciation," an adjustment is made both for the difference between depreciation costs allowed to be deducted from income for the payment of taxes and the depreciation estimated as the economic life of the asset (which is longer than the tax life), and for the effect that changing prices of capital goods have on the cost of replacing plant and equipment. This capital consumption adjustment (CCAdj) has changed considerably in recent years, mainly as a result of the more rapid depreciation allowed in the Economic Recovery Tax Act of 1981, and to a very limited extent as a result of the slowdown in inflation. For example, the corporate capital consumption adjustment went from − $17 billion in 1980 to $58 billion in 1985, a shift of $75 billion over five years. Based on an income tax rate of 46 percent on corporate profits, corporations had $35 billion more available in purchasing power after the payment of income taxes in 1985, basically because of the faster depreciation. Thus, the CCAdj is an important factor in assessing the impact of tax laws and inflation on the financing capacity of business cash flow.

How has the business income tax cut resulting from faster depreciation write-offs of plant and equipment in the Economic Recovery Tax Act of 1981 as modified by the partial business tax increases in the Tax Equity and Fiscal Responsibility Act of 1982, affected plant and equipment investment? Studies have given conflicting results. An econometric macro analysis concluded that about 20 percent of the increase in spending for producers' durable equipment from 1982 (4th quarter) to 1984 (3rd quarter) resulted from the tax legislation of the early 1980s; the study also found that lower interest rates accounted for about 15 percent of the 1982–84 increase in investment, and that the remaining 55 percent was attributable to economic growth and all other factors.[10]

However, a micro analysis of the investment behavior from 1981 to 1983 of 238 nonfinancial corporations from a sample of the Fortune 500 and from other identifying information on large companies, concluded that there was no relationship between tax rates and plant and equipment investment.[11] In that study, the 50 lowest-taxed companies reduced their capital investment by 22 percent, while the 50 highest-taxed companies increased their investment by 33 percent from 1981 to 1983. The study also indicated that lower-taxed companies increased dividends more than higher-taxed companies, an indication that tax reductions were used more for investor income than for plowing back into plant and equipment investment.

Another study of the effect of the business tax cuts on the components of plant and equipment investment concluded there was no relation between the size of the tax cuts and investment in particular items.[12] Thus, while 93 percent of the increase in equipment investment from 1979 to 1984 was in office equipment and business automobiles, the 1981 tax laws increased the tax rate on computers (office equipment), and decreased only slightly the taxes on automobiles. In the case of plant, moreover, while commercial buildings (offices, stores, warehouses) were given the same tax cuts as industrial buildings (factories), spending from 1979 to 1984 increased for commercial buildings and decreased for industrial buildings. The study indicated that in assessing the effect of costs on investment, the tax cuts were outweighed by several factors: the relative decline in capital goods prices compared with other prices, returns on alternative investments (opportunity costs), and differences in the resale value of particular assets (for example, the greater resale value of commercial buildings than industrial buildings).

On balance, although their conclusions on the importance of tax cuts vary significantly, these studies of tax incentives in the first half of the 1980s indicate that taxes are a secondary factor driving plant and equipment investment. Generally, the macro assessment suggested that the tax cuts had a greater effect on investment than the micro and detailed component analyses.

*In assessing business profits for their relation to plant and equipment investment, the analyst should consider any substantial shifts in business income tax laws for their effect on plant and equipment investment. While taxes do not appear to be a major factor affecting capital investment, they may influence particular types of investment in certain periods.*

### Future Indicators of Investment Spending

In contrast to the effects of the underlying factors—economic growth, profits, and cash flow—on plant and equipment spending, other economic indicators focus on actions taken by business early in the investment process. This section notes the main characteristics of these indicators and gives guidelines for monitoring their movements for clues to future investment trends. They are discussed in the sequence they have in the investment process: capital appropriations for investment spending, nonresidential construction contracts and capital goods orders, and projections of plant and equipment spending.

CAPITAL APPROPRIATIONS FOR MANUFACTURING INVESTMENT: In large companies, intentions to invest in plant and equipment become more specific when capital budget funds are appropriated. Capital appropriations are the *earliest* indicator of business sentiment for future capital spending.

The Conference Board provides the only regularly reported information on companies' capital appropriations. It obtains quarterly survey data from the nation's 1,000 largest manufacturing corporations, which had approximately 75 percent of all manufacturing corporations' assets in 1979. In recent years, investment by all manufacturing companies accounted for close to 40 percent of plant and equipment spending in all nonfarm industries. Thus, capital appropriations by the companies surveyed represent about 30 percent of all private nonfarm capital investment spending. The capital appropriations data are available about two months after the quarter in which the decision to appropriate the funds was made.

Capital appropriations pay for all or part of an investment project, but they do not indicate when the spending will occur. They are not necessarily commitments for actual spending, as they can be deferred or cancelled depending on business conditions and perceptions of the future; in addition, the spending patterns vary among individual projects depending on the lead times required for their completion. As a result, trends in appropriations reveal manufacturers' confidence in the growth prospects for their products, but they do not give estimates of planned spending over time.

There are two main series on appropriations, one on the backlog of cumulated appropriations from previous periods that have not yet been spent or cancelled, and the other on newly approved appropriations in the current quarter. The backlog is about six times larger than the new appropriations in constant dollars, and also has smoother trends than the short-term, up-and-down gyrations of the new appropriations. The backlog is the basic source of future spending. The new appropriations indicate the effect that the most recent patterns of business confidence (in terms of initiating new investment projects) have on increasing or lowering the backlog.

*The analyst should use the capital appropriations information as a qualitative indicator of manufacturers' intentions to invest in plant and equipment. Because some investment projects included in the appropriations data are postponed or cancelled, and others have long lead times, appropriations are best used as only one factor in assessing future trends in capital investment spending. Capital appropriations data are a guide to business perceptions of growth prospects in an important segment of the economy, but they cover only about 30 percent of all nonagricultural investment plant and equipment.*

CONTRACTS AND ORDERS FOR PLANT AND EQUIPMENT: The second stage in the investment process is the decision to start the acquisition of capital facilities. This results in the commitment of funds to begin work on the investment project, which in turn will result in spending (payments) for the work done. The commitment of funds in construction contracts and equipment orders is a firmer action than the appropriation of capital funds, as a construction contract or equipment order is subject to less chance of postponement or cancellation. Monthly data on the commitment of funds for plant are derived from contract award information on nonresidential construction of the McGraw-Hill Information Systems Company; monthly data on new equipment orders received by nondefense capital goods manufacturers are based on surveys by the Bureau of the Census in the U. S. Department of Commerce. The two series are shown separately and also are combined into one, in current and constant dollars, in *Business Conditions Digest*.

A few basic differences between the data on construction contracts and equipment orders on the one hand, and plant and equipment spending on the other, should be kept in mind. First, the contract and order information (as in the case of capital appropriations) are for part or all of an investment project, but they do not specify when the spending for the project will occur. This is particularly pertinent for large-scale projects with lead times of more than one year. Second, the order data do not give a precise coverage of equipment purchases by American business because the orders exclude U.S. imports of machinery and other capital goods that are part of investment spending, while they include U.S. exports that are not part of investment spending. Third, while the combined contract and order data in constant dollars are one of the major leading indicators of overall economic activity (see Chapter 8), they show sharp monthly movements and must be observed for about six-month periods to tell whether their direction is increasing, decreasing or level.

The data on construction contracts and equipment orders denote a key point in the investment process when financial commitments are made to proceed with plant and equipment projects. The data are a relatively reliable indicator of the willingness of business to proceed with capital investment projects. However, in using the data to anticipate the trend of plant and equipment spending, the analyst should treat them as broad orders of magnitude. They are limited by the absence of a time span over which the contracts and orders are spent, inconsistencies between plant and equipment spending for exports and imports, and month-to-month gyrations.

PROJECTIONS OF PLANT AND EQUIPMENT EXPENDITURES: Business spending for plant and equipment in the GNP, referred to as nonresidential fixed investment, is based on data from the Census Bureau's monthly surveys of the value of construction and manufacturers' shipments of equipment. It is analogous to, but not completely consistent with, investment data obtained from a quarterly survey by the Bureau of Economic Analysis of businesses' actual and planned expenditures on plant and equipment. Because the expenditure survey provides quarterly and one-year projections of plant and equipment outlays as well as actual spending in past periods, its data are particularly useful for anticipating investment trends. In studies over the past decade, the investment projections in this survey were found to be more accurate than those in similar surveys conducted in the private sector or in projections developed from large-scale econometric models.[13]

Differences between the GNP investment and the survey estimates for plant and equipment reflect variations in the industries covered and timing of the measures.[14] For example, farm investment and outlays for drilling oil and gas wells are both included in the GNP and excluded from the survey data; additionally, GNP measures investment as occurring when the construction work is done and when the manufacturer ships the equipment, while the survey measures investment as occurring when the payments are made for these purchases, which tends to be after the work is done.

Even when the two investment series are adjusted to make them comparable, their movements over time are not always consistent. For example, after the series were made conceptually comparable, GNP investment in 1982 increased by 4.6 percent while the survey investment increased by 5.6 percent; in 1983, GNP investment increased by 3.4 percent and survey investment *decreased* by 6.7 percent. Thus, the relationship of the series changed significantly between the two years. This pattern of year-to-year variability also occurred in previous years.

Using business investment plans, the plant and equipment survey makes projections of investment at various times during the year for one and two quarters ahead and for one year ahead.[15] Based on several years' experience in which the projections were systematically higher or lower than the actual figures, the survey data are adjusted to correct for systematic biases. Over 1955–83, the average difference between actual and projected spending, without regard to whether the projection was lower or higher than the actual, ranged from 2 to 3 percent. As expected, the projections are less accurate the further out they extend in time:

**Average Difference Between Actual and
Projected Plant and Equipment Investment**

| One quarter ahead: | 1.8% |
| Two quarters ahead: | 2.6% |
| One year ahead: | 3.0% |

The long-term averages also are indicative of the accuracy in any particular year, although occasionally the differential was substantially higher. For example, in the yearly projections, differences greater than 5 percent occurred only in 1958 and 1982.

*The survey of plant and equipment expenditure is a useful tool for projecting expected business investment outlays in the GNP, if it is tempered by other information on future investment, such as profits, capital appropriations, and nonresidential construction contracts and nondefense equipment orders. In translating the projected expenditures in the survey to the fixed investment component of the GNP, the analyst should allow for potential differential growth rates in the two series of about 10 percentage points. An allowance also should be made for inaccuracy in the survey projections of about 3 percent.*

## Residential Construction

The residential construction component of private investment covers the value of new construction of privately owned single-family and multifamily housing units, mobile homes, dormitories and other group quarters, as well as additions, alterations, and major replacements to them. Construction of new housing dominates the category of private residential fixed investment in the GNP (64 percent in 1985), which also includes real estate commissions on the sale of new and existing housing, furniture and other consumer durables provided in furnished apartments, and the net purchase of existing residential structures between the private and public sectors. After reviewing overall trends based on residential fixed investment, this section will focus on the construction of new housing units—single-family homes, apartments, and mobile homes.

Residential fixed investment has not grown as fast as the rest of the economy over the long run. For example, from 1950 to 1985, real GNP increased by 198 percent while residential investment increased by 104 percent. Thus, residential investment as a proportion of the GNP declined from 5 to 6 percent in the 1950s to 4 to 5 percent in the first half of the 1980s. This long-term relative decline reflects the slowdown in population growth, from increases of over 28 million in the 1950s, to about to 23 million in the 1970s, to a decade rate of 22 million in the first half of the 1980s.

Although the residential investment share of the GNP is small compared with other components, it has secondary and cyclical impacts that are not apparent from size alone. The secondary impacts result from the tendency for the purchase of a new home to generate additional spending on household appliances, furniture and other consumer durables. The cyclical impact has two aspects. In terms of timing, the number of housing starts, building permits issued by local governments for housing, and the value of residential fixed investment in constant dollars are all classified as leading indicators of the overall economy—turning up in a recession before the expansion begins and turning down in an expansion before a recession begins. However, in terms of the size of the increases and decreases in spending for residential fixed investment over the business cycle, there is no clear evidence that residential construction acts as a stabilizing or destabilizing factor on the overall economy. Figures 12a and 12b show that residential investment increased faster than real GNP in five of the nine postwar expansions, and decreased more than real GNP in four of the eight postwar recessions.

## Factors Affecting New Housing Demand

The market for new housing construction is driven by *long-term* national and geographic demographic trends and—to a much smaller extent—by the replacement of substandard housing and that destroyed by fire and flood. It is also driven by *short-term* cyclical movements of economic growth, personal income, and interest rates. These influences on the value of new construction, along with the effect of shifts in the average size and cost of housing units, are discussed below.

LONG-TERM FACTORS: The typical annual construction of new housing units (the number of single-family homes, townhouses and dwelling units in apartment buildings) has averaged about 1.5 million over the postwar period. It has generally ranged from 1.1 to 2 million (the peak was 2.4 million in 1972), but there is no long-term upward or downward trend in these data.

Future demographic trends are mainly determined by the age distribution of the existing population, birth rates, and migration from foreign countries. These in turn are affected by attitudes toward marriage and family size and by political conditions abroad.

The demand for new housing is mainly related to trends in the number of new households (a household includes a family, a single person living alone, or unrelated individuals sharing a house or apartment). Subsidiary factors affecting demand are the replacement of housing lost to demolition, fire, or flood, and the purchase of vacation and other second homes. Projections by the Joint Center for Urban Studies of MIT and Harvard University indicate an increase of 14 million households in the 1980s and 12 to 13 million in the 1990s. This projection reflects

Figure 12a. **Business Cycle Movements of Real GNP and Residential Fixed Investment: Expansions**

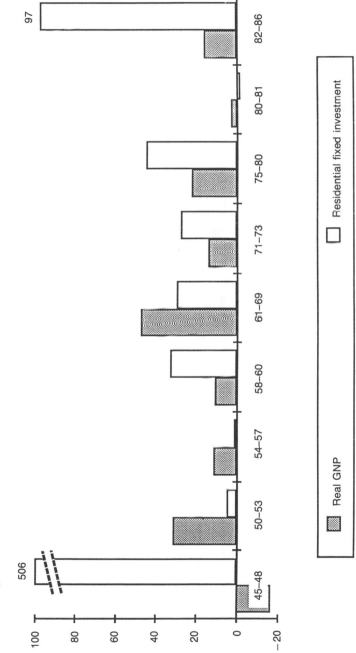

*Note:* Based on Bureau of Economic Analysis data. All figures are in 1982 dollars.

Figure 12b. **Business Cycle Movements of Real GNP and Residential Fixed Investment: Recessions**

Percent change

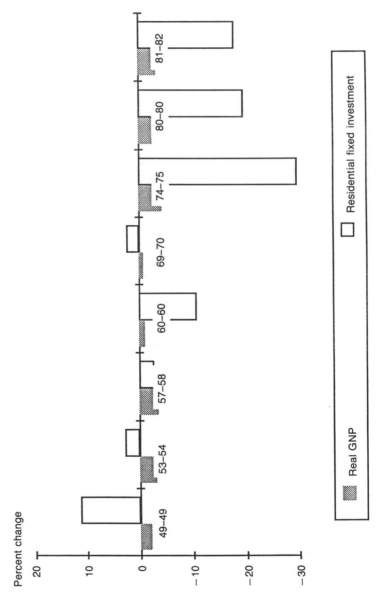

*Note:* Based on Bureau of Economic Analysis data. All figures are in 1982 dollars.

a continuing trend of lower increases since the 1970s, when the number of households increased by 17 million,[16] and is similar to the Census Bureau projections published in 1986. Based on these projections, no increase in the rate of new housing construction and purchases of mobile homes to accommodate new households would be expected over the next five to ten years. For example, the Joint Center for Urban Studies has forecast average annual construction of 1.5 million new housing units in the 1980s and 1.4 to 1.5 million units in the 1990s—down from 1.8 million in the 1970s—and annual purchases of 250,000-300,000 mobile homes in the 1980s and 1990s, similar to the trends in previous decades.[17] *These projections seem reasonable unless there are major, unanticipated geographic shifts of the population within the United States, or significant changes in the formation of new households, that stimulate housing construction independent of increases in the national population.*

Another long-term factor affecting housing demand is the replacement or rehabilitation of housing that has major structural, heating, plumbing, or other physical defects. The Joint Center for Urban Studies estimated that in 1981, almost 12 million households lived in physically inadequate housing.[18] It also estimates that a minimum annual construction of 250,000 new or substantially upgraded housing units are needed to replace or improve substandard housing in the 1980s and 1990s, which still would leave a significant amount of substandard housing in the year 2000.[19] The Joint Center estimate of existing substandard housing is noticeably higher than that in the American Housing Survey conducted by the U.S. Department of Housing and Urban Development. However, regardless of which figure is used, it is a problematic aspect of the projection because it depends on an unforeseen increase in governmental assistance programs.[20] While improvements in substandard housing also occur under private auspices, such as through gentrification in low-income neighborhoods, this upgrading creates additional housing needs for the low-income residents who have been displaced.

SHORT-TERM FACTORS: While housing demand from year to year reflects the long-term underlying demand noted above, it also fluctuates in the short term. These movements are largely due to the effects of business cycle expansions and recessions on employment, inflation, and interest rates.

In expansions, as employment and income increase, more households have sufficient income to qualify for mortgage loans to buy housing or to rent costlier new apartments, both of which stimulate new construction. This increase in purchasing power is partially offset during expansions by higher inflation and mortgage interest rates and the resultant higher cost of housing, but the net effect is increased housing demand and construction. The opposite occurs in recessions when falling employment lessens the demand for housing, although the decline is tempered by less inflation and falling interest rates and the accompanying slower increase or decline in housing costs.

Figure 13 shows trends in real disposable personal income per household,

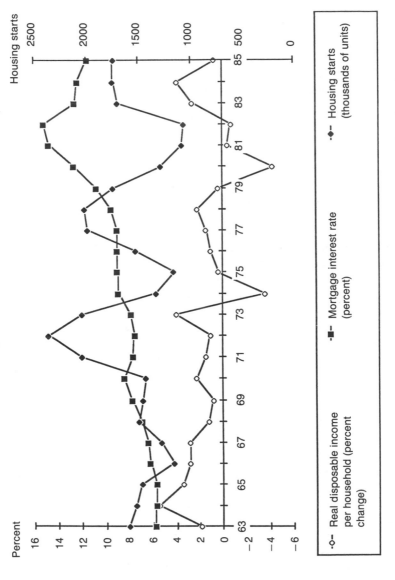

Figure 13. **Housing Starts vs. Real Disposable Personal Income and Interest Rates**

*Note:* Based on Bureau of Economic Analysis, Federal Home Loan Bank Board, and Bureau of the Census data.

mortgage interest rates, and construction starts of new housing units. The disposable income data (income after the payment of income and Social Security taxes) reflect changes in the purchasing power of household incomes resulting from trends in employment, wage rates and inflation. Interest rates in the figure are for mortgages on new single-family homes (interest rates for new multifamily housing have similar movements). *Real disposable income is more important than interest rates in determining housing demand, but interest rates play a significant role.*

As a broad gauge of the effect of interest rates, the National Association of Home Builders estimates that a 2 percent increase in interest rates on a 30-year, $72,000 mortgage raises the monthly mortgage payment about $100, which in turn prices 3 to 4 million households out of the market.[21] While quantitative thresholds defining the level at which interest rates begin to act as a restraint or stimulus to housing demand are difficult to specify, and in any case change over time, these broad estimates indicate that interest rates significantly affect housing demand (see Chapter 7, on the money supply for a more general discussion of interest rates).

HOUSING UNITS AND DOLLAR VALUE: The preceding discussion of long-term and short-term demand factors affecting the construction of new housing focused on the *number* of housing units. However, it is the *dollar value* of the new construction that is part of the GNP, because it incorporates the size and appointments of the housing as well as the number of units.

Over the postwar period, new single-family detached homes grew both in size (as measured by floor space) and in appointments (as measured by the proportion of homes with such items as two bathrooms and central air conditioning). Thus, the constant-dollar construction value of the average single-family home increased.[22] Part of this increase was offset by the shift from single-family detached homes to single-family townhouses and multifamily apartments, because the latter are typically smaller than single-family detached homes. Apartments increased as a proportion of all new housing units, from 12 percent in the 1950s to 44 percent in 1980–85, and the average apartment in 1985 cost about half as much to build as the average single-family detached home and townhouse put together (separate data on townhouses are being collected for the first time by the Bureau of the Census at this writing). The long-term net effect of this increasing size and upgrading of the appointments in single-family detached homes on the one hand, and the shift from the larger single-family detached units to the smaller multifamily apartments and townhouses on the other, has been an increase in the constant-dollar value of the average new housing unit of 1 percent annually.

\* \* \*

*In anticipating the future demand for housing, the analyst should consider both long-term factors of demographics and government programs and short-term cyclical influences such as real personal income and interest rates. Unless substantial changes are expected in the long-term factors, such as sizable changes in geographic migration and household formation or in government programs to replace substandard housing, the long-run demand is largely determined by current population and household trends. By contrast, the short-term outlook requires an assessment of the cyclical macroeconomic environment for interest rates and the purchasing power of household incomes. Because the dollar value of newly constructed housing units, rather than just the number of the housing units, affects the GNP, it also is important to consider future changes in the size of the average housing unit resulting from shifts in the proportion of new housing between the larger single-family detached homes and the smaller townhouses and multifamily apartments.*

## GOVERNMENT SPENDING AND FINANCES

The money governments spend to satisfy civilian and defense needs comes from taxes, user charges, and borrowing. Because government spending and taxation puts money in and takes money out of the income stream, government budgets are central to economic policies for fostering economic growth, high employment and low inflation. This section focuses on how fiscal policy can use government budgets to moderate the extremes of business cycle expansions and recessions. It doesn't address other important ways that government budgets affect the economy, such as the redistribution of income between low- and high-income people, the effects of defense spending on employment and prices, the incentive effects of tax laws, etc. These aspects affect economic growth, but they are difficult to quantify in terms of the overall impact of government budgets on the economy.

Public spending by federal, state and local governments for education, health, police, income maintenance, transportation, national defense, and all other government functions in 1985 totaled $1.5 trillion or 38 percent of the GNP. The role of government in the economy has expanded considerably over the years, rising from 21 percent of the GNP in 1950 to 33 percent in 1980. The federal government accounted for 66 percent of government spending while state and local governments accounted for 34 percent in 1985. Over the postwar period in general, the federal proportion has ranged from 65 to 70 percent, moving toward the lower end during expansions and the higher end during recessions, with no long-term upward or downward movement.

As noted in Part A of this chapter under ''Government Budgets,'' the measure used for government ''purchases'' in the GNP is lower than government ''spending'' in the official budget figures. This difference is due to the fact that the GNP treats government transfer payments (e.g., Social Security and unemployment insurance benefit payments, and interest) and federal grants to state and local governments as being spent by the recipients rather than by the governments providing the funds. Thus, social security and unemployment benefit payments only enter the GNP when they appear as consumer expenditures, while federal grants to state and local governments only appear as spending by state and local governments.

The category of "government purchases" in the GNP, then, is limited to government spending for wages of government workers and purchases from private industry of materials, equipment and services. Government purchases accounted for 20 percent of the GNP in 1985. While this figure is substantially lower than the above noted 38 percent share for all government spending including transfer payments, it is still the second largest component of GNP, surpassed only by consumer expenditures. However, although GNP's measure of government purchases provides a consistent accounting method to avoid double-counting of spending, it is a limited concept for assessing the total impact of government spending on the economy. Therefore, this section focuses on government budgets, which include all spending and the financing of the spending.

## *Government as a Cyclical Stabilizer*

Use of the federal budget for managing the economy—in other words, fiscal policy—is secondary to the main purpose of government spending and taxation, which is to provide for the nation's needs and to finance the spending programs in the most equitable and efficient manner (see the "Economic Policies" section in Chapter 2). Still, one of the main attributes of government budgets, and in particular the federal budget, is the use of overall spending and taxations levels as tools to restrain economic growth and inflation in business cycle expansions and to stimulate growth and employment in recessions.

Government budgets function in two ways to moderate the peaks and valleys of expansions and recessions. The first is through "automatic stabilizers." This term refers to the built-in institutionalized aspects of government budgets that cause government spending and tax collections, without any direct intervention of new government programs, to move in the opposite direction or in less extreme patterns than trends in the overall economy. For example, the inherent nature of unemployment insurance is to put more money in the income stream in recessions than in expansions. Budget outlays for unemployment insurance increase in recessions and decrease in expansions. The progressive income tax removes proportionately more income from households in expansions and less in recessions. Thus, these stabilizers automatically move consumer purchasing power in the direction desired in recessions and expansions.

The second way government budgets affect on the economy is through their use as an analytic fiscal policy tool. The federal budget's basic posture may be assessed in terms of the size of its surplus or deficit (receipts less expenditures) independent of whether the economy is in an expansion or recession, based on hypothetical budgets that focus on whether the budget inherently stimulates or restrains overall economic activity. These hypothetical budgets are referred to as the "cyclically adjusted budget" or the "high-employment budget," depending on the statistical measures used to develop them. Experience with each of these budget measures over the postwar business cycles is discussed below.

### Stabilizing Effect of Government Budgets

How well have government budgets performed as automatic stabilizers? One way of assessing their performance was covered in the earlier discussion of consumer purchasing power in the "Consumer Expenditures" section. That review of the postwar cyclical trends in personal income and disposable personal income indicated that unemployment insurance payments were more important than the progressive income tax in shoring up income in recessions, and that income taxes were more effective in moderating income increases in expansions than in cushioning income decreases in recessions. This section takes a broader approach and assesses the automatic stabilizing aspect of government budgets by analyzing the extent to which all government spending and taxation puts money in or takes money out of the income stream over business cycles.

The result of a budget surplus (receipts exceeding spending) is to take money out of the income stream, while a budget deficit (spending exceeding receipts) puts money into the income stream. Figures 14a and 14b show this experience for all governments, federal, state, and local, in the postwar business cycles. In relating government budgets to the overall economy, the figures depict the change in the budget surplus or deficit for each expansion (from trough to peak) and for each recession (from peak to trough) in relation to the average level of national income in the period.[23] If the budget surplus increases or the deficit decreases, the change is positive; and if the deficit increases or the surplus decreases, the change is negative. *Thus, this analysis focuses on the direction of the change of the surplus or deficit, not whether the budget is in surplus or deficit.*

The federal and the state and local budgets typically moved in the general direction of restraining income growth in expansions and boosting incomes in recessions, which fits the concept of the stabilizing role. The budgets moved in the stabilizing direction in seven of the nine expansions and in all eight recessions.

The impact of the surplus and deficit shifts in relation to national income in expansions showed the federal budget having a more stabilizing role in the first six expansions. In the most recent expansions of 1975–80, 1980–81, and 1982–86, however, the state and local budgets were more stabilizing. In recessions, the federal budget was far more stabilizing than the state and local budgets.

These patterns reflect the combined effects of the level of economic activity, changes in tax laws, and the rate of inflation on tax receipts and spending. The general stabilizing movements of both the federal and the state and local budgets result from different patterns of spending and tax receipts. At both levels, expenditures continually increase in expansions and recessions. However, in

Figure 14a. **Change in Government Budgets Toward a Surplus (+) or Deficit (−) as a Percent of National Income: Expansions**

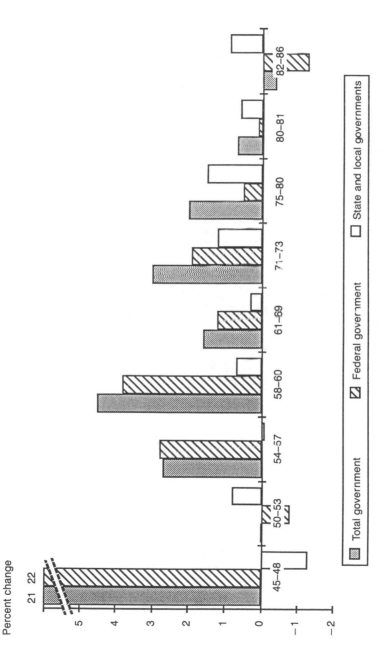

*Note:* Based on Bureau of Economic Analysis data. All figures are in current dollars.

Figure 14b. **Change in Government Budgets Toward a Surplus (+) or Deficit (−) as a Percent of National Income: Recessions**

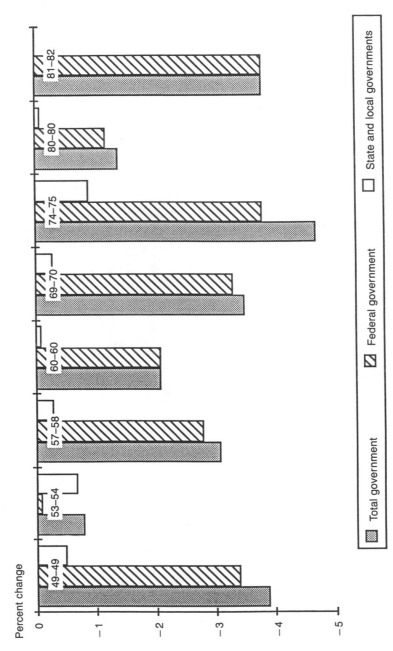

Percent change

*Note:* Based on Bureau of Economic Analysis data. All figures are in current dollars.

recessions federal revenues decrease and state and local revenues increase. Federal revenue falls in recessions because of the greater reliance on income taxes as a source of revenue. High unemployment and low business profits cause tax collections to drop. This decrease is heightened by the progressivity in the federal income tax, in which proportionately higher (lower) taxes are paid as income increases (decreases). By contrast, a much greater share of state and local tax collections comes from sales and property taxes, which are not as cyclically sensitive as income taxes. For example, in 1985, the personal income tax accounted for 43 percent of federal budget receipts and only 12.5 percent of state and local budget receipts. In addition, because unemployment insurance benefit payments are part of the federal budget but are not included in state and local budgets, they raise federal but not state and local outlays in recessions, which heightens the stabilizing impact of the federal government in recessions.

The opposite effect occurs in expansions, when federal tax receipts increase more than spending. This didn't happen in the 1982-86 expansion, however, because of the sharp drop in tax rates under the new tax laws. The stabilizing patterns of state and local budgets result from the effects of cyclical changes in both spending and tax receipts, as neither spending nor tax receipts appear to have a dominant cyclical role.

The overall result for the combined budgets of all governments—federal, state, and local—is that the government sector was a stabilizing factor in postwar business cycles. The government sector moved in the direction of a budget surplus in seven of the nine expansions (the exceptions were 1950-53 when the budgets were balanced, and 1982-86, when the budgets were in deficit), and the budgets moved in the direction of a deficit in all eight recessions. The federal budget has had a greater influence than state and local budgets on the total government sector in the expansions until the most recent ones of 1975-80, 1980-81 and 1982-86, and in all the recessions; this tendency would be expected from the fact that the federal government accounted for 65-70 percent of all government spending over the postwar period. However, it is noteworthy that in the three most recent expansions, state and local governments' budgets have had a greater cyclical stabilizing role in the overall economy.

The experience of the automatic stabilizing effect of government budgets over the postwar business cycles suggests the following:

*1. While the federal budget generally has a more dominant cyclical role than the aggregate of all state and local government budgets, the growing cyclical importance of state and local budgets in the most recent expansions suggests that the analyst should give more attention to the total government sector in future expansions.*

*2. Unless state and local governments shift a much greater share of their tax*

*collections to an income tax system, their budgets are not likely to have signifi-
cantly different impacts on stabilizing the economy in future recessions.*

*3.  The analyst should be alert to the macroeconomic results of indexing
federal income tax payments for inflation. The indexing, which began with 1985
income, will tend to make the federal budget more stabilizing in recessions and
less stabilizing in expansions (see earlier section on "Consumer Expenditures").*

### The Federal Budget in a Growing Economy: A Fiscal Policy Tool

The discussion of automatic stabilizers focused on the variable effects of
government budgets in expansions and recessions. Tax collections and unemployment insurance benefit payments in expansions increase the budget surplus or
decrease the deficit, while the effect in recessions is to lower the budget surplus or
increase the deficit. These automatic movements in the budget surplus and deficit
stem from the *effect of the economy on the budget*. The modified income flows
from this process then tend to moderate the extremes of high economic growth in
expansions and low or negative economic growth in recessions.

The federal government's role in the economy may also be assessed from a
fiscal policy perspective not appropriate to state and local governments.[24] When
viewed as an *active influence that drives the economy rather than reacting to it*,
the federal budget becomes a tool for managing the economy. To do so, hypothetical budgets for obtaining high economic growth consistent with a low or nonaccelerating rate of inflation are developed.

These hypothetical budgets abstract from short-term cyclical shifts in budget
surpluses and deficits to postulate the size of the surplus or deficit that would
occur in a steadily growing economy in which there were no cyclical expansions
or recessions. They are used as a basis for analyzing the inherent posture of
current and future budgets as a stimulus or restraint on economic growth in terms
of the money they put into or take out of the income stream. The analyses center
on the budget implications of government spending programs that are not tied to
the cyclical ups and downs of the economy and of tax laws that specify the tax
rates and the income, wealth, sales, or other items to be taxed.

Economic theory about how best to balance rapid economic growth and low or
nonaccelerating inflation has evolved over the years. In the 1960s a "fully
employed" economy (defined as 3 to 4 percent unemployment) was regarded as
desirable, and "full employment surplus" budgets were developed and used as a
tool of fiscal policy. Because the budget surplus generated from such high employment was found to be a "fiscal drag" on economic growth, it was a basic
rationale for the tax cuts of the early 1960s. During the 1970s the model was
moderated to the "high employment" budget, which raised the minimum unemployment rate believed consistent with low inflation to 5 to 6 percent. The

spiraling inflation of the 1970s moderated the model further. The "cyclically adjusted budget" of the 1980s doesn't specify minimum unemployment rates at all, and focuses only on filtering out cyclical impacts of the budget.

The main difference among these various budgets lies in the measurement of the high economic growth rate. The full or high employment budgets refer to what the GNP and federal budget receipts and expenditures would be at unemployment rates associated with full or high employment, such as unemployment ranging from 3 to 6 percent.[25] These measures are associated with developing a "potential GNP" that would occur at the assumed full or high employment levels. But quantifying the optimal relationship between employment and economic growth is difficult. The tendency in the evolution of the full and high employment budget estimates for the assumed unemployment rate to rise over the years is discussed further in Chapter 5.

On the other hand, the cyclically adjusted budget uses the GNP long-term growth trend and connects the midpoints of the expansion periods to abstract from specific unemployment rates.[26] The midpoint is the average of the middle expansion phase of the upturn, which is defined to include up to 12 quarters after the recovery from the previous recession surpasses the real GNP at the peak of the previous expansion. This "trend GNP" is treated as the GNP level from which to measure the budget surplus or deficit that would be generated in a steadily growing economy based on historical rates of growth. The implied unemployment varies depending on the unemployment rate associated with the trend GNP at a point in time. In 1985, for example, the implied unemployment rate was 7.4 percent, which was close to the actual rate of 7.2 percent. The cyclically adjusted budget is an appropriate technique for assessing budget surpluses and deficits according to the stage of the business cycle. While it is not suitable for setting fiscal policy guidelines because it is based on actual GNP growth rates rather than on goals for economic growth, it is useful for measuring the stimulating or restraining impact of fiscal policies.[27]

Regardless of the approaches used in these alternative measures, they provide a view of the inherently stimulating or restraining effects of the federal budget on economic growth. Two measures are published quarterly in the *Survey of Current Business*. One is based on the cyclically adjusted middle expansion trend GNP, the other on the GNP trend at a 6 percent unemployment rate. Table 6 shows these trends annually from 1981 to 1985. These indicate that the posture of the budget shifted from a neutral or small restraining position in 1981 to a considerable and increasing stimulus in the following years, although the increase in the stimulus in 1985 was about 10 percent less than it was in 1984.

The sharp increase in the budget stimulus to the economy starting in 1982 stemmed mainly from the tax cuts in the Economic Recovery Tax Act of 1981, as partially modified by the tax increases in the Tax Equity and Fiscal Responsibility Act of 1982 and the Deficit Reduction Act of 1984, and from the continued increases in spending for programs independent of those linked to the rate of

Table 6

## Cyclically Adjusted Federal Budget
## Surplus ( + ) or Deficit (-)
## (billions of dollars)

|  | Middle expansion trend GNP | | 6 percent unemployment rate trend GNP | |
|---|---|---|---|---|
|  | Level | Change from preceding year | Level | Change from preceding year |
| 1981 | − 55.6 | + 4.9 | − 27.5 | + 9.9 |
| 1982 | − 88.4 | −32.8 | − 59.5 | −32.0 |
| 1983 | −126.1 | −37.7 | − 97.1 | −37.6 |
| 1984 | −166.5 | −40.4 | −135.8 | −38.7 |
| 1985 | −203.3 | −36.8 | −170.7 | −34.9 |

*Source*: Thomas M. Holloway, ''The Cyclically Adjusted Federal Budget and Federal Debt: Revised and Updated Estimates,'' *Survey of Current Business*, March 1986, Tables 3 and 6, pp. 14 and 17, and *SCB*, August 1986, Table 2, p. 19.

economic growth. A secondary factor contributing to the budget stimulus was the net effect of the reduction in inflation on the deficit, which slowed the increase in tax receipts more than it slowed the increase in spending. This occurred because (a) incomes (and therefore tax collections) did not rise to higher tax brackets as rapidly as in the past because wage adjustments for inflation were lower, and (b) this slowdown in inflation related tax collections was not offset by proportionate reductions in spending.

This increase in the cyclically adjusted budget deficit substantially exceeded the growth in the GNP. As a percent of the middle expansion GNP, the cyclically adjusted deficit rose from 1.8 percent in 1981 to 5.1 percent in 1985. Figure 15 shows that between 1955 and 1981, the first year for which these calculations are available, the percentage was below 2.5 percent except for 1967 (3.2 percent) and 1975 (2.7 percent). While some economists maintain that the large deficits do not affect interest rates, others indicate they do raise interest rates for two reasons: (a) the large demand the deficits create for borrowed funds to finance them raises rates, and (b) lenders perceive the large deficits as meaning that inflation is not under control, and consequently charge higher rates to ensure that the purchasing power of the loans is maintained when they are repaid.[28]

A corollary of the persistently higher budget deficits is that they cumulate to a considerable increase in the federal government's debt, which may impact on business investment. Because the refunding requirements of the debt provide investment opportunities in U. S. securities that have no risk attached, they may result in redirecting investment activity toward government debt instruments and away from business investment such as in plant and equipment and new ventures. This is the ''crowding out'' effect of government borrowing.[29]

Figure 15. **Cyclically Adjusted Federal Budget Surplus (+) or Deficit (−) as a Percent of Trend GNP**

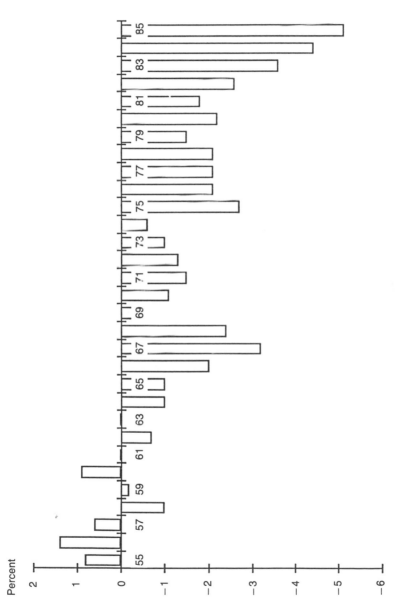

*Note:* Based on Bureau of Economic Analysis data. All figures are in current dollars.

The following considerations are suggested for using cyclically adjusted budgets in assessing the federal budget's impact on the economy:

1. Because the relatively high percentages of cyclically adjusted federal budget deficits to trend GNP are a recent development of the 1980s, there is little historical guidance on the implications of these percentages for economic growth and inflation. *In anticipating the impact of these percentages, the analyst should be alert to signs in credit markets when changes in the competing demands for funds between private industry and the federal government raise or lower interest rates, or for signs that lenders view the inflationary implications of high deficits differently in periods of slow and rapid economic growth.*

2. The refunding of considerable amounts of risk-free U.S. debt stemming from the cumulative federal budget deficits could result in some diversion of investment funds away from new plant and equipment or business ventures, which could lower economic growth rates. *The tendency for such diversion would not necessarily be evident from data on actual investment trends, but in assessing the impact of the federal debt on the economy, the analyst should monitor credit markets for evidence of significant amounts of such diversion.*

## EXPORTS AND IMPORTS

Foreign trade in goods and services has become increasingly important in the American economy since World War II. This internationalization of the economy has also made it more subject to economic and political developments in other countries. As a proportion of the GNP, both exports and imports of goods and services averaged 11 percent in the 1980–85 period. This was twice the share for exports and two and a half times the share for imports in the 1950s. In dollar volume, exports and imports are both larger than consumer spending for durable goods and residential construction investment.

There have also been shifts between the goods and services components of exports and imports, reflecting changes in the competitive position of American business. Goods are agricultural, mineral, and manufactured products, while services include travel, transportation, insurance, telecommunications and other business services as well as profits on foreign investments. Goods make up the bulk of foreign trade, accounting for 59 percent of exports and 76 percent of imports in 1985.

However, long-term trends in export/import shares indicate the inroads made by foreign businesses in trade in goods. The export trends indicate that American business increasingly is investing abroad to take advantage of the lower costs of production and to comply with requirements in some countries that certain items be produced locally (domestic-content laws). For example, while goods declined from 69 percent of all exports in the 1950s to 60 percent in 1980–85, income from investment abroad rose from 15 percent of all exports in the 1950s to 23 percent in 1980–85. The import trends show an increasing share for goods, rising from 66 percent of imports in the 1950s to 76 percent in 1980–85. Yet, this increase was accompanied by a rise in profits from investment in the United States, from 4 percent of all imports in the 1950s to 15 percent in 1980–85. These trends reflect the tendency of foreign business to invest in the United States because of the large markets and, more recently, because of the possibility of higher import barriers such as tariffs and quotas resulting from American protectionist sentiment.

As noted in Part A of this chapter under "Net Exports," exports and imports are recorded in the GNP as a net figure, exports minus imports. This results in a very small number, ranging from about –1 to +1 percent of the GNP, the sign depending on whether exports are larger or smaller than imports. This bookkeeping technique to avoid double counting in the GNP does not indicate the importance of foreign trade in the economy. On the other hand, the net figure is relevant for assessing America's competitive position in the world economy, the foreign exchange value of the dollar, and possibly the extent of protectionist sentiment, which in turn have a large effect on exports and imports.

There are several versions of international transactions in the "current account" of balance of payments data, which are similar but not identical to the figures on exports and imports of goods and services in the GNP. The main differences are the treatment of gold, capital gains and losses of affiliates of U.S. and foreign companies, U.S government interest payments to foreigners, and money sent to relatives and others living abroad who qualify for American pensions. In addition, international transactions in the balance of payments cover "capital" movements for foreign investments, money flows in payment for the current account exports and imports, and government reserve assets of gold and assets with international monetary organizations. While the capital movements are not directly part of the GNP, they record economic activity that affects the foreign exchange value of the dollar (which in turn affects exports and imports as discussed below), and thus indirectly impact on the GNP.

A problem with the balance of payments data in recent years has been the large difference between the sum of the current account exports, imports and foreign investments on the one hand, and the recording of the money flows to finance these transactions on the other.[30] Conceptually these are identical. More accurate reporting of these transactions could affect the picture of some international aspects of the American economy (discussed below with respect to external debt) and would allow more reliable analysis of trends in money and investment flows between the United States and other nations.

## Demand for Exports and Imports

The volume of exports and imports is determined by three general economic factors: economic activity at home (for imports) and abroad (for exports), relative prices for competing U.S. and foreign goods and services, and the foreign-exchange value of the dollar (which reflects relative prices of currencies). The ways in which these factors work is summarized below. In addition, exports and imports are affected by the quality of U.S. and foreign goods and services and other nonprice factors, including tariffs, quotas, and nontariff barriers such as domestic-content laws requiring that imported goods contain minimum proportions of dometically produced items.

---

### Directional Impact of Factors Affecting Foreign Trade

| Demand Factor | Exports | Imports |
|---|---|---|
| Economic activity abroad | Higher activity, higher exports | — |
| Economic activity in U.S. | — | Higher activity, higher imports |
| U.S. prices relative to foreign prices | Higher U.S. prices, lower exports | Higher U.S. prices, higher imports |
| Value of the dollar | Higher dollar, lower exports | Higher dollar, higher imports |

---

The relationship of exports and imports to American business cycles is more tenuous than that of the other GNP components because of factors outside the United States that affect foreign trade. For example, economic activity and prices in the United States are not always paralleled in other countries, and the value of the dollar is affected by factors only partially influenced by American actions, such as interest rate differentials between the United States and other countries or political stability abroad.[31]

Figures 16a and 16b show exports and imports in relation to real GNP over the postwar business cycles. In the expansions, both exports and imports typically increased faster than GNP, which is consistent with the long-term growing importance of foreign trade noted earlier. The exceptions to this general pattern came in the first half of the 1980s, when exports declined. In the recessions, exports showed no general pattern, increasing in four cases and decreasing in four cases, while imports decreased in six of the eight cases. This tendency of imports to follow business cycle movements more closely than exports reflects the stronger link of imports to economic activity in the United States.

### Relative Importance of Demand Factors

In assessing the importance of the three general factors driving exports and imports—economic activity at home and abroad, relative prices in the United

Figure 16a. **Business Cycle Movements of Real GNP, Exports and Imports: Expansions**

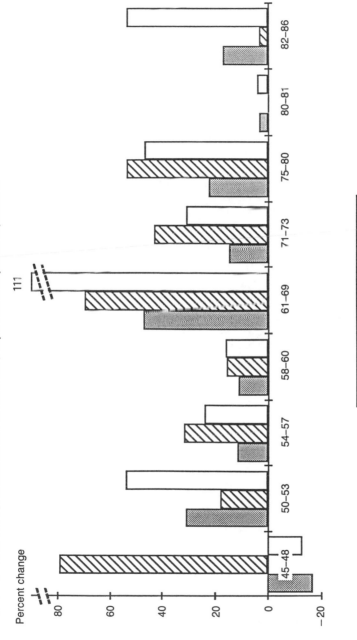

*Note*: Based on Bureau of Economic Analysis data. All figures are in 1982 dollars.

Chart 16b. **Business Cycle Movements of Real GNP, Exports and Imports: Recessions**

Percent change

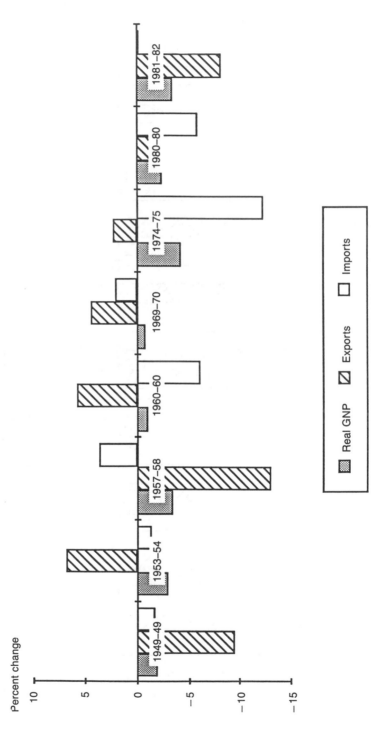

*Note:* Based on Bureau of Economic Analysis data. All figures are in 1982 dollars.

States and foreign countries, and the value of the dollar—it should be noted that there are relationships among them which are difficult to quantify. For example, while exports are directly related to economic activity abroad, they also indirectly reflect economic activity at home: when business is booming in the United States, American companies may be less aggressive in marketing exports, while in recessions they may be more aggressive. Another interaction occurs between prices and exchange rates, as an anticipated high rate of inflation in a country may reduce the value of its currency.

Other factors such as the threat of future import barriers may also affect foreign trade, as in the case of the voluntary limitations of exports of Japanese cars to the United States. However, such export limitations may be implemented in ways that offset at least part of the intended effect. For example, while Japan controls the *number* of cars exported to the United States, an increasing proportion of the cars are more expensive models, raising the *dollar value* of each exported car. The limitations on the number of cars, which Japan establishes annually, have also been raised since they were introduced—from the initial level in 1981 of 1.7 million to 2.3 million in both 1985 and 1986.

The analyst should keep these qualitative aspects in mind during the following discussion of the impact of the three demand factors on export/import levels.

ECONOMIC ACTIVITY AND PRICES: Several studies comparing the effect of economic activity (such as real gross domestic product) and prices on exports and imports have indicated that economic activity is two to four times as important as prices for periods up to one year, and that this differential is significantly lessened although not eliminated for longer periods.[32] Because these relationships are based on several studies which use varied estimating techniques, they are not fully consistent, and thus suggest magnitudes rather than specific numbers.

VALUE OF THE DOLLAR: Changes in the value of the dollar affect relative prices between the United States and other countries. Thus, changes in the dollar have the same relative importance to economic activity as was noted above for prices. According to one widely cited theory, over the long run the value of the dollar is established according to the concept of purchasing power parity (PPP). This theory starts with a hypothesized period in which the American and other economies are considered to be in balance, with relatively little excess in unemployment, inflation, and foreign trade balances. The prices of goods and services in the United States and other countries, which are reflected in the value of the dollar in relation to the currencies of those countries during this "equilibrium" period, are used as the base from which to calculate future price changes. As subsequent price movements in the United States and other countries diverge (for example, U.S. prices rise faster than prices in England), the value of the dollar would fall proportionate to the relative rise of American prices in order to maintain the PPP of the base period between the dollar and the pound.

One recent approach is to cite 1980 as the base period, on the premise that it roughly represents the average foreign exchange value of the dollar since the floating exchange rate replaced the Bretton Woods system of fixed exchange rates in 1973. Theoretically, the divergence of the foreign exchange value of the dollar from the 1980 relationships will give a measure of its under- or overvaluation. However, 1980 was also a year of recession, with high inflation and high interest rates, and if the period from 1974 to 1983 is used as an average base period, the dollar appears to be *undervalued* by over 10 percent in 1980.

Despite the appeal of the theory, foreign currency values do not typically move in accord with the PPP concept because (a) it is difficult to determine the base period when economies were in balance, and (b) the base period may become obsolete due to changes in such areas as productivity, investment opportunities, new resource supplies like North Sea oil, interest rates, and political stability. Hence the PPP concept is difficult to implement in practice, particularly during periods when substantial changes occur in international economic relationships.[33] But because of its basic rationale, if used as a broad approximation of underlying currency values, it seems to provide a useful measure from which to account for factors causing variations between the actual and theoretical value of the currency.

A refinement of the pure PPP approach to assessing the relative value of the dollar is to determine for any period what the dollar's exchange rate would have to be over the business cycle to bring the current account flows of foreign trade into balance with the capital flows, without restrictive foreign trade measures to affect the balance of payments. The extent of the dollar's under- or overvaluation is determined by comparing the actual rate to this hypothetical rate, which is referred to as the "fundamental equilibrium exchange rate."[34] This methodology has more conceptual refinement than the simpler PPP base-period approach, but considerable judgment is required in estimating adjustments for the current stage of the business cycle and between the current accounts and capital transactions in the balance of payments; it is thus subject to an unknown range of estimation error.

In assessing alternative PPP estimates of the value of the dollar, the various indexes used in comparing the dollar against the combined currencies of selected European countries, Canada and Japan should be considered. For example, three commonly cited indexes—prepared by the Federal Reserve Board, International Monetary Fund, and Morgan Guaranty Trust Company—have different weighting schemes, based on the volume of foreign trade, for combining the currencies of other countries. They give noticeably different results, even simply in determining the actual value of the dollar. For example, the value of the dollar declined from the peak level in the first quarter of 1985 to the second quarter of 1986, but this decline ranged from 25 percent for the Morgan Guaranty index to 32 percent for the Federal Reserve index; and according to a newly constructed index from the U. S. International Trade Commission, the dollar declined by only 19 percent over the same period. Therefore, any comparison of the alternative PPP measures should use the same measure for the actual value of the dollar.

Depending on which PPP concept and measure of the actual value of the dollar is used, in mid–1986 the dollar is estimated to be overvalued in the range of 10 to 30 percent. This overvaluation is generally attributed to several factors: higher real interest rates (market interest rates adjusted for inflation) in the United States than abroad, which attracted considerable foreign funds; faster economic growth and investment opportunities with higher profit potentials in the United States; favorable prospects for low U.S. inflation rates; and the political stability of the United States as a haven for funds from nations with unstable governments.[35]

In assessing whether this recent decline is a tendency for the dollar to verge closer to a PPP-type measure, the underlying forces in the economy are relevant. Thus, just as the "overvaluation" is perceived to have been a result of the factors just listed, these "fundamentals" driving the value of the dollar would have to change if the dollar were to fall further.

In analyzing the effect of the value of the dollar on foreign trade, it also is important to distinguish the foreign exchange trends for individual countries. While the indexes that combine the currency values for several European countries, Canada, and Japan into a single figure in relation to the dollar show a considerable decline in the dollar's value in 1985 and the first half of 1986, the declines were much smaller—or even showed a depreciation in terms of the dollar—for other countries in Asia and South America, along with Mexico and Canada, that have significant trade with the United States and which export to it substantially more than they import. Consequently, the currency relationships for particular countries outside of Europe and Japan also have important effects on American foreign trade.

BALANCE OF PAYMENTS DEFICITS AND EXTERNAL DEBT: When exports of goods and services exceed imports, the balance of payments is in a surplus, and when imports exceed exports, the balance of payments is in a deficit. Since 1982, imports have increasingly exceeded exports, resulting in large balance of payments deficits. There are two main measures of these balances. One is the balance of payments, which includes both goods and services. A second measure of such flows is the balance of trade, which only includes goods. The two measures do not always show the same patterns. For example, the balance of payments first went into a deficit in 1982; by 1985, the deficit had risen substantially, to $103 billion. By contrast, the balance of trade had been continuously in deficit since 1977, and in 1985 that deficit was $124 billion. (The balance of payments figure is lower because profits on American investments abroad exceed profits of foreign investment in the United States.) However, since 1982 there has been the same pattern of large and increasing deficits in both measures. A third measure of the balance, the current account balance of payments measure—which, as noted previously, includes transactions in gold, U.S. government interest payments abroad, money sent to relatives abroad and other technical items—had deficit of $118 billion in 1985.

These deficits result from faster economic growth in the United States and from the sharp increase in the value of the dollar, both of which stimulate imports relative to exports. The cumulation of the annual deficits changed the United States from a creditor to a debtor nation in 1985.[36] In borrowing from abroad to finance the deficits, Americans for the first time since before World War I owe more money to foreigners than foreigners owe to Americans. The most recent figures show that from the end of 1982 to the end of 1985, the United States went from being a creditor of $138 billion to a debtor of $107 billion. Unless there is a basic change in the relative economic growth rates and in the value of the dollar between the United States and its major trading countries, this external debt will likely increase for at least several years.

American industry's general problem competing in world markets has been a long-term postwar development. The resultant growing external debt will put increasing strains on the American domestic economy.[37]. The shift to a debtor position causes concern for several reasons. It will result in a net flow of money out of the United States to pay interest on the debt. With annual balance of payments deficits of well over $100 billion expected in future years, foreigners may become disenchanted with financing the deficits unless American interest rates rise.

The deficit heightens the problem for the Federal Reserve Board in balancing monetary policies to promote economic growth and moderate inflation. Tightening the availability of credit to raise interest rates will bolster the foreign exchange value of the dollar and thereby hold down inflation, but the higher interest rates and value of the dollar will also cause problems of slower economic growth and less employment in the United States. One proposal for giving greater stability to the value of the dollar is for the Federal Reserve Board to lessen the movement of dollars between the U.S. and other countries by instituting reserve requirements on branches of American banks abroad.[38] This would moderate loans by American banks abroad based on their dollar deposits (called Eurodollars) just as American banks in the U.S. are subject to limits on their loans (see Chapter 7 for a discussion of reserve requirements).

The continuing high balance of payments deficits are also likely to encourage protectionist sentiment. Industries, unions, and localities hurt by high imports will press for increased tariffs and other trade barriers to stave off further losses in domestic markets for American products and to save jobs threatened by imports. Such a trend toward protectionism is considered undesirable because of the societal benefits associated with free trade. New American import barriers would provoke retaliation by other countries with a consequent contraction of world trade, less efficient allocation of resources, and higher prices to consumers.

Theoretically, a fall in the value of the dollar would tend to lower the balance of payments deficit by increasing exports (through lower U.S. prices) and lowering imports (through higher foreign prices). However, several caveats are in order here. First, the short-run effect (six months to one year) of a large change in the value of the dollar is likely to have opposite effects on the deficit from those expected in the long run, because of the time lag in adjusting contracts and trade habits to the new price situation. For example, in the short run a large depreciation of the dollar probably would lead to a larger balance of payments deficit, because the price effects would dominate the volume effects, lowering the value of exports and raising the value of imports. But in the long run (after a year or longer), this pattern would be reversed. This phenomenon is known as the "J" curve.

Second, countries with large investments in industries that are dependent on exports to the United States are likely to reduce prices or slow their increase in order to remain competitive in the large American market. Third, American companies that have gone out of business or discontinued product lines because of import competition are not likely to be replaced soon after the international price situation improves: there will be concern that the decline in the dollar is temporary, and time is required to develop the new production facilities. Fourth, changes in import barriers at home and abroad can take complex patterns, and their effect on the balance of trade and the feedback effect on the value of the dollar are hard to quantify. Such changes may range from a general reduction in import barriers in the spirit of free trade to increased protection for particular American industries, which may lead to retaliation from other countries on American exports.

\* \* \*

In anticipating the role of exports and imports in the American domestic economy, the analyst should focus on three broad issues:

*1. For periods up to one year, greater weight should be given to changes in economic activity (e.g., real gross domestic product) than to relative prices at home and abroad for their effect on the volume of export and import trade, given similar percent changes in economic activity and prices. For longer periods, although economic activity is still more important, a smaller distinction should be made between economic activity and prices. If there is a large change in relative prices, such as one resulting from a sizable depreciation of the value of the dollar, the price effect could be larger than changes in economic activity.*

*2. The foreign exchange value of the dollar is related to a variety of mea-*

*sures associated with the purchasing power parity concept. While these are useful constructs, they are difficult to quantify in practice, and the estimates they yield on "undervaluation" or "overvaluation" of the dollar as a guide to its future direction should be considered as rough magnitudes. In addition, indexes that combine the currencies of several countries into one figure in terms of the dollar should be supplemented by analyses of the currency values for particular countries that have large foreign trade with the United States.*

*3. Several factors inhibit a decline in the value of the dollar from resulting in automatic increases in American exports and decreases in American imports. These are the lagging effect of the "J" curve, the tendency of foreign exporters to adjust their prices to remain competitive in the American market, and a delay by American industry in entering markets that were previously lost to import competition.*

## SUMMARY

Analyses of GNP trends may take both an overall top-down perspective and a building-block approach focusing on the main components. Total GNP and alternative summary GNP measures provide the overall view; the household, business, government, and international components give insight into the factors driving the overall movements.

### Total GNP and Alternative
### Summary GNP Measures

The summary measures of the national accounts besides GNP are final sales, final sales to domestic purchasers, gross domestic product, command GNP, and GNP on the income side. The GNP and the alternative summary GNP measures differ in the way they treat inventories, foreign trade and statistical errors. The main difference in these measures over the nine expansions and eight recessions of the postwar period lies in the effect additions and depletions of business inventories have on total GNP. While inventory increases in expansions are not nearly as important as inventory declines in recessions, it is important to monitor inventories in the expansion to determine if the buildup appears to be in balance or excessive in relation to sales. Reports in the press in recent years that business is maintaining better inventory controls—which, if sufficiently widespread would moderate the extremes of expansions and recessions—are not supported in the data on inventory and sales trends.

For periods shorter than the entire expansion or recession, the alternative GNP measures sometimes give slightly different pictures of overall trends in economic activity. Consider, for example, the slowdown in the expansion from mid–1984 to mid–1986.

## GNP Components

The four main GNP components are consumer expenditures, private investment, government spending, and exports and imports. When observing these components, the analyst should remember the key linkage of income to spending. For example, consumer spending is affected by personal income; plant and equipment investment is affected by business profits; government spnding is affected by tax receipts; and exports are affected by income abroad and imports by income in the U.S.

*Consumer expenditures* for durable goods, nondurable goods and services account for the bulk of the GNP, and have also tended to be a stabilizing factor in business cycles. Of the three kinds of consumer expenditures, spending for consumer durables (items that ordinarily last at least three years, such as cars, furniture and household appliances) is by far the most cyclical. The cyclical stability of consumer spending could be affected by shifts in the relative importance of durables, nondurables, and services, which could make consumer expenditures either more or less stabilizing in expansions and recessions.

The main source of financing for consumer spending is disposable personal income. Consumer purchasing power over the business cycle tends to be stabilized through the net effect of: (a) the increase in unemployment insurance payments in recessions, and (b) the increase in tax collections in expansions and decrease in recessions, because the federal government's progressive income tax takes proportionately more money out of the income stream as individual incomes rise to higher tax brackets. The indexing of federal income taxes for inflation starting with 1985 income will probably enhance the cyclical stability of disposable income in recessions and lessen it in expansions.

Other important factors affecting consumer spending are how consumers view the macroeconomic environment for employment and inflation, the relationship of consumer installment credit to personal income, and personal saving rates.

*Private investment* for business plant and equipment and residential construction, along with inventory accumulation and depletion discussed previously with the alternative summary GNP measures, has the most extreme cyclical movements of all GNP components. *Plant and equipment investment* for new buildings and machinery is often dtion, along with inventory accumulation and depletion discussed previously with the alternative summary GNP measures, has the most extreme cyclical movements of all GNP components. *Plant and equipment investment* for new buildings and machinery is often deferrable, as business can "make do" with the existing facilities. This, plus the fact that business profits—the mainmotivation for plant and equipment investment—have extreme cyclical movements in their own right, causes investment in capital facilities to increase much more in expansions and to decline much more in recessions than GNP. Trends in business capital appropriations, contracts and orders for plant and equipment, and projections of plant and equipment spending provide advance indicators of plant and equipment investment.

Another source of funding for plant and equipment investment is the depreciation allowances for wear and tear and obsolescence of plant and equipment, deducted as an expense in business income tax returns. Recent tax cuts related to the accelerated depreciation allowances in the Economic Recovery Tax Act of 1981 were intended as an incentive for plant and equipment investment. Taxes do not appear to be a major influence on investment in factories and machinery; however, they may have a greater impact on certain other investments such as office buildings and shopping centers.

*Residential construction* of single-family homes and townhouses, multifamily apartment buildings, and hotels, motels and dormitories is relatively small compared with other GNP components, but it is important for two reasons. It has a secondary impact on economic activity by generating consumer spending for items such as furniture and household appliances, and it tends to lead business cycles, turning down before a general recession begins and turning up before recovery.

The long-term demand for housing construction is mainly determined by population trends and household formation. Demographic projections indicate an annual average of 1.4 to 1.5 million new housing units through the 1990s, unless there is a sharp change from recent trends in household formation rates and government programs to replace substandard housing. However, the year-to-year short-term demand for new housing fluctuates considerably, mainly in response to movements in real disposable income per capita, but also to an important extent in response to the rise and fall in interest rates.

*Government spending* by federal, state, and local governments for civilian and defense needs has grown considerably over the postwar period. Government spending and taxation have a greater stabilizing effect on the overall economy through the "automatic stabilizers" of income taxes and unemployment insurance, which take proportionately more money out of the income stream in expansions and put proportionately more money into the income stream in recessions. The federal budget has had a greater stabilizing role than state and local budgets in the postwar expansions and recessions, but in recent expansions state and local governments have had a greater stabilizing impact.

The federal budget is also used as a fiscal policy tool through the concept of the "cyclically adjusted" or "high employment" budgets. These indicate whether the federal budget's posture at any given time, as well as whether its direction from year to year, is inherently stimulating (deficit) or restraining (surplus) on the income stream. One of the recent major changes in the federal budget, even after markets for indications of their impact on interest rates, lenders' views of the inflation, and diversions of investments away from plant and equipment and new ventures and toward investment in government debt instruments.

*Exports and imports* of goods and services including profits from foreign investments have accounted for a growing share of foreign trade in the American economy over the postwar period, which also makes the economy more subject to economic and political developments abroad. Three main factors determining the demand for exports and imports are economic activity at home (imports) and abroad (exports), relative prices of competing American and foreign goods and services, and the foreign exchange value of the dollar. Several studies indicate that economic activity is more important than prices in determining the volume of exports and imports. This is particularly evident for periods up to a year, and is valid for longer periods as well, although prices have an increasing importance with the passage of time. Because the foreign exchange value of the dollar affects relative prices in the United States and abroad, it has the same secondary importance to economic activity as was noted for prices.

The value of the dollar gets particular attention because of its effect on the American competitive position in foreign trade. Various measures indicating that the dollar is overvalued should be treated as rough magnitudes rather than precise numbers when using them as guides to future trends in the value of the dollar. While a decline in the value of the dollar theoretically would increase exports and reduce imports, several factors inhibit such an automatic cause-and-effect relationship.

## NOTES

1. Use of demand and supply terminology refers to the distinction between the components of the GNP on the product and income sides. In total, both sides measure "production." The difference between the two is in the demand and supply nature of the components.

2. "Nominal" and "real" are the terms commonly used to denote the distinction in GNP measures with and without inflation. Some may object to these words as misleading; there is nothing nominal about GNP in current prices because this is the only actual GNP, and there is nothing real about GNP in constant prices because in the everyday world items are bought and sold in today's prices, not in the unchanged prices of a particular year.

3. Because the growth rates are calculated from similar stages of the business cycle in which the final years of the comparisons—1948, 1959, 1969, 1979, and 1985—are years of economic expansion, they provide a consistent representation of long-term trends; calculating the rates from terminal periods that include both expansion and recession years would have distorted the averages.

4. As a technical note to the treatment of housing in the GNP, housing rents are included in consumer spending because they are current services, but purchases of new or existing housing are treated as a business, and consequently are in the investment component of the GNP, which is discussed in a later section.

5. Because personal income includes nonhousehold investment income of life insurance companies and nonprofit organizations, which account for 3 percent of personal

income, the saving rate is 0.15 to 0.25 percentage points lower than it would be if the nonhousehold items were not included, assuming saving rates of 5 to 8 percent. This is a relatively small absolute amount, and because these components as a share of personal income are relatively stable, they do not significantly affect the saving rate over time.

6. Charles A. Luckett and James D. August, "The Growth of Consumer Debt," *Federal Reserve Bulletin*, June 1985, pp. 400 and 402.

7. *Ibid.*, pp. 390–396. "The Growth of Consumer Debt" uses disposable personal income rather than personal income as used here in the denominator of the consumer debt burden measure. The use of disposable personal income raises the proportion by about 2.5 percentage points, but the movements over time in both figures are similar. Personal income is used here because it is regularly charted in *Business Conditions Digest*.

8. *Ibid.*, p. 391.

9. Depreciation is almost all of the capital consumption allowance category in the GNP, the remainder being accidental damage to capital facilities.

10. Leonard Sahling and M. A. Akhtar, "What is Behind the Capital Spending Boom," *Quarterly Review* (Federal Reserve Bank of New York), Winter 1984–85, p. 27.

11. Robert S. McIntyre and Dean C. Tipps, *The Failure of Corporate Tax Incentives* (Citizens for Tax Justice, January 1985).

12. Barry P. Bosworth, "Taxes and the Investment Recovery," *Brookings Papers on Economic Activity*, 1985:1.

13. Herman I. Liebling, Peter T. Bidwell, and Karen E. Hall, "The Recent Performance of Anticipation Surveys and Econometric Model Projections of Investment Spending in the United States," *Journal of Business*, October 1976; Karen Bradley and Avril Euba, "How Accurate are Capital Spending Surveys," *Quarterly Review* (Federal Reserve Bank of New York), Winter 1977–78; and J. Steven Landefeld and Eugene P. Seskin, "A Comparison of Anticipatory Surveys and Econometric Models in Forecasting U. S. Business Investment," paper presented at the 16th Centre for International Research on Economic Tendency Surveys (CIRET) Conference, Washington, D. C., September 21–24, 1983.

14. For more detail on these differences, see Eugene P. Seskin and David F. Sullivan, "Revised Estimates of New Plant and Equipment Expenditures in the United States, 1947–83," *Survey of Current Business*, February 1985, pp. 24–25.

15. *Ibid.*, p. 21 (text) and pp. 38–45 (tables).

16. These projections are incorporated in the report by the National Association of Home Builders, *Housing America—The Challenges Ahead*, 1985, pp. 2–3.

17. *Ibid.*, p. 19.

18. *Ibid.*, p. 24.

19. *Ibid.*, p. 19

20. *Ibid.*, "Executive Summary," p. 7.

21. *Ibid.*, p.21.

22. The Bureau of the Census price index for new homes provides for these changing characteristics in estimating construction costs, which are used in calculating the value of construction in constant dollars.

23. National income covers employee compensation, business profits, rental income, and net interest, and is basically the same as GNP on the income side except that it excludes depreciation allowances and sales and property taxes. National income is used here because it centers on income flows to the labor and capital factors of production, which are directly affected by the stage of the business cycle, although the results of the analysis would not differ if current dollar GNP were used.

24. In the American federal system, it is impractical to use state and local budgets as a fiscal policy tool because (a) each state or local economy is heavily influenced by economies in the surrounding region as well as by national economy; (b) institutional aspects

vary considerably—there are differing constitutional limitations on debt, legislatures meet at different times of the year or every other year, and fiscal years cover different 12-month periods; and (c) it is not politically and economically feasible to have a coordinated fiscal policy for even the 5 or 10 largest states (abstracting from the other states and the over 3,000 localities)—the complexity is far greater than that of the federal budget, which itself becomes quite complicated merely in the dealings between Congress and the President.

25. The Full Employment and Balanced Growth Act of 1978 (Humphrey-Hawkins Act) set an unemployment goal of 4 percent and inflation goal of 3 percent by 1983, with a further inflation goal of zero percent by 1988, provided that achieving the inflation goal would not impede achieving the unemployment goal. These goals are to be reported on in the annual *Economic Report of the President.* (Joint Economic Committee of Congress, *Employment Act of 1946, As Amended, with Related Laws*, October 1985, Section 4, pp. 5–7).

26. Frank de Leeuw and Thomas M. Holloway, "Cyclical Adjustment of the Federal Budget and Federal Debt," *Survey of Current Business*, December 1983.

27. *Ibid.*, p. 30.

28. Vito Tanzi, "Federal Deficits and Interest Rates in the United States: An Empirical Analysis," *International Monetary Fund Staff Papers*, December 1985.

29. This idea focuses on the fact that the ratio of the capital stock of existing plant and equipment to GNP is inversely related to the ratio of government debt to GNP. It was introduced in "Cyclical Adjustment of the Federal Budget and Federal Debt," *op. cit.*, and is elaborated in Frank de Leeuw and Thomas M. Holloway, "The Measurement and Significance of the Cyclically Adjusted Federal Budget and Debt," *Journal of Money, Credit, and Banking*, May 1985.

The "crowding out" of private investment due to large amounts of government borrowing is associated with two conditions: (a) periods of full employment when, because of low unutilized plant and equipment capacity and low unemployment (Chapters 4 and 5), additional demand for credit raises prices and interest rates rather than economic growth (Chapters 6 and 7), and (b) periods of less than full employment when, even though unutilized capital and labor resources are available to increase production, the Federal Reserve Board does not accommodate the increasing demand for credit because of concern that it will ignite inflation. "Crowding in" occurs during periods of less than full employment when the government deficit stimulates economic growth and thus private investment.

A refinement of the effect of the cyclically adjusted budget surplus or deficit on the economy relates to the fact that in periods of less than full employment, accompanied by budget deficits and high inflation and interest rates—as in the late 1970s and early 1980s—adjusting the deficit for the high inflation and interest rates would greatly reduce it, or even put the budget in surplus. Thus, Robert Eisner considers the conventionally measured budget deficits in the late 1970s and early 1980s to have misled economic policymakers into slowing economic growth to contain inflation: they instituted restrictive fiscal and monetary policies, which resulted in the severe recession in 1981–82. See Robert Eisner, *How Real is the Federal Deficit?* (The Free Press, A Division of Macmillan, Inc.: 1986).

30. This difference, which is referred to as the statistical discrepancy, was $23 billion in 1985. It has been relatively high in recent years, exceeding $20 billion during 1979–85 except for 1983, and reaching $36 billion in 1982. The difference is disconcerting because it shows substantially more money coming into the country than is recorded in the statistical reporting systems.

31. The importance of the United States as a political haven for funds from other countries in driving up the value of the dollar is difficult to quantify and has also been questioned on pragmatic grounds. See Peter Isard and Lois Stekler, "U.S. Intenational Capital Flows and the Dollar," and Richard N. Cooper's "Discussion Paper" in *Brook-*

*ings Papers on Economic Activity*, 1985:1, pp. 226–227 and 246–247.

32. Morris Goldstein and Mohsin S. Khan, "Income and Price Effects in Foreign Trade," *Handbook of International Economics*, Volume II, edited by R. W. Jones and P. B. Kenen (Elsevier Science Publishing Co., Inc.: 1985), particularly pp. 1076–1086.

33. David Bigman, "Exchange Rate Determination: Some Old Myths and New Paradigms," in David Bigman and Teizo Taya (editors), *Floating Exchange Rates and the State of World Trade Payments* (Ballinger Publishing Company, Division of Harper & Row, Publishers, Inc.: 1984).

34. John Williamson, *The Exchange Rate System*, Policy Analyses in International Economics 5 (Institute for International Economics), September 1983, revised June 1985, particularly pp. 11–36 and 78–85.

35. International Monetary Fund, *World Economic Outlook*, April 1985, pp. 31–37. See its footnote 30 for references questioning the relevance of the United States as a political haven for funds.

36. Russell B. Scholl, "The International Investment Position of the United States in 1985," *Survey of Current Business*, June 1986, p. 26 and Tables 1 and 2, pp. 27–28. A note by Jack Bame to the previous year's similar article, in the June 1985 *Survey*, indicates that because of inadequacies in the reporting of international capital transactions associated with the statistical discrepancy cited in Footnote 30 above, the balance of payments data may obscure the fact that the United States was a debtor nation before 1985.

37. C. Fred Bergsten, "The Second Debt Crisis is Coming," *Challenge*, May/June 1985, and Stephen N. Marris, "The Decline and Fall of the Dollar: Some Policy Issues," *Brookings Papers on Economic Activity*, 1985:1.

38. Howard M. Wachtel, *The Money Mandarins: The Making of a New Supranational Economic Order* (Pantheon Books, a division of Random House Inc.: 1986), pp. 95–104 and 209–211.

# 4 • Industrial Production and Capacity Utilization

The industrial production index and industrial capacity utilization rates are monthly indictors provided by the Federal Reserve Board. They encompass manufacturing, mining, and electric and gas utilities, which account for over 25 percent of the gross national product. The production index measures the quantity of nonfarm goods and energy produced; the capacity utilization rate measures the proportion of plant and equipment used in that production.

The industrial production and capacity utilization indicators focus heavily on cyclically sensitive markets such as business inventories, consumer durable goods, plant and equipment investment, and residential construction—demand in these markets increases faster in expansions and declines more sharply in recessions than other GNP components (see Chapter 3). Thus, both indicators are dominated by the most cyclical aspects of the economy. The production index measures output strengths of the components of the economy that play the dominant role in business cycles. The capacity utilization rates suggest future plant and equipment investment.

This chapter is divided into two sections, which treat respectively the industrial production index and the capacity utilization rates.

## INDUSTRIAL PRODUCTION INDEX

The industrial production index (IPI) provides a monthly measure of the *percent change in the quantity of output* in manufacturing, mining, and electric and gas utilities. This index thus focuses on the relative movement of the quantity of production; because it excludes the effect of price changes, it doesn't measure the value of production. Manufacturing dominates the index, accounting for 84 percent of the total output; mining accounts for 10 percent and electric and gas utilities, 6 percent. These industries are among the most capital-intensive in the economy—in their production operations, they use much more plant and equipment relative to labor than other industries, and consequently are the source of most plant and equipment spending. In 1985, the industries covered in the IPI generated 26 percent of the gross national product, but accounted for 56 percent of the nation's private nonfarm plant and equipment investment.

The IPI measure is provided from two perspectives, although the total is the same for both. One measures production by market groups, distinguishing types of product by end use; the other measures production according to the industry in which the product is made. The market groupings have three broad categories: (a) final products, encompassing consumer durable and nondurable goods, business equipment, prefabricated homes, drilling for oil and gas wells, and defense and space equipment (45 percent of the total); (b) intermediate products, encompassing construction materials that become part of residential and nonresidential structures, and business supplies such as commercial energy produced and animal feeds (13 percent); and (c) materials, encompassing raw materials, parts, containers, and fuels (42 percent). The IPI industry measure centers on which industries produce these products—manufacturing (84 percent), mining (10 percent) and utilities (6 percent).

From an economic perspective, the market measure focuses on the *demand* for products in the consumer, business and government markets (export markets are not separately identified, although some of the products are sold as exports). The industry measure focuses on the *supply* of the products provided by the producing industries. Demand for the different types of products accounted for in the market measure determines the growth rates of the particular industries supplying the goods.

## PART A: ESTIMATING METHODOLOGY

The IPI is a composite of detailed components that are weighted by their relative importance.[1] (General issues regarding index numbers were discussed in Chapter 2).

The base period of the index is 1977 = 100, which means that the index for any period represents the percent change from the 1977 average. For example, the index in December 1984 was 122.7, representing a 22.7 percent increase from the 1977 average, and the index in June 1985 was 123.6, representing a 23.6 percent increase since 1977. The change between two dates is therefore figured as the percent change between the two index levels. For example, between December 1984 and June 1985, the IPI increased by 0.7 percent (123.6/122.7 –1.0 x 100).

The weights used for combining the components into the index since 1977 are based on the costs and profits that each industry added to the value of the products it sold in 1977. This "value-added" measure counts the wages, depreciation, purchased services, and profits in each producing industry;

Table 7

**Estimating the Industrial Production Index for June 1985**
**(1977 = 100)**

| (1)<br>Industry | (2)<br>1977 weights | (3)<br>Ratio Change,<br>1977 to June<br>1985 | (4)<br>June 1985<br>proportions<br>(2) × (3) |
|---|---|---|---|
| Manufacturing | 84.21 | 1.261 | 106.19 |
| Mining | 9.83 | 1.106 | 10.87 |
| Utilities | 5.96 | 1.095 | 6.53 |
| Total | 100.00 | — | 123.59<br>(Total index) |

in this way it avoids double-counting the value of goods each industry buys from other industries, although it does double-count purchased services.[2] The weights always sum to 100 and are updated based on the most recent five-year ecomic censuses of American industry, which are conducted by the Census Bureau for the years ending in 2 and 7. When the 1982 economic censuses are incorporated in the IPI sometime around 1990, the 1977 weights will be used for 1977 to 1981, and the 1982 weights will be used for 1982 and later years. (Similarly, the weighting scheme for the years before 1977 is based on new patterns every five years—for example, the 1972–76 IPI is based on 1972 weights.) These "general" or "benchmark" revisions include statistical improvements such as the inclusion of new industry categories and updated industry classifications to reflect the most current technologies, and updated seasonal adjustment factors (the general process of revisions was discussed in Chapter 2).

Table 7 shows in summary form how the IPI is figured for the major industry categories in May 1985. Although much more component detail is used in developing the index (for manufacturing, over 100 component industries are weighted), the basic procedure for deriving the index is simple. In this example, value-added weights for the broad industry categories are multiplied by the relative change in production in each of the industries since the base period. The sum of the products of the industry components is the index for the new period—in this case, 123.6 for June 1985.

## Current Period Revisions

Ideally, current movements in the index are based on data for the actual items of output. However, because direct data are not available monthly for all items, indirect data based on employee hours and electricity consumption are also used for some industries. The indirect data are converted to estimates of production based on projections of technological trends and changes in labor productivity and electricity use per unit of output in the different industries. Direct product data account for approximately 50 percent of the IPI estimates; the other half is almost equally divided between the indirect electricity and employment information. This results in revisions to the current index when more complete direct data on output become available, replacing the indirect estimates.

The IPI for each month is first published in the third week of the following month, and is subsequently revised in each of the next three months as underlying information on which the indexes are based becomes available. About half of the time, the revision from the first to the fourth estimate is plus or minus 0.3 percent—from a first estimate of 125.0, for example to a fourth estimate of between 124.6 and 125.4 (the typical revision for monthly movements is also 0.3 percent). The indexes are also revised yearly to incorporate still more complete underlying data and also to update the seasonal adjustment factors.

## Effect of Changing Weights

Revisions in the weights affect mainly long-term rates of output growth rather than the short-term monthly and quarterly movements.[3] For example, in the 1985 revision, which incorporated new weights for 1972 and 1977, the main change to the IPI affecting cyclical expansions and recessions occurred in determining the start of the 1974–75 recession. The pre–1985 index showed the third quarter of 1974 as the peak of the previous expansion, rather than the end of 1973 as is now shown in the revised index; however, both indexes moved in a narrow range for most of 1974, and then clearly declined in the last quarter of 1974 and first quarter of 1975. For longer periods, the annual growth rates of the two differed. Between 1967 and 1977, the old rate was 2.9 percent compared to the new rate of 3.1 percent; for the 1977–84 period, the old rate was 3.4 percent compared to the new rate of 2.9 percent. Thus, the revision from 1967 to 1977 was small, but the revised trend for 1977–84 showed a noticeably slower growth rate than previously depicted.

The revised growth rate for 1977–84 was influenced by the higher oil prices resulting from the first major price action of the Organization of Petroleum Exporting Countries (OPEC), in 1973–74. These prices were not incorporated in the IPI until 1985, when the 1977 weights began to be used. The same pattern is likely to occur when the second round of higher OPEC oil prices in 1979 is incorporated in the 1982 weights, which will be used in the next IPI revision about 1990. If so, the business cycle expansion starting at the end of 1982 will appear less strong than it does in the mid–1980s, which could affect subsequent retrospective analyses of the impact of fiscal and monetary policies in the 1980s.

# PART B. ANALYSIS OF TRENDS

As noted previously in this chapter, the IPI focuses on the most cyclically sensitive markets of the economy. This is apparent in the postwar business cycle patterns of the IPI and real GNP (Figures 17a and 17b). In the nine postwar expansions, the IPI typically increased 50 to 100 percent more than the GNP; in the eight postwar recessions, the IPI typically declined three to four times more than the GNP. The estimate of "GNP Goods," which is similar definitionally to the IPI, is more cyclical than total GNP. Nevertheless, the IPI also has significantly greater cyclical movements than GNP Goods, although the differential is smaller than between the IPI and GNP. In expansions, the IPI typically increases by 25 to 75 percent more than GNP Goods, and in recessions the IPI typically declines 75 to 100 percent more than GNP Goods.[4]

The relationship between the IPI and GNP corresponds more closely, however, during periods of slow economic growth (typified by real GNP increasing at an annual rate of 3 percent or less) such as occurred from mid-1966 to mid-1967, throughout 1979, and from mid-1984 to mid-1986. Table 8 shows that in the 1966-67 and 1979 slow-growth periods, GNP rose only slightly less than the IPI, and that in 1984-86 GNP rose more than the IPI. The IPI and GNP are similar during such periods because the less cyclical aspects of the economy, which represent most of the GNP (72 percent in 1985), are more prominent in times of slow growth.

The IPI closely reflects extreme cyclical movements in the economy because of the importance in its makeup of consumer durable goods, business equipment, construction supplies, and materials (inventories that are reprocessed into other goods). As indicated in Chapter 3, these markets dominate the cyclical movements of the economy. The IPI excludes the more cyclically stable markets such as consumer services and government employment.

While the manufacturing, mining and utilities industries covered in the IPI account for a relatively small portion of the GNP—only 26 percent in 1985—they have wide secondary impacts. First, service industries are affected by movements

---

Table 8

**IPI and GNP in Slow Economic Growth Periods
(Annual percent change)**

|  | IPI | Real GNP |
|---|---|---|
| 1966:2 - 67:2 | 3.0 | 2.4 |
| 1979:1 - 79:4 | .9 | .6 |
| 1984:3 - 86:3 | 1.4 | 2.5 |

*Note*: Number after the colon is the quarter of the year.

Figure 17a. **Business Cycle Movements of Industrial Production and GNP: Expansions**

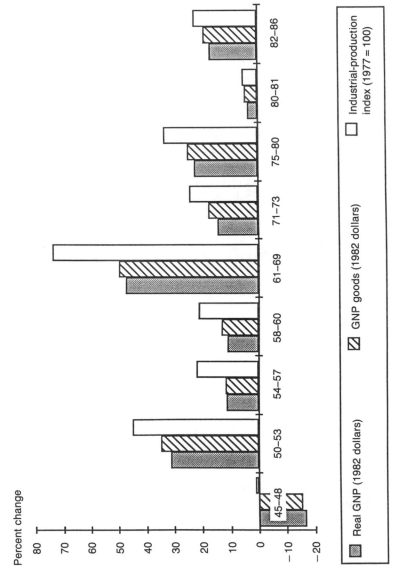

*Note:* Based on Federal Reserve Board and Bureau of Economic Analysis data.

Figure 17b. **Business Cycle Movements of Industrial Production and GNP: Recessions**

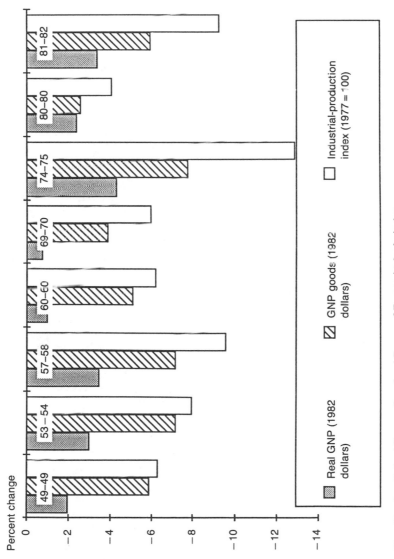

*Note:* Based on Federal Reserve Board and Bureau of Economic Analysis data.

in the IPI because the IPI industries generate a significant amount of business for service industries. When production is high, manufacturers use more transportation, communication, finance, insurance, repairs and personnel services that when production is low. Second, because the IPI industries account for the major share of investment in plant and equipment, they impact heavily on the demand for machinery, trucks, building materials and construction workers. Third, because average incomes of workers in the IPI industries are higher than those in other industries, consumer spending is affected proportionately more by changing levels of IPI production than by changing production in other industries.

*In relating the IPI to the GNP, the analyst should allow for the IPI's more extreme cyclical movements. If the IPI is projected to rise or fall significantly, the GNP movements are likely to be less pronounced—typically one-half to two-thirds of the IPI rise in expansions, and one-fourth to one-third of the IPI decline in recessions. By contrast, there tends to be a closer relationship between the IPI and GNP in periods of slow economic growth. On average, an annual growth in the IPI of at least 6 percent is necessary to generate sufficient GNP growth to lower the unemployment rate (see Chapter 5 for the GNP/unemployment relationship).*

## CAPACITY UTILIZATION RATES

Capacity utilization rates (CURs) are monthly indicators of the relation of actual production to productive capacity for the same industries as the IPI covers— manufacturing, mining, and electric and gas utilities. The Federal Reserve Board CUR measures are the most widely used figures and are the focus of this section.

CURs indicate the amount of unused capacity that industrial facilities could bring into production. For example, if a factory with the plant and equipment capacity to produce 1,000 cans of paint a month actually produces 800 cans a month, its utilization rate is 80 percent and its unutilized capacity is 20 percent. Unutilized plant and equipment is analogous to the unemployment of workers in the job market (see Chapter 5) as both measures indicate available resources that could be used to expand production. This doesn't imply that the two are equated, however, because on a social basis unemployment of workers is a more serious problem than unused industrial facilities.

Theoretically, the direction and level of CURs indicate the demand for plant and equipment investment and the degree of inflationary pressure in the economy. Rising CURs tend to *reduce* unit costs for a time as the existing plant and equipment investment (fixed costs) produces a larger volume of goods. The cost advantage of the larger volume (increasing returns to scale) continues until the utilization rate reaches a level at which further increases in production *raise* unit costs because of machinery breakdowns, increasing use of older and less efficient equipment, hiring of less productive workers as unemployment falls, and laxness by managements in holding down costs.[5]

The specific point at which the turnaround occurs on costs, and consequently on plant and equipment spending, varies among industries and is hard to quantify with precision. A comparison of Federal Reserve Board CURs with figures on industry plant and equipment spending indicates that the turnaround typically occurs in the 80 to 85 percent range. This observed turnaround zone is based on movements of the figures—it docsn't mean that company decisions to invest are linked to a particular CUR zone. (As discussed below, CUR measures provided by the Census Bureau are noticeably lower; comparing Census CURs to capital spending would therefore indicate a lower turnaround zone.) The rising production costs at the higher utilization rates are a stimulus to companies to reduce costs by increasing capacity through new investment in plant and equipment. By contrast, relatively low and falling CURs reduce business incentives to expand capacity, and replacements of rundown and outmoded capacity account for greater shares of plant and equipment investment during such periods.

## PART A: ESTIMATING METHODOLOGY

CURs are provided for the total of all manufacturing, mining, and utility industries and for the component industries within each of these groups; the figures are available for manufacturing industries since 1948 and for mining and utilities since 1967. Separate CURs are provided for industrial materials—minerals, manufactured materials, parts, components and containers, and fuels—that are further processed in the production of finished goods such as food, clothes, appliances, buildings, and equipment.

A CUR is the ratio of the IPI to industrial plant and equipment capacity. Consolidation of component industries to broader industry categories and the total CUR is based on the value added weights used in the IPI. Because the IPI (in the numerator) was discussed earlier in this chapter, the following discussion concentrates on the capacity estimates as used in the denominator.[6]

$$\text{Capacity utilization rate} = \frac{\text{Industrial production index}}{\text{Industrial capacity}} \times 100$$

An industry's capacity, while partly a result of its capital plant and equipment facilities, is also determined by the length of the typical working day and week. The capacity measures assume an eight-hour day and five-day working week for most industries, but these measures are higher for some industries such as steel, petroleum refining, and utilities, which maintain production around the clock. As in the case of the IPI, manufacturing dominates the movement of the CUR, accounting for 84 percent of the component industries. For manufacturing and gas utilities, capacity measures are developed through an indirect estimating procedure:

(a) Year-end capacity levels are established by dividing the IPI by surveys of company capacity utilization conducted by McGraw-Hill, Inc., the Census Bureau, and other government and private sources.

(b) The annual movements of the implied capacity measures are modified in (a) to be consistent with alternative figures on capacity data obtained from government agencies and private organizations, such as information on physical units (e.g. tons of steel), the dollar value of existing capital facilities (capital stocks), and direct surveys of capacity, and to allow for peak capacity to meet seasonal needs.

(c) To derive monthly capacity estimates for previous years, the year-end capacity levels are connected and the monthly trends for each year are the prorated rate of change between the two year-end monthly levels. Monthly estimates in the current year are based on continuing the rate of growth in the previous year.

Different estimating procedures are used for electric utilities and mining. For electric utilities, Edison Electric Institute data on kilowatt generating capacity are used. These take into account the need for reserve capacity for outages as well as power to meet peak summer and winter needs. For some mining industries, the capacity estimates are based on information from the U.S. Departments of the Energy and the Interior. For others, where such information isn't available, capacity figures are inferred from long-term production trends based on connecting the production expansion peaks of business cycles.

## CURs and Capacity: Measurement Problems

Figure 18 details the movements of the Federal Reserve Board figures for capacity, industrial production, and the CUR for all industries. While the CUR follows the cyclical pattern of the IPI, which is the numerator of the CUR ratio, capacity itself differs considerably from the highly cyclical IPI. Capacity increases at a relatively steady rate with no cyclical ups and downs because in any period, capacity is composed mainly of existing facilities, with only marginal net changes made for the addition of new investment and deduction of depreciated facilities. The overall CUR usually ranges from 75 to 85 percent, toward and above the upper end during expansions and toward and below the lower end during recessions. The range of CURs for individual industries varies from this overall average.

The overall CUR typically does not approach or exceed 100 percent. The

Figure 18. **Industrial Production, Capacity, and Capacity Utilization**

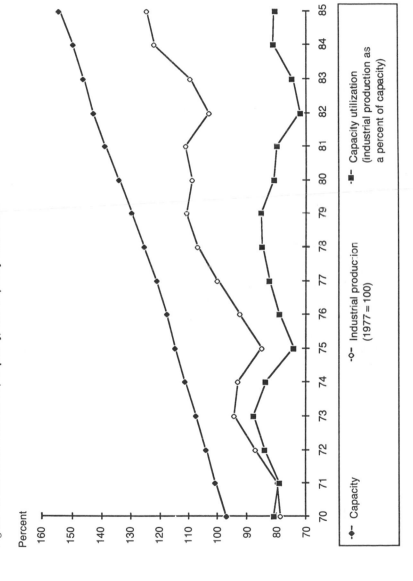

*Note:* Based on Federal Reserve Board data. Figures cover manufacturing, mining, and utilities.

major exception is high mobilization during wars, when industry undergoes a widespread conversion to two and three eight-hour shifts a day. Because such multiple shifts are not considered typical capacity levels that can be sustained over long periods in peacetime, they don't result in an upward adjustment in the estimated capacity levels; thus CURs theoretically may reach the 100 percent range. However, industry would probably operate at this level only during a full-scale war, and perhaps not even then. For example, the peak manufacturing CURs in the Korean and Vietnam Wars were 92 percent. There are no estimates for World War II because CURs were not developed until 1948. It remains unclear whether even a full-scale war would raise CUR's to the 100 percent range.[7]

Productive capacity is an elusive concept to define and measure. Theoretically, the ultimate capacity of a business is the output it could produce if operated seven days a week, 24 hours a day, with allowance for maintenance of existing equipment, shortage of materials, or other downtime. This level of operation is referred to as "engineering capacity." Other than in wartime, it is realistic only for industries with continuing process operations in which it is more efficient to operate around the clock. "Practical capacity" refers to the usual operations schedule that is realistically maintained on a continuing basis. These vary among industries from single and multiple eight-hour shifts over a five-day week to continuous operations seven days a week.

Practical capacity is the implied measure in the Federal Reserve Board figures. However, the measure isn't always explicitly defined in the source data used for the estimates. For example, the McGraw-Hill CUR company surveys do not define the capacity measure for the respondents.[8] This probably leads to inconsistent reporting by companies—for example, some may assume engineering capacity as practical capacity. This is less of a problem for the capacity figures that are based on Census Bureau data, because Census provides respondents with qualitative definitions of capacity in terms of typical operational schedules; however, as noted below, the lack of quantitative definitions is still felt to cause some inconsistency.[9]

Another continuing problem with any statistical measure of capacity is whether plants that are closed down in recessions are considered permanently removed from production, or if this capacity is considered "found" and available again in expansions.[10] While the Federal Reserve uses consistency checks with alternative data and statistical procedures to modify aberrant movements in the capacity figures, there is a considerable amount of indirect estimating associated with the preparation of the capacity figures. Finally, the capacity figures do not include imports, which are an important source of added supply in some industries and which in effect increase capacity. *For these reasons, the capacity figures should be considered orders of magnitude rather than precise numbers.*

The difficulty of developing an operational measure of capacity is apparent in the varying CUR levels in different surveys. As noted previously, the Census Bureau's CUR measures for manufacturing industries are used for some industry

Table 9

**Alternative Capacity Utilization Rates for Manufacturing**
**(Percent of practical capacity)**

| Fourth Quarter | (1) Federal Reserve | (2) Census Bureau | (3) Difference (1)–(2) |
|---|---|---|---|
| 1975 | 74 | 67 | 7 |
| 1976 | 79 | 68 | 11 |
| 1977 | 82 | 72 | 10 |
| 1978 | 86 | 74 | 12 |
| 1979 | 83 | 75 | 8 |
| 1980 | 79 | 68 | 11 |
| 1981 | 75 | 66 | 9 |
| 1982 | 68 | 58 | 10 |
| 1983 | 77 | 64 | 13 |
| 1984 | 81 | 67 | 14 |
| 1985 | 80 | 65 | 15 |

*Note*: The Federal Reserve data are seasonally adjusted, and the Census Bureau data are not seasonally adjusted.

capacity estimates in the Federal Reserve Board figures.[11] The Census figures, which are for the fourth quarter of the year, are available in the third quarter of the following year. They are based on surveys of small companies and of divisions of large companies (sometimes referred to as "establishments"); the measure of capacity is qualitatively defined for the survey respondents. The Federal Reserve data are provided on a current monthly basis; they are based in part on indirect estimating techniques using company-level rather than divisional reporting for large companies, and in part on vaguely defined measures of capacity. Even with the qualitatively defined Census capacity measures, some survey respondents may assume practical capacity to be the same as around-the-clock engineering capacity. While some changes are made in the process of reviewing the survey reports to make them conform to the definition of practical capacity, there remains an inherent subjective element in the figures because of the difficulty of specifying quantitative definitions of practical capacity.[12]

Table 9 shows that the yearly *movements* of the two series are similar. However, their *levels* are substantially different. The Federal Reserve figures are typically at least 10 percentage points higher than the Census data, and in the first half of the 1980s the differential has been increasing. This discrepancy may be due to differences in the way that divisions of large companies (from which the Census figures are obtained) as contrasted with company headquarters (on which the Federal Reserve figures are based) treat interplant shipments of products within the same company and bottlenecks caused by materials shortages or equipment breakdowns in assessing current capacity, but these factors have not been quanti-fied. Differences due to the use of Federal Reserve seasonally adjusted data and Census unadjusted data are insignificant because fourth-quarter production for the total of all industries has very little seasonal variation. On balance, both CUR series have measurement problems, but because the Federal Reserve data are available promptly every month, they are more applicable to ongoing macroeco-nomic analysis. *As in the case of the capacity figures, the CURs should be considered as orders of magnitude rather than precise figures.*

### Digression on Preferred Operating Rates

The Census Bureau also provides a "preferred" operating rate for manufac-turing for the fourth quarter of the year.[13] The preferred rate is based on the level of operations that companies report they would like to maintain over the long run. It is calculated as the ratio of actual production to preferred production. In the measure, preferred production may equal but not exceed practical capacity. This level is presumed to be the level at which profits are maximized (marginal revenue equals marginal cost). A theoretical conclusion is that if the preferred rate is less than 100, there is room to expand production and maximize profits; conversely, if the preferred rate exceeds 100, production should be reduced or capacity expand-ed to maximize profits.

$$\text{Preferred operating rate} = \frac{\text{Actual production}}{\text{Preferred production}} \times 100$$

However, there are inconsistencies in the survey reports for the production and capacity figures used in developing the CURs and preferred operating rates. In addition, the assumption in compiling the data that the preferred production cannot exceed practical capacity may not always reflect business realities, be-cause in some short-term cases the desired production may exceed practical capacity. These data problems are significant limitations in using the preferred operating rate for clues to inflationary pressures and future investment in plant and equipment. Because of these problems, the preferred rate is not used in macroeconomic analysis; it is discussed here merely to acquaint the reader with the concept because it is sometimes included in assessments of investment needs.

## PART B: ANALYSIS OF TRENDS

This section profiles the CUR trends since the late 1940s and compares them to trends in plant and equipment spending. It also considers the relationship between the CURs and price movements. Because manufacturing accounts for 84 percent of the industries covered in the CUR total, there is little difference in the

Table 10

## Capacity Utilization Rates

|  | Total (Manufacturing, Mining and Utilities) | Manufacturing |
|---|---|---|
| 1967 | 87.1 | 86.7 |
| 1968 | 87.4 | 87.0 |
| 1969 | 87.4 | 86.7 |
| 1970 | 80.9 | 79.2 |
| 1971 | 79.0 | 77.4 |
| 1972 | 84.0 | 82.8 |
| 1973 | 87.9 | 87.0 |
| 1974 | 83.6 | 82.6 |
| 1975 | 74.1 | 72.3 |
| 1976 | 78.8 | 77.4 |
| 1977 | 82.4 | 81.4 |
| 1978 | 84.8 | 84.2 |
| 1979 | 85.2 | 84.6 |
| 1980 | 80.9 | 79.3 |
| 1981 | 79.9 | 78.3 |
| 1982 | 72.1 | 70.3 |
| 1983 | 74.7 | 74.0 |
| 1984 | 81.0 | 80.5 |
| 1985 | 80.4 | 80.1 |

*Note*: Data are available for manufacturing since 1948 and for mining and utilities since 1967.

*movements* of the CUR combined total for manufacturing, mining, and utilities and the manufacturing component (Table 10). There also is only a slight difference in the *levels* of the combined total and the manufacturing component—the combined total tends to be 0.5 to 1.0 percentage point higher. Thus, because manufacturing is dominant, the following discussion of CUR trends deals mainly with manufacturing industries.

CURs give important clues to future plant and equipment investment, but they are difficult to apply for analyzing potential inflationary pressures. Figure 19 shows the CUR and the plant and equipment spending (in 1982 dollars) trends for all manufacturing industries for 1948–85. The manufacturing CUR averaged 82 percent, peaking at 91 percent in 1966 (the early part of the Vietnam War buildup) and falling to its lowest level, 70 percent, in the 1982 recession year. The CUR has been in a downward trend since the mid-1960s (abstracting from cyclical expansions and recessions): in the 1980–85 it averaged 77 percent. This downward trend is consistent with the slowdown in economic growth over the period (see Chapter 3).

Although there is not a one-to-one relationship between the CUR and investment in plant and equipment, trends in manufacturing suggest similar movements of the two measures over three- to five-year periods, with a CUR of about 80 percent as the turnaround zone for capital investment (horizontal line at 80 percent on Figure 19). Some analyses have located the turnaround as a single level at about 83 percent, which is sometimes referred to as a "flash point." However, reference to the turnaround zone as a point is misleading because it suggests a precision and short-term response between capacity utilization and investment that don't exist.

With the above caveat, the analyst may interpret the CUR movements as follows. *When the CUR is below 80 percent or when it tends downward toward 80 percent for three to five years, there typically is a decline or little growth in investment; by contrast, when the CUR exceeds 80 percent or rises toward 80 percent for several years, investment tends to increase, sometimes substantially.*

On the other hand, despite the theoretical basis for a relationship between prices and the CUR, there is no observable relationship over the postwar period (Figure 20). While the CUR moved up and down cyclically, producer prices for finished goods always increased (although at differing rates). Prices drifted upward from 1948 to 1972 (at an accelerated rate starting in the latter 1960s), rose sharply in the intense inflation of 1973 to 1981, and increased much more slowly in 1982–85.

An empirical relationship may be established for periods when the CURs were sustained for several years at substantially lower or higher levels than is typical for the postwar period—for example, if they average above 85 percent or below 75 percent. It may also appear for particular manufacturing industries as distinct from the manufacturing total. *However, because of the lack of an observable relationship between the CURs and price movements at the overall manufacturing level, experience with the component industries is not pursued further here.*

## CUR's and Investment for Component Industries

Focusing on investment in key component industries within manufacturing plus the utilities industries may help assess the reasonableness of the economy-wide investment analysis discussed in Chapter 3. Total manufacturing accounted for 38 percent of all private nonfarm plant and equipment investment in 1985. While this is a minority share, it is a highly cyclical segment of the economy and is sufficiently large to be of interest in viewing the investment behavior of the main component industries that affect the grand total. The manufacturing industries with the largest investments are petrolem refining, nonelectrical machinery, chemicals, electrical machinery, motor vehicles, food and paper (28 percent of all capital investment in 1985). The other industries covered in the IPI and CURs with the largest investments are electric, gas and sanitary utilities (13 percent of all 1985 plant and equipment investment).

Figure 19. **Capacity Utilization and Plant and Equipment Investment: Manufacturing**

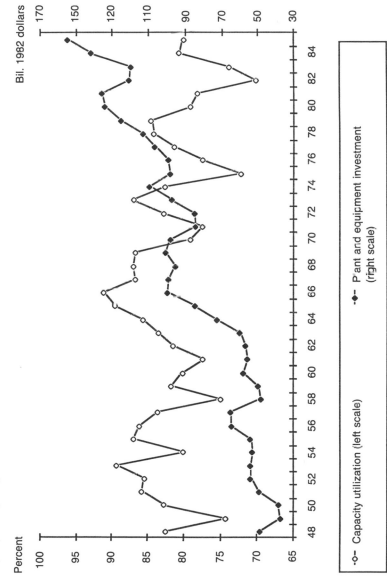

Percent                                                                 Bil. 1982 dollars

-o- Capacity utilization (left scale)          -●- Plant and equipment investment
                                                   (right scale)

*Note:* Based on Federal Reserve Board and Bureau of Economic Analysis data.

Figure 20. **Capacity Utilization and Finished-Goods Prices: Manufacturing**

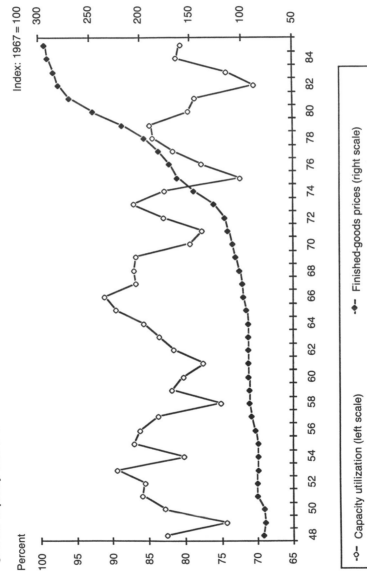

*Note:* Based on Federal Reserve Board and Bureau of Labor Statistics data.

-o- Capacity utilization (left scale)    -•- Finished-goods prices (right scale)

Figures 21 to 28 show the relationship between CURs and investment (in 1982 constant dollars) for the seven manufacturing industries over 1948–85 and for the electric and gas utility total during 1967–85. The highlights of these comparisons are summarized below (1985 investment in current dollars is in parenthesis).

*Petroleum Refining ($26.7 billion)*: No obvious relationship between the CUR and investment emerges. The investment decline in 1968–73 and the investment increase during 1974–81 are not clearly related to the CUR movements or levels.

*Chemicals ($16.5 billion)*: Yearly investment tends to follow the CUR movements of the previous year.

*Nonelectrical machinery ($16.0 billion)*: Investment tends to follow the CUR movements as the CUR rises above or falls below the 80 percent zone. This typically occurs in two- and three-year periods.

*Electrical machinery ($15.6 billion)*: Investment tends to follow the CUR movements as the CUR rises above or falls below the 75 percent zone. This typically occurs in two- and three-year periods.

*Motor vehicles ($14.5 billion)*: Yearly investment tends to follow the CUR movement of the previous year.

*Food ($10.8 billion)*: Investment tends to follow the CUR movements as the CUR rises above or falls below the 80 percent zone. This typically occurs in two- and three-year periods.

*Paper ($8.5 billion)*: Investment tends to follow the CUR movements as the CUR rises above or falls below the 85 percent zone. This typically occurs in two- and three-year periods.

*Electric and gas utilities ($48.7 billion)*: Investment tends to follow the CUR movements as the CUR rises above or falls below the 85 percent zone.

This review of the high-investment industries indicates a broad relationship beween the CURs and investment that is consistent with the theoretical supposition. The exception is petroleum refining, in which other factors dominate investment spending. In most of the industries—nonelectrical machinery, electrical machinery, food, paper and utilities, as well as in total manufacturing—the relationship is operative as the CURs move above or below certain zones. Such a turnaround zone is not apparent for chemicals, and motor vehicles, perhaps because the influence of new products for chemicals and style changes, including vehicle size, for motor vehicles override the significance of a turnaround zone.

Figure 21. **Capacity Utilization and Plant and Equipment Investment: Petroleum Refining**

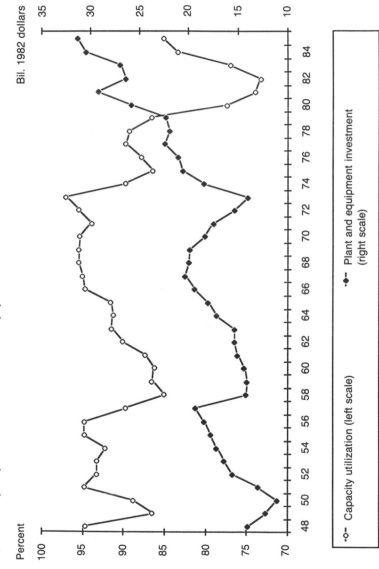

*Note:* Based on Federal Reserve Board and Bureau of Economic Analysis data.

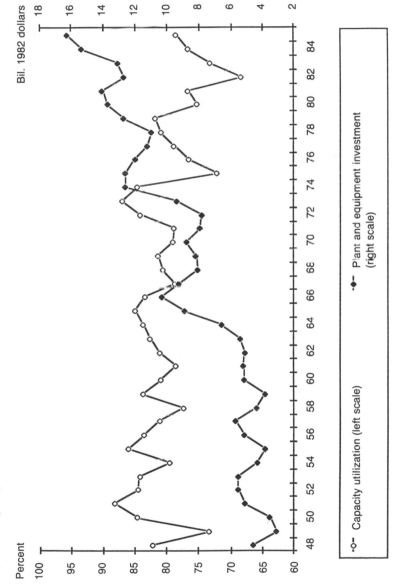

Figure 22. **Capacity Utilization and Plant and Equipment Investment: Chemicals**

Percent

Bil. 1982 dollars

- Capacity utilization (left scale)
- Plant and equipment investment (right scale)

*Note*: Based on Federal Reserve Board and Bureau of Economic Analysis data.

Figure 23. **Capacity Utilization and Plant and Equipment Investment: Nonelectrical Machinery**

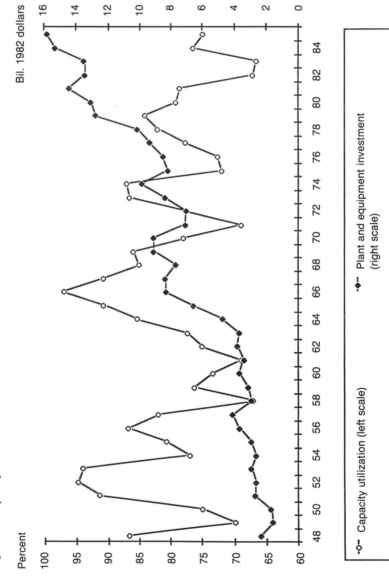

*Note*: Based on Federal Reserve Board and Bureau of Economic Analysis data.

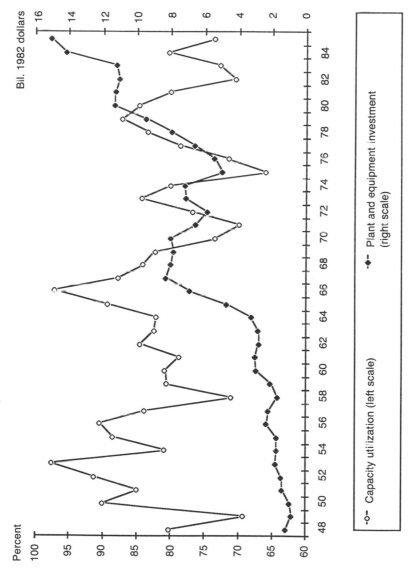

Figure 24. **Capacity Utilization and Plant and Equipment Investment: Electrical Machinery**

Percent

Bil. 1982 dollars

-o- Capacity utilization (left scale)

-●- Plant and equipment investment (right scale)

*Note:* Based on Federal Reserve Board and Bureau of Economic Analysis data

130

Figure 25. **Capacity Utilization and Plant and Equipment Investment: Motor Vehicles**

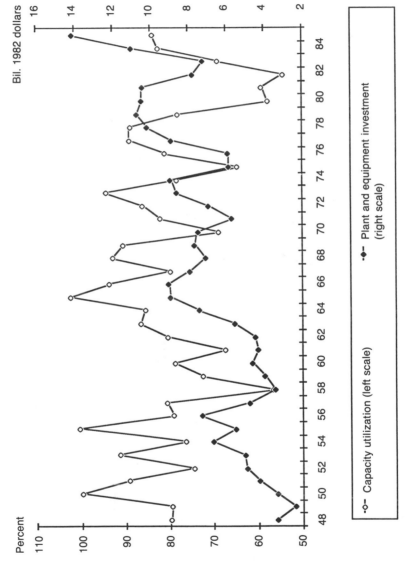

*Note:* Based on Federal Reserve Board and Bureau of Economic Analysis data.

Figure 26. **Capacity Utilization and Plant and Equipment Investment: Food**

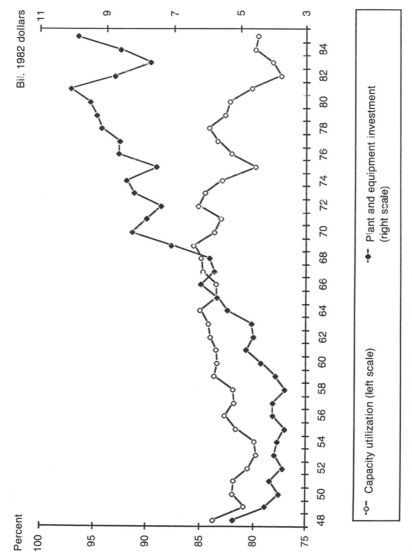

*Note:* Based on Federal Reserve Board and Bureau of Economic Analysis data.

Figure 27. **Capacity Utilization and Plant and Equipment Investment: Paper**

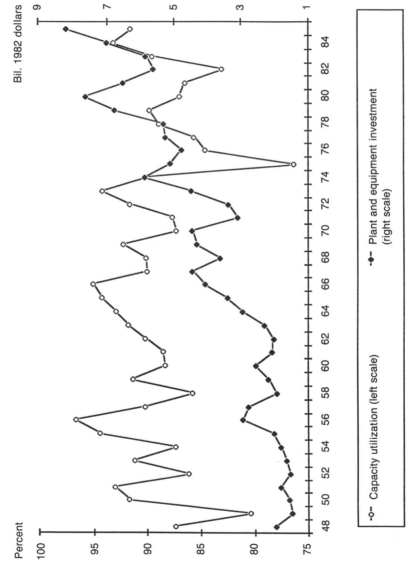

*Note*: Based on Federal Reserve Board and Bureau of Economic Analysis data.

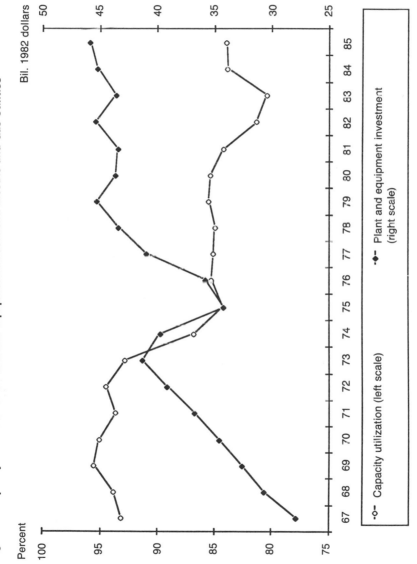

Figure 28. **Capacity Utilization and Plant and Equipment Investment: Electric and Gas Utilities**

*Note*: Based on Federal Reserve Board and Bureau of Economic Analysis data.

The import of this assessment is that CURs offer clues to future trends in investment spending in the cyclically volatile industries with large capital investments, but only as a supplement to the investment determinants discussed in Chapter 3. *In using the CUR investment assessments as a supplement to the economy-wide investment outlook in Chapter 3, the analyst should relate the CUR-based estimates to the comparable industry components of the economy-wide projections. This is particularly appropriate when the economy-wide projections are based on industry components, such as the anticipated investment reported in surveys of business plans for plant and equipment spending. Because the CUR industry coverage is a partial although important segment of the economy, their use is limited to the CUR-covered industries.*

## SUMMARY

The IPI covers the most cyclically volatile segments of the economy. While the manufacturing, mining and utilities industries covered in the IPI represent only one-fourth of the GNP, they generate a significant amount of business for service industries and account for the bulk of investment plant and equipment. They therefore have a large secondary impact on the entire economy. Compared to the GNP, the IPI increases much more in expansions (other than periods of slow economic growth) and decreases much more in recessions. The analyst should account for these contrasts in relating the movements of the IPI (which dominate cyclical fluctuations) to the GNP. On average, an annual growth rate in the IPI of at least 6 percent is needed to generate sufficient GNP growth to reduce the unemployment rate.

The CUR provides a theoretical basis for assessing future demand for plant and equipment investment and inflationary pressures. Experience over the post-World War II period indicates that the CURs are related to capital investment, and on a selective industry basis may be used to supplement the economy-wide investment projections. However, no empirical relationship is apparent between the CUR and price movements.

## NOTES

1. For a summary discussion of the construction of the index based on the general revision using the new 1977 weights, see Joan D. Hosley and James E. Kennedy, "A Revision of the Index of Industrial Production," *Federal Reserve Bulletin*, July 1985. A more detailed description of the methodology is available in Board of Governors of the Federal Reserve System, *Industrial Production 1986 Edition: With a Description of the Methodology*, December 1986.

2. These weights are based on Census Bureau value-added data. They differ from GNP value-added measures which do not double-count purchased services or purchased goods, but include sales and property taxes.

3. "A Revision of the Index of Industrial Production," *op. cit.*, pp. 488 and 490 (Table 3).

4. For several technical reasons (among them footnote 2), attempts to "reconcile" differences in the cyclical movements of GNP Goods and the IPI by modifying the definitions to make the two indicators conform more closely have only been partially successful.

5. In prosperous times, managers probably have less pressure to seek more efficient operations and eliminate marginal activities than in periods of slow growth or recessions, when businesses tend to be more aggressive in cutting costs. These practices over the business cycle are difficult to quantify, but they are intuitively plausible and also appear anecdotally in the press. They are related in the economic literature to the idea of "X-Efficiency," which typically associates differences in competitive pressures in monopolistic and more competitive industries. See Harvey Leibenstein, "Allocative Efficiency vs. 'X-Efficiency'," *American Economic Review*, June 1966, and F. M. Scherer, *Industrial Market Structure and Economic Performance*, Second Edition (Rand McNally College Publishing Company: 1980), pp. 464–466.

6. Richard D. Raddock, "Revised Federal Reserve Rates of Capacity Utilization, *Federal Reserve Bulletin*, October 1985.

7. One analyst suggests that even in a major mobilization it is unrealistic to expect CURs in the 100 percent range. See Zoltan E. Kenessey, "Capacity Utilization Statistics: Further Plans," Board of Governors of the Federal Reserve System, *Measures of Capacity Utilization: Problems and Tasks* (Staff Studies 105), July 1979, pp. 245–248.

8. "Revised Federal Reserve Rates of Capacity Utilization," *op. cit.*, p. 763.

9. Bureau of the Census, U.S. Department of Commerce, "Survey of Plant Capacity, 1984," *Current Industrial Reports*, September 1985.

10. "Revised Federal Reserve Rates of Capacity Utilization," *op. cit.*, pp. 761–762.

11. Survey of Plant Capacity, *op. cit.*

12. *Ibid.*, p. B 1.

13. *Ibid.* The preferred operating rates are included in the same report as the conventional capacity utilization rates.

# 5 • Unemployment, Employment, and Productivity

Labor is the dominant source of household income. It is also the dominant cost item to business and governments in producing the nation's goods and services: employee compensation (wages and fringe benefits) accounts for about 60 percent of the GNP (see Chapter 3). Hence, trends in employment and unemployment have tremendous economic significance.

This chapter focuses on the main labor indicators of unemployment, employment, and productivity. The basic data for these indicators are provided monthly and quarterly by the Bureau of Labor Statistics. The unemployment rate, probably the most familiar indicator, is discussed first, followed by employment (which includes hours worked and wage rates) and productivity (which includes the relationship of unit labor costs to inflation).

The discussion of trends in employment and unemployment is limited to what they indicate about economic growth and material living conditions. However, the analyst should note that these trends may also affect the economy in more intangible ways, such as the effect they may have on personal satisfaction and social stability. While, strictly speaking, these factors are not "economic," they can affect economic developments. For example, voters experiencing high unemployment are more likely to vote for politicians who offer new economic theories and the promise of job creation. While such cause-and-effect relationships are difficult to quantify, the analyst should bear them in mind when considering the economic policy implications of employment data.

## UNEMPLOYMENT

The unemployment rate (UR) is the proportion of the nation's working population 16 years of age and older that is out of work and looking for a job. It functions as a relative measure of the degree of slack in job markets. A relatively high UR indicates that production may be expanded without generating inflation, because the available labor supply will tend to moderate wage rate increases and in some cases reduce wage rates. Conversely, in periods of low unemployment, rapid economic growth will frequently raise wages—the tighter labor supply pushes up wages as more jobs are filled with less experienced and less productive workers. It should be noted, however, that the overall UR may mask significant differences among local labor markets, occupations and industries, and demographic groups.

## PART A: ESTIMATING METHODOLOGY

There are several measures of unemployment. All are calculated by figuring the number of unemployed persons as a proportion of the labor force, which is defined as the sum of employed plus unemployed persons. The basic difference among the various measures is the definition of the unemployed.[1]

$$\text{Unemployment rate} = \frac{\text{Unemployed persons}}{\text{Employed plus unemployed persons (Labor force)}} \times 100$$

The most widely accepted UR measure defines the labor force as consisting of persons at least 16 years old who have a job or are actively seeking work. There are two variants of this conventional definition, one covering both civilian and armed-forces employment and the other including only civilian employment. The employment component includes full-time and part-time jobs as paid employees, self-employment, and persons working at nonpaid jobs in a family business for at least 15 hours a week. All persons are counted equally if they are paid for an hour or more of work per week. If a person has two or more jobs, the job with the most hours worked in the week is the only one counted in the figures. (The effect of this treatment is compared with a different employment measure in the next section on employment.) Unemployed persons are those who looked for a job at least once in the previous four weeks and specify an acceptable job search (for example, answered a newspaper advertisement or checked with an employment agency, employer, friends or relatives).

Persons under 16 years of age (regardless of their employment status) and those with no job who are not actively seeking work are "not in the labor force" and therefore are not included in the UR figures. For example, "discouraged workers"—persons 16 and older who are not looking for a job because they believe there are no available jobs in their area or in their line of work, or because they believe that they would not qualify for existing job openings—are not included in the labor force or UR measures because they are neither working nor looking for work. Discouraged workers usually equal about 1.0 to 1.5 percent of the labor force, tending toward the lower figure in expansions and the higher in recessions.

The information used in deriving the UR is obtained from a monthly survey of a sample of about 60,000 households, conducted for the Bureau of Labor Statistics by the Census Bureau. The survey covers the calendar week that includes the 12th day of the month. Because the sample may not be fully representative of the demographic and economic characteristics of America's 63 million households, the chances are that in two of three cases, the error in the level and monthly movement of the UR is plus or minus 0.1 percentage point.[2] For example, if the UR is 7 percent, it most likely is in the range of 6.9 to 7.1 percent. Because of this sampling error, a single month-to-month change of 0.1 percentage point is not statistically significant, but a change of 0.2 percentage point or more is statistically significant. By the same token, cumulated changes in the UR in the same upward or downward direction of 0.1 percentage point a month for two or more months in a row are statistically significant. If the reliability range is raised to 19 of 20 cases—thus raising the accuracy of the figures from the above example of two out of three cases—the sampling error for the level and change increases to 0.2 percentage point, and the above examples are increased accordingly. Thus, a UR of 7 percent would have an error range of 6.8 to 7.2 percent, an a monthly change would have to be at least 0.3 percentage point to be statistically significant.

Some economists believe that the measured UR is too high because the labor force figures do not include persons working in the underground economy (see Chapter 1 for a general discussion of the underground economy). In a review of the literature on the problem published in 1984, the Bureau of Labor Statistics questioned the validity of estimates by other analysts, such as that in 1978 the official UR was overstated by 1.5 percentage points.[3] They concluded that there are no sound estimates of the effect of the underground economy on the UR, and that their analysis of the household survey data did not substantiate the claims of a significant effect on the UR. However, this is still an unresolved issue, and the analyst should follow new findings on the topic. If such estimates are developed, they also would affect the employment figures discussed in the next section.

## Alternative UR's

The BLS provides eight alternative URs based on the household survey (Table 11). The lowest UR is associated with persons unemployed for 15 weeks or longer The highest includes persons working part-time who would work full-time if jobs were available, plus "discouraged" workers who do not look for work because they think there are no jobs for them. The range between these extremes is considerable—2 to 10.4 percent in the fourth quarter of 1985, with the conventional definitions at 7 percent. URs are also calculated from the household survey for components of demographic groups by age, race, ethnic origin, sex and family

Table 11

## Alternative Unemployment Rates Using Varying Definitions of Unemployment and the Labor Force (in percent)

|  |  | 1985: 4[a] |
|---|---|---|
| U–1 | Persons unemployed 15 weeks or longer as a percent of the civilian labor force | 1.9 |
| U–2 | Job losers as a percent of the civilian labor force[b] | 3.5 |
| U–3 | Unemployed persons 25 years and over as a percent of the civilian labor force | .5.4 |
| U–4 | Unemployed full-time jobseekers as a percent of the full-time civilian labor force | 6.7 |
| **U–5a** | **Total unemployed (16 years and older) as a percent of the labor force, including the resident armed forces** | **6.0** |
| **U–5b** | **Total unemployment (16 years and older) as a percent of the civilian labor force** | **7.0** |
| U–6 | Unemployed persons seeking full-time jobs plus 1/2 of unemployed persons seeking part-time jobs plus 1/2 of employed persons who are working part-time for economic reasons as a percent of the civilian labor force less 1/2 of the part-time labor force[c] | 9.4 |
| U–7 | U–6 plus discouraged workers as a percent of the civilian labor force plus discouraged workers less 1/2 of the part-time labor force[c] | 10.4 |

[a]Fourth quarter of 1985.

[b]Job losers are unemployed because because they were laid off or fired.

[c]"Part-time for economic reasons" refers to persons who wish to work full-time but who are working less than 35 hours a week because of slack work, materials shortages, or other factors beyond their control.

*Source*: Bureau of Labor Statistics, U. S. Department of Labor, "The Employment Situation: February 1986" (News Release), March 7, 1986, Table A–5.

responsibility to highlight variations that different segments of the population have in obtaining work. In addition, there is a measure of unemployment based on unemployment insurance data, although as discussed below, it isn't comparable to the eight URs.

The two conventional URs that are the most widely accepted (U–5a and U–5b in Table 10) are the "official" measures. These two are the most neutral in terms of value judgments related to the widely accepted labor force definitions. They include all unemployed workers and give equal weight to each unemployed person. The only difference between them is the inclusion of the resident armed forces (those stationed in the United States) as a portion of the labor force in the 5a measure. Typically, their measures differ by only 0.1 percentage point—the UR (5a) including the armed forces being lower than the civilian UR (5b).

Although their movements over time are similar, the different UR definitions indicate a varying absolute range of slackness in the economy.[4] They therefore tend to be cited selectively by persons characterizing the extent of unemployment, depending on social or political perspectives. For example, those who wish to emphasize the economy's success in generating employment highlight the U-1 end of the spectrum giving the lower URs, and those who wish to emphasize the economy's failure to provide jobs highlight the U-7 end giving the higher URs.

## Unemployment Associated with Unemployment Insurance

A different measure of unemployment based on persons collecting unemployment insurance benefit payments is provided weekly and monthly by the Employment and Training Administration in the U.S. Department of Labor. Its main use for macroeconomic analysis is that the figures on persons filing initial claims for benefit payments when they become unemployed are a component of the composite index of leading indicators (see Chapter 8).

The basic problem with the unemployment insurance data is that their coverage is limited to persons filing claims for unemployment insurance benefits and consequently is a much less comprehensive measure of unemployment than those based on the household survey discussed above. In 1984, for example, on average 2.6 million unemployed workers were insured by state and federal unemployment insurance programs, compared with 8.5 million workers counted as unemployed in the household survey; thus, data on insured unemployment represented only 31 percent of all unemployment. Similarly, in 1984 the insured UR was 2.8 percent compared to the household UR of 7.5 percent.[5]

Many unemployed persons cannot receive unemployment insurance because benefits are only payable to those who (a) lost their job, (b) previously worked long enough to be eligible for benefit payments (e.g., six months), (c) applied for benefit payments, and (d) have not exhausted the period (e.g., 26 weeks) during which they may collect the payments. Thus, insured unemployment excludes such groups as young persons looking for their first job after graduation, former workers who are re-entering the labor force, and those who are otherwise ineligible or have exhausted their unemployment benefits.

In addition, the proportion of unemployed persons covered by unemployment insurance has declined over time. This falloff was gradual from the mid–1950s to 1980, and accelerated after 1980. A recent study suggested that the gradual decline until 1980 was caused by the changing demographic composition of the labor force—males 24 years and older, who historically accumulate more unemployment benefits from longer work experience, are a declining proportion of the labor force—and by the shift of industries from manufacturing, construction and mining (industries with high unemployment insurance coverage) to services (an area in which coverage is low, even after insurance coverage was extended by federal law).[6] This study also suggested that the decline quickened since 1980 mainly because of new laws taxing unemployment benefits, and to a lesser extent because of (a) reductions in unemployment benefits to older unemployed workers who then retire and receive Social Security and private pensions, (b) reductions in extended benefits (federal payments available during recessions to unemployed workers whose 26-week state payments have run out), and (c) cutbacks in funding for state unemployment insurance offices.

However, because the insured UR data are available weekly and because their monthly movements (the average of the four weeks) tend to be similar although not identical to those for the household UR, they are sometimes used as a clue to the forthcoming monthly household UR. *The analyst should treat these clues as suggestive only, because the weekly trends do not always indicate the more comprehensive household UR movements.*

## Dynamic Factors in Labor Force and UR Analysis

Long-term and short-term movements in and out of the labor force complicate UR analysis. As previously stated, the labor force is the sum of employed and unemployed persons. The "labor force participation rate" represents the number of persons in the labor force as a proportion of the population 16 years of age and older.

Long-term demographic cycles are important in assessing UR trends over several years. Population changes resulting from long-term birthrate cycles have the most pronounced impact on the labor force over long-run five- and 10-year periods, mainly because of the lag in the effect of birthrates in previous decades on the working-age population. (Changing immigration, emigration, and death rates are less important factors affecting the working-age population.) For example, the low birthrates of the depression in the 1930s led to a low compounded annual increase of the working-age population in the 1950s of 1.1 percent; the baby boom of the latter 1940s and the 1950s resulted in faster average annual increases in the working-age population of 1.6 percent in the 1960s and 2.0 percent in the 1970s. The subsequent drop in birth rates extending from the mid–1960s through the mid–1980s lowered the annual working age population increases in 1980–84 to 1.2 percent.[7]

Changes in the labor-force participation rate over the long run mainly reflect changes in life-style. These are typified by the tendency for increasing proportions of women to pursue a career while greater proportions of men have shortened their working careers by going to school longer and retiring earlier. The overall effect of these tendencies on the combined civilian participation rate for men and women has changed since 1950; while this total rate increased from only 59.2 percent to 60.4 percent from 1950 to 1970, the relatively large growth of women in the labor force during the 1970s raised the total rate in 1980 to 63.8 percent. In the early 1980s, the influx of women slowed as the total rate in 1985 reached 64.8 percent, although the influx was still faster than in 1950–70.[8] On balance, the long-run factors of a rising rate for women and a declining rate for men have resulted in an upward trend in the total rate.

Over shorter cyclical periods, changes in the participation rates of persons entering and leaving the labor market are more likely to respond to short-term economic conditions. Typically, more people enter the labor force in expansions than in recessions, as the prospects of finding a job are higher in expansions than in recessions. Yet even in recessions there tends to be a general upward thrust in participation because of the underlying upward trend.

Monthly and quarterly movements of the participation rate are key items affecting the short-run UR, because they indicate how individuals perceive their immediate chances of finding work. Intuitively, one would expect that more persons would enter the labor force during expansions than during recessions because they would be more hopeful of getting a job when the economy is growing. However, short-term movements in and out of the labor force do not always follow such expected patterns. For example, in recessions it isn't clear what the typical behavior is if one member of a family loses a job—whether this causes another family member to seek work to supplement the family's income (the added-worker effect), or if the declining job market discourages the second family member from seeking work (the discouraged-worker effect).[9] These alternative responses introduce an uncertain short-term factor into the labor force and the UR. At the extremes, a greater optimism about job prospects could cause a rise in the UR at the same time that employment is rising if more people enter the labor force than can be hired; conversely, if declining employment causes large numbers to withdraw from the labor market because of the pessimistic outlook for jobs, the UR could decline along with the falling employment (although this is more hypothetical than experiential, since unemployment has always increased in recessions).

In some months these movements in and out of the labor force result in changes in the UR that outweigh changes in employment. In these cases, large numbers of persons leaving the labor force lower the UR while large numbers of persons entering the labor force raise the UR. Thus, UR trends may give a different picture of the economy than employment trends. In 1986, for example, the UR increased in May and decreased in June, although employment increased in both months. *Therefore, in evaluating UR movements, the analyst should consider the monthly effects of flows in and out of the labor force.*

# PART B.  ANALYSIS OF TRENDS

Over the post-World War II business cycles, the UR moved as expected—declining in expansions and rising in recessions. The only exception was the expansion from 1945 to 1948; the exceptionally low UR of 1.9 percent in 1945 was not sustained in the subsequent demobilization of war production and the reduction of the resident armed forces (from 11.4 million in 1945 to 1.5 million in 1948). Thus, the UR averaged 3.9 percent in 1946 and 1947 and 3.8 percent in 1948. In retrospect, these were the lowest "peacetime" URs in the postwar period, as discussed below. The relatively low URs in 1946–48 resulted from the strong civilian economy noted in Chapter 3, and from the return of many veterans to full-time schooling, which removed them from the labor force.

Several features of the UR movements are noteworthy. First, unemployment levels have worsened over time, drifting upward so that typically the low point at the peak of each expansion is higher that it was at the peak of the previous expansion. Second, the UR has not been below 3 percent other than in the 1952–53 Korean War period, and since then it was below 4 percent for a sustained period only in the 1966–69 Vietnam War period. Third, the goal of achieving, through fiscal and monetary policies, a minimum level of unemployment, corresponding to a notion of "full employment," without causing inflation has changed. In the 1960s it was believed the lowest feasible UR was 3 to 4 percent; in the 1970s this figure was raised to 5 to 6 percent, and there has been little discussion of minimum unemployment goals in the 1980s.

## Upward Drift in URs

Figure 29 shows the UR at the peaks and troughs of the postwar expansions and recessions. A long-term upward movement in the UR occurs when the UR is increasingly higher at the peaks of the succeeding expansions and at the troughs of succeeding recessions (a correspondingly downward movement occurs when the UR has decreasingly lower peaks and troughs). Following an upward creep in the 1950s and a sharper decline in the 1960s, the UR generally rose from 1970–85. From slightly below 4 percent at the end of the 1960s, it drifted upward in succeeding expansions to around 7 percent in the 1980s. There was a similar upward drift in the UR at the troughs of recessions: it rose from 6 to 7 percent at these troughs through 1970 to 9 and 10.6 percent in 1975 and 1982 (the intervening 1980 recession trough was 7.8 percent).

This upward drift in the UR is primarily the result of (a) a declining rate of economic growth since the 1970s, and (b) the changing demographic composition of the labor force since the 1960s. The slowdown in the real GNP growth rate (see Chapter 3) damaged the economy's ability to absorb the increasing number of persons seeking jobs. The changing composition of the labor force that raised unemployment rates—the relatively large increase in the teenage population due to birthrate cycles and, less importantly, the increasing participation of women in the labor force—are elaborated in the following sections on minimum URs.

## Minimum URs

A major policy interest in the UR has been finding the lowest level that could be

Figure 29. **Unemployment Rate for All Civilian Workers**

Percent

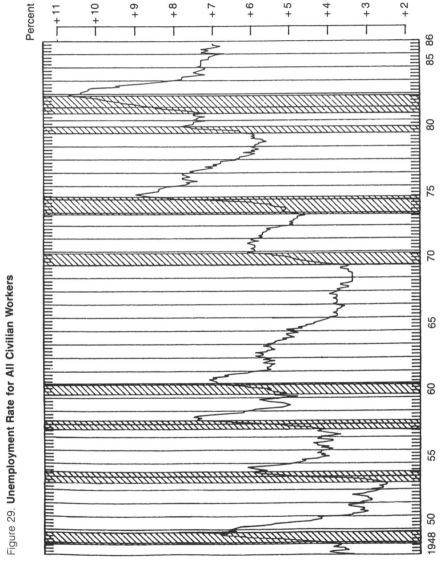

*Note:* Based on Bureau of Labor Statistics data. Lined bars are recession periods.

sustained over long periods without causing inflation. Over the years this concept has been referred to variously as "full," "maximum" or "high" employment, "natural" unemployment, and the "nonaccelerating inflation rate of unemployment." Regardless of the terminology, the intent is to establish an employment level toward which the nation should strive. There are two major issues relevant to developing a minimum UR: determining an "acceptable" rate of inflation and adjusting the UR for the changing composition of the labor force.

With respect to inflation, a minimum UR raises the question of what rate of price increase accompanying minimum unemployment goals is acceptable. The 1956 UR of 4 percent and 1.5 percent increase in the consumer price index were sometimes referred to as a desirable goal because that was the lowest peacetime UR since the Korean War. However, one year later, when the UR rose only slightly, to 4.2 percent, inflation rose much more (contrary to economic theory), to 3.6 percent, which emphasizes the poor rationale of using one year as an ideal. The 1962 *Economic Report of the President* cited a 4 percent minimum UR as an interim goal, implying that it could be driven below 4 percent, but did not specify the accompanying rate of inflation.[10] Nor did commentaries in the 1970s that mentioned minimum URs of 5 to 7 percent specify the inflation rate. Then in 1978 the Full Employment and Balanced Growth Act (Humphrey-Hawkins Act) established a UR goal of 4 percent and an inflation goal of 3 percent by 1983, with a further reduction of inflation to zero by 1988; however, the Act permits the inflation goals to be relaxed if they would hinder achieving the unemployment goal. In mid–1986, inflation was increasing at an annual rate of 2 percent and the UR was 7 percent; thus, inflation was slightly closer than unemployment to the 1988 goals.

In estimating a minimum UR, it is recognized that there will always be some unemployment, for two reasons. First, there is never a perfect match between persons in the labor force and the skills required by employers, because of residual outmoded skills from declining industries, lack of training, geographic immobility of workers, or age, race, sex, and other discrimination in hiring (structural unemployment). Second, there is an inherent time lag in finding a job whether persons are newly entering the labor force or whether they have lost their job (frictional unemployment).[11] In practice, determining a minimum UR that would accommodate this structural and frictional unemployment has been based on past relationships between unemployment and inflation rather than on an analysis of what the inherent structure of the economy would generate (this approach is referred to as the "Phillips curve" and is discussed in Chapter 6). Although a structural analysis is theoretically more appealing, it would require an assessment of the micro transactions of buyers and sellers in product, labor, and financial markets that could be translated into the overall macro economy. This is a monumental task, and the methodology of economics is not yet capable of it (see the "Macro vs. Micro Analysis" section in the Introduction). There is also a view held by "monetarist" economists (who are discussed in Chapter 7) that the trade-off between unemployment and inflation occurs only in the short run; in the long run, according to this view, there is no trade-off, as all attempts to stimulate economic growth will only increase inflation without lowering unemployment. [12]

## Demographic and Growth Factors Affecting Minimum URs

As noted previously, the targeted minimum URs have drifted upward from 3 to 4 percent in the 1960s to 5 to 7 percent in the 1970s, with much less discussion of an actual figure in the 1980s (see Chapter 3 on government spending and finances). The upward drift reflected the perception that because teenagers and adult women, who had higher URs than men, were accounting for an increasing proportion of the labor force, this demographic change alone would increase a minimum UR over time. In a study of the effect of these demographic changes, the Bureau of Labor Statistics estimated that if the composition of the labor force between 1957 and 1977 had remained the same, the civilian UR would have been 0.8 of a percentage point lower than it was in 1977 (6.3 percent compared with the actual 7.1 percent). [13] The study also found that most of the increase in unemployment due to the demographic factors over the period resulted from the increased number of teenagers in the population rather than from the increasing labor force participation rates of women: there is a great disparity between adult male URs compared with teenage URs, while adult male and female UR's are much closer. Examples of these URs from 1957 to 1985 (during four expansion years) are shown below.

|                           | 1957 | 1967 | 1977 | 1985 |
|---------------------------|------|------|------|------|
| Adult men (20 years + )   | 3.6  | 2.3  | 5.2  | 6.2  |
| Adult women (20 years + ) | 4.1  | 4.2  | 7.0  | 6.6  |
| Teenagers (16 to 19)      | 11.6 | 12.9 | 17.8 | 18.6 |

However, the upward creep in the UR due to the demographic shifts was reversed in the mid–1970s. As a result of the birthrate cycle discussed in Part A, the teenage proportion of the labor force, which had increased from 6.4 percent in 1957 to 9.6 percent in 1974, fell to 6.8 percent in 1985. Although updated calculations of the effect of these demographic changes since the late 1970s have not been made, they would result in lowering the minimum UR. In fact, the study cited above projected a 0.4 of a percentage point decline in the UR between 1979 and 1990 due to demographic changes of this type that had already occurred. Thus, the demographic changes in the labor force which until the mid–1970s increased the measure of a minimum UR over time have now been reversed. In addition, the lower birthrates of the baby-boom parents will continue the decline in the minimum UR in the 1990s because of the resultant lower proportion of teenage workers.

UR trends also indicate that, independent of the demographic compositional shifts, unemployment levels within each group have risen significantly (for example, the adult-male UR increased from 3.6 in 1957 to 6.2 percent in 1985). In addition, while the adult-female UR typically is higher than the adult-male UR, in the recent years of 1982 and 1983 (not shown above) the adult-female UR was lower. These trends reflect the slower rates of economic growth in 1970–85 (see Chapter 3) and the higher unemployment in the 1982 recession in manufacturing industries (which have a high concentration of male workers) than in service industries (which have a high concentration of female workers).

Figure 30 shows the average annual total UR from 1970 to 1985 (annual URs are 12-month averages; thus, particular months during the year are above and below the average). The figure also shows constant URs of 4, 5 and 6 percent as horizontal lines, which represent the range of minimum URs as discussed above. Because actual URs rose over the 15-year period, the gap between them and the minimum UR goals also increased. URs were at their lowest level in 1970–74, and yet at 5 to 6 percent were always above the 4 percent interim goal of the 1960s; in the 1975–79 period, after rising to over 8 percent in 1975, they declined to the 6 percent range by 1978–79; and in 1980–85 they ranged cyclically from 7 to 9.5 percent.

Minimum unemployment goals are difficult to quantify and are the core of the debate on appropriate economic policies. Typically, liberals emphasize lowering unemployment and allowing for some increase in prices, while conservatives concentrate on holding down inflation and allow for some increase in unemployment. There is also the question of how effective fiscal and monetary policies as discussed in Chapters 2, 3 and 7 can be in lowering unemployment without igniting inflation unless active employment programs are provided—that is, education and training to raise the skill levels of the labor force, along with child care in order to match the skills of the labor force with actual job openings. While minimum unemployment goals are not prominent in economic policy in the mid–1980s, they are likely to re-emerge as an important policy instrument.

## Economic Growth and Unemployment: Okun's Law

Economic growth is a key factor affecting unemployment: rapid economic growth lowers the UR, and slow or declining growth raises the UR. These relationships have been studied by comparing economic growth, as represented by movements in the real GNP, to changes in the UR. Such relationships develop a break-even point indicating (a) the level of growth required for maintaining a steady UR, and (b) the unemployment effects of growth rates above and below the break-even point. This is referred to as "Okun's Law" after Arthur Okun, who developed

Figure 30. **Total Unemployment Rate Annual Averages and Constant Unemployment Rates**

Percent

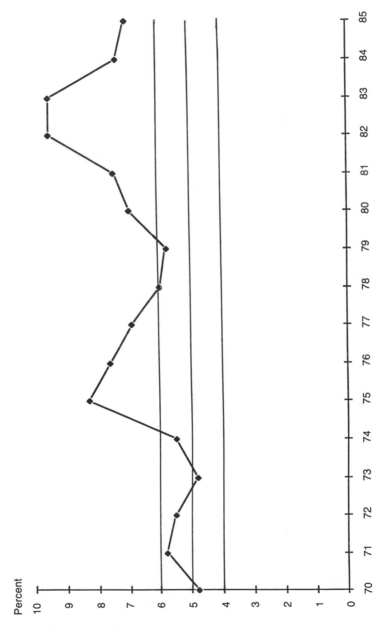

*Note:* Annual figures are based on Bureau of Labor Statistics data. Horizontal lines are constant unemployment rates.

such relationships in the 1960s.

Figure 31 shows the UR/GNP relationship from 1972–85. It indicates the basic inverse relationship:as GNP increases the UR falls, and vice versa. Graphically this appears in the direction of the lines connecting the UR and GNP points for each year, which slope downward to the right. This general relationship is expected from economic theory. However, it is also apparent from the differential slopes of the lines on the chart that the relative movements are not the same in all years. For example, in 1975 the GNP growth rate declined by –1.3 percent and the UR increased by 2.8 percentage points, for a change in the UR of more than twice the change in the GNP; but in 1985, the GNP increased by 2.2 percent and the UR dropped by 0.3 of a percentage point, for a change in the UR of only one-eighth the rate of the GNP change.

A 1984 study by the Federal Reserve Bank of New York that updated the quantification of Okun's Law relationship suggested that the break-even point is an annual real GNP increase of 3 percent. This figure is in line with other estimates using different methodologies—the break-even point in the other estimates is typically 0.3 of a percentage point higher. [14] At the 3 percent growth rate, the UR tends to be stable; and for every percentage point of annual GNP growth above or below 3 percent, the UR tends to decrease (increase) by 0.4 of a percentage point over the year. These relationships are averages and, consistent with the discussion of Chart 31, do not hold for every annual period. The study also noted that while divergences in the actual UR from what is expected from Okun's Law cancel out over the years, the divergences were greater from 1974–83 than from 1960–73.

Several factors complicate the use of Okun's Law. GNP is driven directly by employment, weekly hours worked, and productivity, and these factors do not always move in tandem with the UR trends. As noted previously, short-term monthly movements of unemployment are not always consistent with the movements in employment. Both weekly hours and productivity are discussed below, but their impacts on Okun's Law are noted briefly here. The response of weekly hours worked to changes in economic activity, while tending to lead overall economic activity at the business cycle turning points, fluctuates considerably during the expansion and recession phases, and thus does not always move in the expected direction of increasing in expansions and decreasing in recessions. Productivity shows noticeable changes in longer-term rates of growth that impact on GNP movements, which do not necessarily parallel UR movements.

In addition, the long-run break-even point of a 3 percent annual growth rate in real GNP to maintain a stable unemployment rate may be too high for the 1980s. This is due to the demographic trends, previously noted, that have led to a declining proportion of teenagers (who have very high unemployment rates) in the labor force. Thus, as evidenced by the experience of 1985 and 1986 in which real GNP grew by less than 3 percent and the UR also declined, the declining share of teenage workers that began in the mid-1970s may have reduced the

Figure 31. **Okun's Law: 1972-85**

All-worker unemployment rate, annual change
(percentage points)

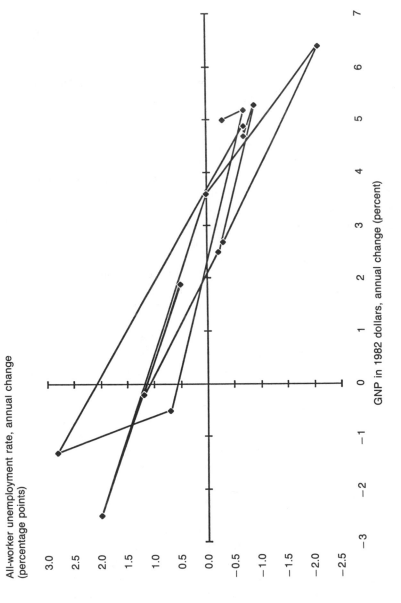

GNP in 1982 dollars, annual change (percent)

*Note:* Lines connect the same year points of unemployment (vertical scale) and GNP (horizontal scale).

break-even point in the mid-1980s to a real GNP growth rate of 2 to 2.5 percent.

*With these caveats, Okun's Law provides an overall perspective for linking economic growth with unemployment. In assessing these trends, the analyst should observe special conditions that may cause large divergences from the the long-run trend for particular periods. In addition, the long-run relationship should be reviewed every few years to determine if there are significant changes that should be brought into the analysis.*

## Digression on Job Vacancies

One approach for assessing the magnitude of unemployment is to compare it with available job vacancies. To make such a comparison meaningfully, it would be necessary to match the distribution of job skills among the unemployed with those required in the available jobs. Only with appropriate data on both of these factors would it be plausible to make unemployment-vacancy comparisons at the overall macro level. If there were a reasonable match, it could be assumed that part of the unemployment could be absorbed. Such an analysis could provide a clearer perspective on the extent of unemployment requiring fiscal and monetary policies or special job programs.

However, no such information on job vacancies is available that would allow absolute comparisons with unemployment levels. Previous attempts by the Bureau of Labor Statistics to collect such data were discontinued in the 1970s because the poor quality of the information obtained prevented its use for job-placement programs or for matching with the employment and unemployment survey figures.[15] The BLS found it very difficult to get a representative sample of employers to cooperate in reporting job vacancies.

As an alternative to collecting job vacancy data from employers, there are the Conference Board figures from help-wanted newspaper advertisements. They are collected from one newspaper in each of 51 cities defined by the Bureau of Labor Statistics as major labor-market areas; this sample is raised to an estimated national total by the proportions of national employment accounted for by the sample cities. The data are provided monthly as an index of the percent change in the number of jobs advertised. The Bureau of Economic Analysis publishes this index, as well as the ratio of the job vacancy index to the percent change index of unemployment, in the *Business Conditions Digest*. These two data series are classified in the *Digest* as a leading indicator at business expansion peaks (turning down before the overall economy slides into a recession), and as a lagging indicator at business recession troughs (turning up after the overall economy moves into a recovery), although they are not part of the composite index of leading indicators (see Chapter 8).

The help-wanted data seem to provide reasonable estimates of the relative change in job vacancies with respect to their timing at expansion and recession turning points. However, they are not comprehensive or representative enough to be used as absolute levels for comparisons with the actual number of unemployed persons, because many jobs are not advertised in newspapers. In fact, the long-run trends in the indexes suggest that the newspaper advertising of job vacancies may be declining. The help-wanted figures also do not distinguish job vacancies by occupational skills, which as noted above is necessary for matching with unemployment skills.

Thus, while some job vacancy figures are available, problems with the data prevent their use at this time for assessing the overall magnitude of unemployment.

## EMPLOYMENT: PERSONS, HOURS, AND WAGES

This section covers three aspects of employment: the number of employed persons, the hours per week they work, and the wages they earn.

### *Employed Persons*

There are two monthly estimates of the number of persons with jobs: (a) the household survey discussed in the previous section on unemployment, and (b) the survey of workers on employer payrolls. They are based on different definitions and data collection methods, and as a result sometimes show noticeably different monthly and cyclical trends. Therefore, it is important to know which figures are used in analyses of trends.

The definitional differences in the two employment surveys also result in each providing different types of detailed data. A basic distinction is that the employer survey provides a count of jobs with considerable industry detail, while the household survey counts unemployed persons, with a focus on demographic characteristics. The household survey provides information not available in the employer survey on employed persons by age, race, sex, family responsibility, agricultural employment and self-employment, and full-time and part-time work.

## *PART A: ESTIMATING METHODOLOGY*

The employer survey counts all paying jobs of nonagricultural civilian employees. It includes *all* jobs held by each worker (not just the primary one), workers under 16 years old, residents of Canada and Mexico who commute to the United States for work, and institutionalized persons on payroll jobs—all of whom are excluded from the household survey. However, it excludes the self-employed; private household, agricultural, and unpaid family workers; and workers on the job rolls but temporarily not receiving pay such as those on strike or on unpaid vacations or sick leave. All of these are in the household survey. Neither surveys makes any distinction between a full-time and a part-time worker—both are counted as one person—and unpaid work around the house by homeowners and renters is excluded. In addition, there are substantial differences in the sampling and data collection aspects of both surveys.

The net effect of these differences is that the household survey shows more employment that the employer survey—in 1985 the household survey's civilian-employment figure was 107.2 million, while the employer survey showed 97.7 million. Most of this 9.5 million difference is accounted for when both measures are put on a similar definitional basis, although this reconciliation cannot be done fully because of the lack of information on all groups of workers that differ between the surveys.[16] In 1985, the reconciliation resulted in the initial difference of 9.5 million more workers in the household survey being shifted to only 300,000 more workers in the employer survey.

Employment based on the household survey was covered in the section on unemployment; the new information noted here concerns the sampling error of the household employment information. In two cases out of three, the monthly level of employment is within a range of plus or minus 270,000 persons, and the monthly change in employment is within a range of plus or minus 205,000 persons;[17] if the reliability is raised to 19 cases out of 20, these ranges are increased to 540,000 and 410,000 respectively. By way of perspective, civilian employment in the household survey in December 1985 totaled 108.2 million and the monthly change from November was 237,000. The sensitivity of the monthly change to sampling error is apparent from the comparison of the November-December 237,000 change to the sampling error in two of three cases of 205,000. The proportionate sampling error for the monthly change is much greater than that for the monthly level. *Thus, no single month's employment should be considered as establishing a trend, but rather should be considered in light of the movements for several months to indicate if something different is occurring.*

The employment figures based on the employer survey are derived from the records of companies, nonprofit organizations, and governments.[18] A sample of these employers is surveyed for the pay period that includes the 12th day of the month. The surveys are conducted for the Bureau of Labor Statistics by state employment agencies. The survey covers the number of workers employed as well as their paid weekly hours and earnings (discussed in the next section). The monthly sample of 280,000 employer establishments (places of work including individual establishments of large companies) covered 40 percent of all nonagricultural employment in 1985.

The monthly figures go through two sets of revisions. They are initially published as "preliminary" in each of the first two months after the survey is taken, and in the third month are "final" based on the most complete returns from the employer sample. These are subsequently revised annually to conform

Table 12

**Percent Difference between Monthly Survey and Benchmark Nonagricultural Employment**

|  | (+ : benchmark exceeds monthly survey<br>− : benchmark less than monthly survey) |
|---|---|
| 1979 | +.5 |
| 1980 | −.1 |
| 1981 | −.4 |
| 1982 | −.1 |
| 1983 | less than .05 |
| 1984 | .4 |
| 1985 | less than .05 |

*Source*: Bureau of Labor Statistics, U.S. Department of Labor, "BLS Establishment Estimates Revised to March 1985 Benchmarks," *Employment and Earnings*, June 1986, p. 7.

to benchmark figures for the month of March which are based on data from the *universe* of all employers reporting their unemployment insurance payments to the state employment offices. The new March levels are then used to revise the previous 11 months, which were based on data obtained from the *sample* of employers, and extrapolations are carried forward to the most current month as well. The unemployment insurance reports covered 97 percent of all nonagricultural employment in 1984; these are supplemented by other reports for industries exempt from unemployment laws, such as those available from Social Security records. Table 12 shows that over 1979–85, the benchmark revisions for all employees ranged from −0.4 percent to +0.5 percent. They reflect differing revision patterns for individual industries—for example, in 1985 transportation and public utilities was lowered by 1 percent and state governments were increased by 2 percent.

Despite the relatively small revisions in the annual benchmarks, there have been long-standing concerns regarding the quality of the employer survey data. Some question how up-to-date the sample of participating firms is, and whether there are appropriate procedures for checking on the accuracy of the data reported by those firms.[19] For example, because a scientifically representative sample of employers has not been maintained in the survey, there are no estimates of the probable range of error in the figures due to the use of a sample. The existing estimates of expected revision are analogous to a range of error and suggest that a true probability sample would not result in significantly different figures, although a probability sample could result in noticeably different monthly movements during the year. A comprehensive program to raise the quality of the survey is underway, but it will be completed in several years.[20]

## Use of Alternative Employment Surveys

Statistically, both surveys have strengths and weaknesses. The household survey is stronger in terms of general sample survey methodology as it has both a scientifically controlled representative sample and better quality controls to assess the validity of the data reported. This advantage is lessened by the typical undercounting in household surveys of minority-group males, who also have relatively high cyclical employment experience. The information source for the employer survey is better because the data are obtained from employer payroll records, which are used for tax returns rather than from answers by household members, which are not documented. The employer survey also does not have the uncertain seasonal adjustment movements for summer students from June to September that occurs in the household survey.

Over the years, the employer survey has been considered to provide a better measure of the monthly change in the total employment.[21] This is discussed in Part B, which includes guidance for assessing the monthly and cyclical trends.

# PART B. ANALYSIS OF TRENDS

There are noticeable differences in the monthly and cyclical movements of employment as measured by the employer and household surveys. The employer survey has both steadier rates of growth over three to six months, and more extreme cyclical movements in the longer expansion and recession periods, than the household survey.

## Monthly Movements

Figure 32 shows the monthly employment trends of both surveys in 1984 and 1985. The figures from the employer survey increased continually over the two years, while the household survey had short periods of decline in both years—June to August 1984 and March to June 1985. These monthly differences are perplexing. It has been suggested that the employer survey may understate employment growth for short periods because it is slow in identifying new firms for its sample (due to the lag in the paperwork of firms that apply to enter the unemployment-insurance system).[22] However, the experience of 1984 and 1985 was in the opposite direction.

The varying movements of the two surveys over three to six months reflect the difference in coverage and methodology noted in Part A. But it is difficult to say which survey gives a better depiction of the actual economy. *Over any period of months, the analyst should compare the employment movements from both surveys. If they are similar, they may be considered to confirm the trend. If they differ significantly, definitional and statistical differences between the surveys should*

Figure 32. **Monthly Employment of Employer and Household Surveys**

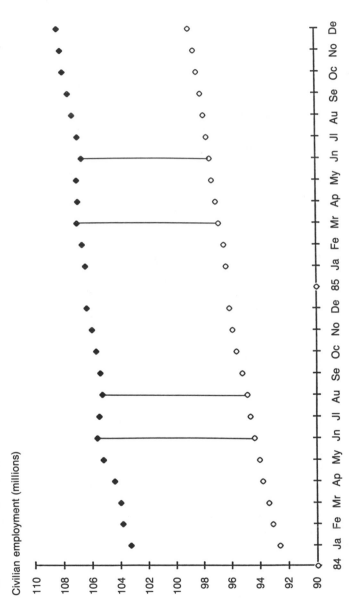

*Note:* Vertical lines highlight periods of differential movements in the two surveys.

*be examined to see if there is a reasonable explanation. If there is no plausible explanation, the trend for that short period may be treated as within the lower and upper range of both survey figures.*

## Cyclical Movements

Figures 33a and 33b show the changes in both employment surveys and in the real GNP during the postwar expansions and recessions (the cyclical turning points are the same as those used in Chapter 3 for the GNP). In all cases, the employer survey showed more extreme cyclical movements, increasing more in expansions and decreasing more in recessions than the household survey. The typical cyclical difference between the two surveys was 1 to 2 percentage points; the exceptional cases of much larger differences occurred in the expansions of 1950–53 (10 percentage points) and 1961–69 (13 percentage points). While the differentials have been relatively stable since the 1970s, the differences in definition and methodology suggest that large variations may again occur, although probably not as great as in 1950–53 and 1961–69.

Employment as measured in both surveys is typically less cyclical than the GNP, rising less in expansions and falling less in recessions. The GNP is more cyclical because in addition to employment, it takes into account weekly hours and productivity, both of which are more cyclical than employment. (They are discussed later in this chapter.)

Explanations of the varying cyclical patterns are based on qualitative assessments of the likely effect of the differences between the two surveys.[23] In recessions, there are two situations that result in employment decreases in the employer survey and no decrease in the household survey. These are cases in which a dual jobholder loses one job, and cases in which a person loses a job with a large employer who is a respondent in the employer survey and switches to a marginal employer who is not in the employer survey (perhaps even switching to the underground economy). In expansions, the reverse situation occurs for persons who had been with marginal employers not in the employer survey and switch as demand increases to larger employers that are in the employer survey; this appears as an employment increase in the employer survey but as no change in the household survey. Another supposition on the greater cyclical volatility of the employer survey is considered more speculative: it is possible that because the persons typically undercounted in household surveys, such as minority males, are those with the greatest cyclical changes in employment, the undercount may reduce that survey's employment fluctuations.

There also are cyclical fluctuations in self-employment, which is included in the household and excluded from the employer survey. Self-employment increases in expansions along with other employment, but in recessions it tends to decline less sharply and to start increasing sooner than wage and salary employment.[24] These countercyclical movements in recessions may result from two

Figure 33a. **Business Cycle Movements of Civilian Employment and Real GNP: Expansions**

Percent change

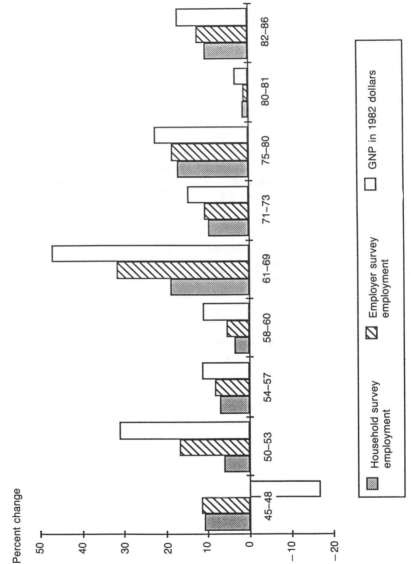

*Note:* Based on Bureau of Labor Statistics and Bureau of Economic Analysis data.

159

Figure 33b. **Business Cycle Movements of Civilian Employment and Real GNP: Recessions**

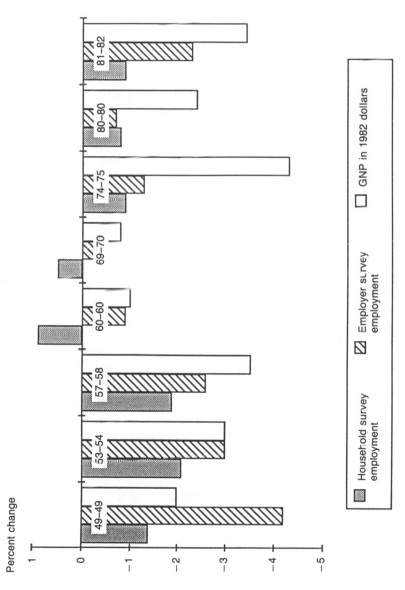

*Note:* Based on Bureau of Labor Statistics and Bureau of Economic Analysis data.

factors: (a) persons who are self-employed as a second job and thus are counted only in their primary job in the household survey, are counted as self-employed when they lose their employee job, and (b) some workers who have lost their jobs and aren't able to find another one try self-employment and thus are still counted in the household survey.

As an overall assessment of which survey is most appropriate for cyclical analysis, the conceptual emphasis in the employer survey on jobs, including dual jobholders, gives a better picture on employment in expansions and recessions than the emphasis on demographic groups in the household survey. Main coverage drawbacks of the employer survey are the exclusion of nonagricultural self-employed and all agricultural workers (these accounted for 10.3 percent of the household survey's civilian employment in 1985), and the fact that the survey does not specify the number of persons (as distinct from jobs) and which demographic groups are gaining and losing. Statistically, the weaknesses in both surveys seem to produce a standoff. *But, on balance, the concept of jobs seems most relevant for assessing cyclical employment trends, which suggests that the analyst should focus on the employer survey.*

## Labor Hours, Earnings and Costs

Wage payments represent income to workers and costs to employers. They affect consumer purchasing power, job security, business profits, and inflation. They also have an impact on wage bargaining.

The total amount of wage payments in the economy reflects three factors: the number of jobs (discussed in the previous section), average hours on the job, and average wage rates of pay. *Weekly hours* represent the average length of the workweek. *Weekly earnings* are the average weekly paycheck, from the combined result of the hourly rate of pay and the weekly hours. Both hours and earnings are averages for all private nonfarm industries and occupations, and thus can change if there is a shift of jobs between industries or occupations that have longer and shorter workweeks or higher and lower rates of pay, such as manufacturing and services or clerks and computer programmers. *Wage costs* represent changes in the average paycheck for all private nonfarm industries, assuming that the distribution of jobs between industries and occupations remains constant. Thus, wage costs measure labor expenses for doing the same kind of work. Weekly hours and weekly earnings are provided monthly, and wage costs are provided quarterly, by the Bureau of Labor Statistics.

The data are based on survey information obtained from employers for the pay period that includes the 12th day of the month for the total of full-time and part-time workers in all private nonagricultural industries. Similar information is available for particular industries. The hours and earnings data are obtained mainly from the employer survey on the number of jobs, covered in the previous section. The indicator on wage costs—the employment-cost index—

is based on a different survey, which is discussed below.

The hours, earnings, and costs are averages for the total of full-time and part-time workers, and of overtime hours that are paid a premium over the straight-time rate in private nonagricultural industries. Technically, they are based on "hours paid for," which includes employees on paid vacations and sick leave, as distinct from the actual working time on the job (hours worked). This is done so that the payments represent the actual earnings and costs, rather than simply the hours worked.

The data on hours and earnings are limited to "production and nonsupervisory workers," which in all industries exclude executives and managers; in manufacturing, construction, and mining, workers engaged in professional, technical, office and sales activities are excluded as well.[25] Thus, the data represent "line" workers as distinct from administrative and support employees. The information on wage costs is more comprehensive on two counts. It includes all workers—production and nonsupervisory workers as well as executives, managers, administrative, and support personnel. The cost figures also include money wages and fringe benefits in a combined total as "compensation." In contrast to the earnings figures, which only cover money wages, the cost data include payments by the employer for Social Security, unemployment insurance, and private health and life group insurance.

## Weekly Hours

The figure for weekly hours is an early indicator of changes in the utilization of labor. Typically, employers change existing employees' hours before hiring new employees when sales turn up in a recession and before laying off workers when sales turn down in an expansion. Because recent sales trends may be reversed in a short period, it is simpler for employers to adjust work schedules first. Hiring new employees involves administrative costs and training time, which may not be justified by future business activity. Laying off workers in temporary downturns may result in losing efficient labor to other employers just as demand picks up. Retaining workers during slack periods that are expected to be of short duration—sometimes referred to as "hoarding"—is one way to avoid this possibility. Other factors encourage employers not to immediately lay off workers before there is a more definitive indication of sales trends. They recognize the importance of the job to the worker and, on a personal level, may be reluctant to lay anyone off. Employers also seek to avoid higher unemployment insurance premiums, which can result from increasing layoffs because the premiums are based on the unemployment experience of the employer.

The figure for average weekly hours in manufacturing industries is so sensitive to changes in demand that it is classified as a "leading" indicator of business activity—turning up before the general economy starts rising from a recession trough, and turning down before the general economy begins declining from an expansion peak. The manufacturing figure is one of the twelve components of the composite index of leading indicators (see Chapter 8). It includes overtime, and typically ranges from 39 to 41 hours; in short periods, typically of one to three months, it has fallen below 39 hours in some recessions, and less frequently has risen above 41 hours in expansions.

On average, it takes at least three months for the weekly hours figures for manufacturing to establish a cyclical upward or downward trend. A one- or two-month upward or downward movement is affected by too many factors to be considered a statistically reliable trend. However, even within the longer expansion and recession periods, the weekly hours series is quite erratic. This characteristic is shared by several components of the composite leading index, including the initial applications for unemployment insurance noted earlier in the section on unemployment. *Consequently, the analyst should consider current trends in weekly hours only as a broad clue to developments in labor markets.*

## Weekly Earnings

The data on average weekly earnings in constant dollars provide trends on the material well-being of all workers from their job earnings after correcting for effects of price inflation. This estimate of the purchasing power of wage income is obtained by modifying the actual income for price changes as measured by the consumer price index (see Chapter 6).

A simplified version of the relationship between income, prices, and spending (assuming no change in saving rates) may be summarized as follows: If both income and prices change at the same rate, income keeps pace with inflation and will have a neutral effect on consumer spending; if income rises faster than prices, the increased purchasing power will be a stimulus for consumers to buy more goods and services, and thus production and employment will increase; and if prices rise faster than income, the decline in consumer spending will result in lower production and employment. Analogous relationships between income and spending occur if prices are declining, although price declines in non-depression periods occur only in occasional months; for example, if income remains the same and prices decline, purchasing power increases. In this schema, income is used synonymously with earnings of each jobholder, although income for the broader household spending unit includes income for all workers in the family plus income from investments and income maintenance programs, as measured in personal income (see Chapter 3 under "Consumer Expenditures"). The assumed one-to-one relationship between purchasing power and spending is also modified by consumers' perception of future job prospects and inflation, as discussed in Chapter 3 under Consumer Expenditures.

Figure 34 shows the trend from 1970 to 1985 of average weekly earnings corrected for price change as an index using 1977=100. Weekly earnings in constant dollars declined from the peak years of 1972-73 to 1980 by 13 percent, and then leveled out between 1980 and 1985 with small year-to-year fluctuations

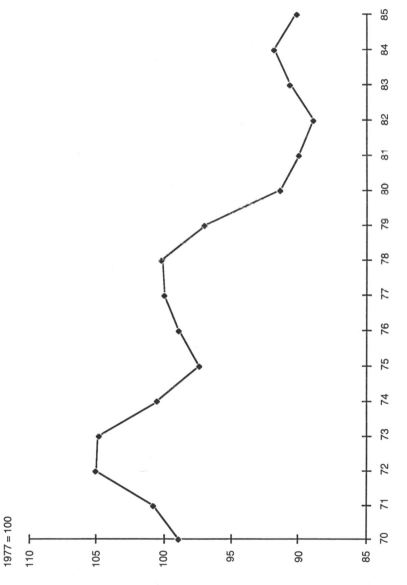

Figure 34. **Real Weekly Earnings for Production and Nonsupervisory Workers in Private Nonagricultural Industries**

1977 = 100

*Note*: Based on Bureau of Labor Statistics data. The author converted earnings in 1977 dollars to 1977=100 index.

and no discernible upward or downward trend. Thus, most of the 1970s were characterized by a decline in workers' material well-being, and the first half of the 1980s continued at the lower level of material well-being reached at the beginning of the decade.

### Labor/Management Wage Bargaining

The analyst is primarily interested in the weekly earnings figures because wages may affect inflation and job security adversely. Unions strive to ensure that wage increases keep pace with inflation and productivity improvement so that the material well-being of workers continually improves. When increases in wages are less than price increases, living conditions decline, and unions will press for greater wage increases to compensate. However, rapidly rising wages may perpetuate inflation or lead to a loss in jobs due to plant shutdowns or to American industry becoming less competitive with imports. Rapidly rising wages may also contribute to a shift of jobs from union to nonunion companies, either in the same region or through plant relocation and the startup of new firms in areas where wages are lower. In assessing the effect of wages on plant shutdowns and shifts to lower-paid nonunion workers, it should be kept in mind that wages are only one factor affecting competitiveness, and not always the dominant one; examples of others are the market for the firm's products, production costs associated with management and labor skills and the utilization of modern equipment, closeness to customers and suppliers, and state and local taxes.

Unions accounted for only 18 percent of all workers in 1985. Although union membership increased continually over the postwar period until the 1980s, this share has declined as the increase in union membership has been slower than the increase in total employment. Actual union membership fell in the first half of the 1980s, which may have weakened unions' bargaining position for increases in wages and fringe benefits (compensation).[26] Such a weakened bargaining position resulting from the declining membership relates to the union movement as a whole, although it does not apply to a few individual unions that have grown in membership, such as those representing teachers.

Despite the fact that unions represent a relatively small percent of American workers, union wage rates and fringe benefits influence wage rates in general. Because unions are the dominant bargaining agent in several industries, their compensation patterns often are a guideline for compensation of nonunion workers in the same industry or company. For example, some nonunion companies make it a policy to increase compensation in accordance with their union counterparts in order to reduce incentives for their workers to join a union, and some union agreements for wage freezes or cuts in the early 1980s had similar provisions requiring "equality of sacrifice" for nonunion counterparts in the same firm. There isn't a one-to-one relationship between union and nonunion compensation; in fact, the trends discussed below indicate they haven't always moved in tandem. However, as the pacesetter for improving workers' incomes, union compensation often is used in efforts to unionize nonunion companies as a standard by which to measure nonunion compensation increases.

Figure 35 compares annual changes in union and nonunion compensation with the consumer price index over 1970–85 based on the employment cost index. This index of wage income is based on maintaining the same distributions of industry and occupational employment, and thus differs from the weekly earnings figures, which incorporate changes over time in the employment distributions of industries and occupations.[27] Maintenance of the same industry and occupational distributions provides a more accurate measure of compensation changes, because shifts in the distributions of employees among low- and high-paying industries and occupations do not affect the measures. From 1970 to 1983, union wage increases typically exceeded nonunion wage increases by 1 to 2 percentage points. Union wages consistently rose faster consistently until 1983, and in 1984 and 1985 nonunion wages increased more than union wages.

The result of these trends is that the spread between union and nonunion wage levels increased considerably from 1970–85, even after the reversals in 1984 and 1985. Rough data available on *absolute* differences of weekly earnings between union and nonunion workers in the same industry generally show significantly higher union wages. For example, in 1984 these data showed union wage levels exceeding nonunion wages in the following broad industry groupings: construction (76 percent); wholesale and retail trade (42 percent); transportation (38 percent); government (20 percent); manufacturing (19 percent); and services (15 percent).[28]

It is clear that nonunion workers suffered the brunt of the decline in real earnings in the 1970s, and that in the 1980s both union and nonunion workers have fared about the same. Because of the widespread use of cost-of-living allowances in union contracts, in high inflationary periods such as the 1970s union wages, are likely to increase faster than nonunion wages which do not have such institutionalized buffers against inflation. From the decline and subsequent leveling off in the purchasing power of the average wage from the early 1970s to 1985, unions would be expected to bargain for higher wages to make up for past declines and to obtain longer-term gains. However, the impact of the union/nonunion wage spread on future wage increases is unclear. The higher wage increases for nonunion labor in 1984 and 1985 may be more than temporary, as unions may hold down wage demands to prevent a further shift to nonunion labor or imports. Yet the wage differential between union and nonunion labor could indicate higher union productivity, which would mitigate against a substantial narrowing of the wage differences.

Management plays a key role in determining wages. Trends in sales, profits and unemployment affect employers' willingness to give wage increases. Following the back-to-back recessions in 1980 and 1981–82 (and other structural changes in American industry, noted below), the bargaining power shifted from

Figure 35. **Annual Changes in Union Wages, Nonunion Wages, and Consumer prices**

Percent change

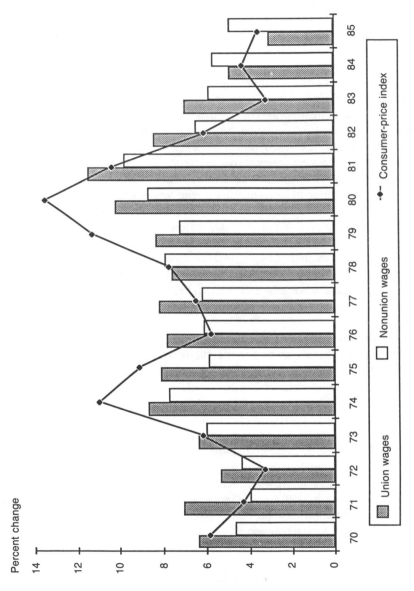

*Note*: Based on Bureau of Labor Statistics data. See Chapter 5, footnote 27 for breaks in wage series.

unions to management, leading to the sharp decline in collective-bargaining wage increases in 1982–85.

Employers in the 1982–85 period have been aggressive and successful in bargaining to hold down the amount of wage increases. This has resulted in two-tier wage scales, which pay new workers lower wages than existing workers in the same job, albeit in some cases the arrangement has a planned phaseout. In some cases, wages have been reduced as "givebacks" to save jobs. Wage costs have also been lowered by changes in work rules, such as using less-experienced workers and contracting out to lower-wage nonunion companies.

The reduced bargaining power of most unions is generally considered the result of the high unemployment and low economic growth of the 1980s; increased import competition due to the high value of the dollar and higher American industry costs; increased growth of nonunion companies, due to industrial shifts to the Sunbelt states that have less forceful laws requiring union representation and to the deregulation of airlines and trucking; and a generally more aggressive posture by employers in hiring nonunion workers to continue operations during strikes.

The magnitude of this shift in bargaining power is difficult to quantify. For example, part of the smaller negotiated wage settlements occurred because inflation dropped substantially starting in 1982—the consumer price index dropped from average annual increases of 12 percent from 1979–81 to 4 percent from 1982–85. The shift is based on a qualitative assessment.

The question in the late–1980s is whether there has been a long-term shift in the bargaining positions of labor and management, or if the recent lower wage increases mainly reflect the high unemployment and slow economic growth of the 1980s.[29] *The analyst should monitor trends affecting both sides of the bargaining table: efforts by unions to make up for losses in the purchasing power of wage income, and the tendency of employers to resist large wage increases. These will be affected by how each side perceives the relationship between wages and jobs. If a strong linkage between wages and jobs is assumed, there would be more of a tendency for lower wage increases or some shift to noncash fringe benefits than if job security were not an overriding issue.*

## Wage Costs

Wage payments as a production cost to the employer are related to prices and profits. Wage costs vary among industries—for example, wages are a higher proportion of total costs in the labor-intensive services than in manufacturing industries that use proportionately more machinery in their production processes. Because of these industry differences, changes in labor costs must be measured over time for the same composition of industries to identify the direct effect of wage-rate changes (for example, hourly or annual wages) on wage costs; otherwise, employment shifts between high- and low-wage industries will affect the analysis. For the same reason, the composition of occupations within each industry must be held constant over time to abstract from the employment shifts between high- and low-paying occupations.

The BLS provides two indicators of wage costs with differing degrees of refinement regarding the composition of employment. One is derived from the monthly employer survey, discussed above, for weekly earnings. This "average hourly earnings index" is adjusted to reflect a constant composition of industry employment based on the 1977 distribution of industry employment, and in manufacturing a 1977-based constant amount of overtime at premium pay. The other is an employment cost index (noted in the previous section in comparing union and nonunion wage increases), which is based on a constant employment composition of both industries and occupations within industries based on the 1970 employment distributions.[30] (These are based on the 1980 employment distributions beginning in 1986.) While these nonproduction and nonsupervisory workers are excluded from the earnings index, the employment cost index includes all workers, including executives, managers, professional, and administrative personnel.

Because the cost index is derived from a sample survey of employers that is 1 percent the size of the employer survey sample, it has much less industry detail than the earnings index. It also is less current than the monthly earnings index; the cost index measures the change in wage costs from one month in every quarter to the following quarter (March, June, September, and December) for the pay period containing the 12th day of the month. The cost index has a more representative sample of companies in the survey, although work is under way to improve the representativeness of the survey sample of the earnings index. The cost index is a relatively new measure, which started in 1977 covering money wages only. It was extended in 1981 to include fringe benefits paid by the employer for Social Security, unemployment insurance, and private health and life group insurance; by contrast, the earnings index excludes fringe benefits. Therefore, analysis of longer-term trends of labor costs must be based on the earnings index.

The most important differences between the two indexes are the treatment of occupations and fringe benefits and their timeliness. The differing sizes of the sample surveys and the representativeness of the companies in the surveys are not important in terms of their use at the economy-wide level for all industries combined. Previous experience in updating base periods in indexes indicates that the varying base periods used in calculating constant employment distributions of the two wage cost indexes are not likely to make much difference.[31]

Figure 36 shows wage cost changes from 1981 to 1985 measured by the hourly earnings index and the employment cost index. Both showed the same general pattern of a substantial decline in the rate of wage cost increases over the period. However, the cost index shows higher annual wage increases and a slower decline in the rate of increase than the earnings index. Thus, annual increases in the cost index ranged from 0.5 to 2 percentage points higher than the earnings index.

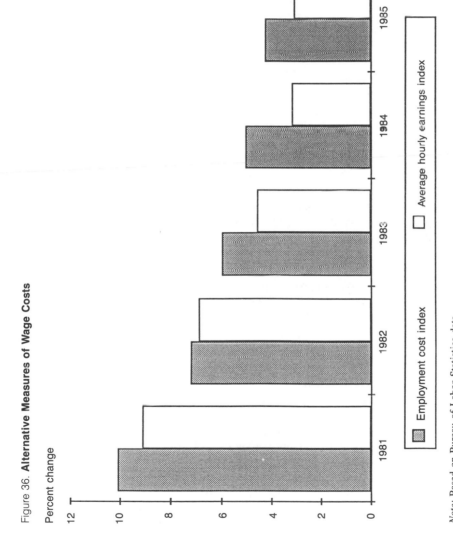

Figure 36. **Alternative Measures of Wage Costs**

Percent change

Employment cost index

Average hourly earnings index

*Note*: Based on Bureau of Labor Statistics data.

These differences reflect the shifts in occupational employment and the effect of fringe benefits.

*In tracking the short-term movements of wage costs, the analyst should consider the employer cost index as a more definitive measure due to its constant distribution of occupations. Because the cost index is available four times a year, compared with the monthly availability of the hourly earnings index, the earnings index provides a more up-to-date assessment of recent trends. But in using the earnings index for very timely trends, an allowance should be made for its tendency to understate the increase in wage costs.*

## PRODUCTIVITY

Productivity is the general term referring to the efficiency of production operations; it is fundamental to improvements in living conditions. Rising productivity is a key factor in increasing total output, and thereby improving the material well-being of the population along with maintaining a secure defense. There are two ways to increase the volume of goods and services available for private and public use: increase the amount of labor and capital equipment used in production, or increase the efficiency of these factors in producing the output. The latter defines the productivity of the economy and is a primary factor determining the total output of the nation. Because new technology causes some workers to be unemployed or to work at lower-paying jobs, however, not everyone shares equally in productivity improvements. This section assesses the effect of productivity on unemployment and inflation.

Productivity is defined as the output produced in relation to the inputs of labor, machinery, materials, and services required for the production. It is economic output per unit of input, and for the economy as a whole is measured as the real gross national product per labor hour (real GNP is covered in Chapter 3, and worker hours are the product of employment and hours, as covered earlier in this chapter). The figures on worker hours include paid employees, the self-employed, and unpaid family workers. The productivity measures are provided quarterly due to their link to the GNP numbers.[32] This is the conventional summary measure of productivity; another measure, called multifactor productivity, analyzes the component contributions of the labor, capital, and other inputs as discussed below.

Because of statistical problems in measuring productivity of government, nonprofit organization and household workers, in the GNP their output is equivalent to their labor input of wages and salaries adjusted for inflation; consequently, there is no statistical change in their productivity. Therefore, the measure of output used in estimating producitivity is real GNP in the business sector which excludes government, nonprofit organization and household output, because to include them would bias the productivity measures downward.

$$\text{Productivity} = \frac{\text{Output}}{\text{Input}} = \frac{\text{Real GNP*}}{\text{Labor hours**}} = \text{Real GNP per worker hour}$$

*Business sector.

**Paid employees, the self-employed, and unpaid family workers.

There are many underlying factors affecting productivity: the skills and effort of workers; use of capital equipment in production; scientific technology in the production process; managerial know-how; level of output; utilization of capacity, energy and materials; organization of production that integrates output, transportation, and distribution; and the interaction of these and all other factors. The measure of productivity above reflects the total effect of all of these labor, capital and other elements.

From 1948 to 1985, productivity in the business sector increased at an annual rate of 2.3 percent. However, it grew at noticeably different rates over the period, with a marked slowdown since the early 1970s. For example, after rising by 2.9 percent annually from 1948–73, the annual increase dropped to 0.8 percent from 1973–81, and then rose to 1.4 percent from 1981–85. It appears that the rebound of 1981–85 (which still had not attained the higher rates of the 1948–73 period) is a cyclical phenomenon of the expansion that began at the end of 1982, rather than a reflection of improvements in the underlying causes of productivity. For example, in 1985 the productivity increase dropped sharply, to only 1 percent, along with the slowdown in economic growth in that year.

Cyclical changes in productivity generally arise from the previously discussed tendency of employers not to make immediate changes to their workforce when business turns down in a recession from the previous expansion peak or when it first turns up in an expansion from the previous recession trough (see the section above on Weekly Hours). Because of this practice, productivity rises more in expansions than in recessions irrespective of changes in labor skills, capital equipment, and other basic factors affecting productivity.[33]

There have been various explanations offered for the 1973–81 slowdown in productivity: decreasing technological advance due to lower research and development spending; less investment in plant and equipment investment as higher energy prices caused business to use more labor relative to energy-using machinery; and more hours paid for than worked because of increases in paid vacations and sick leave. However, actual measures of these and other possible reasons related to multifactor productivity have yielded estimates that account for only about 20 percent of the decline, and the factors causing the slowdown are not well understood.[34]

(Two analysts have suggested that the measured slowdown in productivity growth since 1973 is a statistical illusion associated with the price controls in the early 1970s.[35] Their analysis is based on the assumption that the official price measures used to estimate real GNP in 1973 didn't adequately reflect the price inflation and consequently overstated the 1973 productivity level, thus indicating a productivity slowdown from 1968 to 1973, but no further slowdown after 1973. However, substantiating the extent of the price-measurement problem empirically is difficult. It requires accounting for changes in the quality of goods in determining price changes, a technical aspect discussed in Chapter 3, Part A under "Real GNP and Inflation," and in Chapter 6 on the consumer price index. Because this alternative view hinges on the assumed price-measurement problem that has not been demonstrated empirically, it has not replaced the generally accepted perception that there has in fact been a productivity slowdown.)

Figure 37 shows that the year-to-year measures of productivity fluctuate substantially. This is due to the sharper cyclical changes in the GNP (numerator) than changes in labor hours (denominator). Again, employers tend to delay laying off and hiring workers at the turning points of business cycles. Although not shown in the figure, the same phenomeon occurs in the quarterly trends. However, despite the substantial fluctuations in the measure, the underlying factors driving productivity don't have significant quarterly and annual changes. *Therefore, in assessing the prospect for productivity trends, the analyst should be aware of the differing cyclical and longer-term factors affecting productivity.*

Additionally, as the average for all industries, the overall productivity measure conceals wide variations among individual industries. Figure 38 shows little relationship for several individual manufacturing industries between productivity and output change for 1973–83. Industries with high productivity show both high and low increases in employment, as do industries with low productivity increases or actual productivity declines. Thus, these data do not support the concern that advanced technology, by displacing workers with outmoded skills, results in lower employment. Rather, the net effect on employment seems more closely related to demand for each industry's product.[36] It should be noted, however, that these relationships refer to total employment. Persons with particular or limited skills who lose their jobs because of the introduction of labor-saving machinery, such as factory workers and laborers, are not always able to find new work, and many work at new jobs at lower income levels.[37]

## *Productivity and Inflation*

Prices are determined by both the markets for goods and services (demand) and production costs (supply). Prices tend to rise faster when economic growth is strong than when it is slow or declining, because households and businesses are more willing to buy items at higher prices when employment and incomes are rising rapidly (higher demand). This section, however, focuses on the supply effect of production costs on prices. Price movements are discussed more fully in Chapter 6 on the consumer price index.

Productivity affects inflation through its effect on the costs of producing goods and services. If costs rise, business will be motivated to increase prices in order to maintain profit rates (profits as a percent of sales). If costs remain the same or

173

Figure 37. **Productivity in the Business Sector: Annual Percent Change**

Percent change

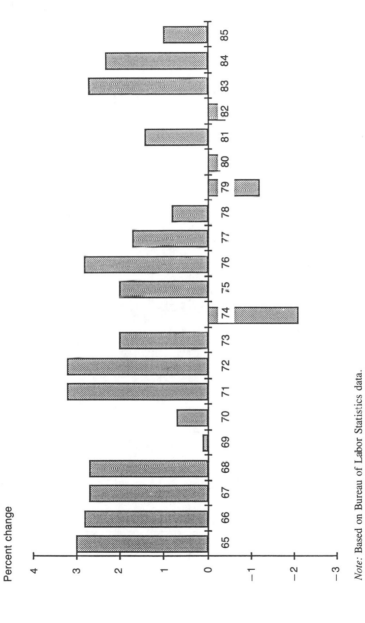

*Note:* Based on Bureau of Labor Statistics data.

Figure 38. **Output Per Employee Hour and Employment in Selected Manufacturing Industries, 1973-83.**

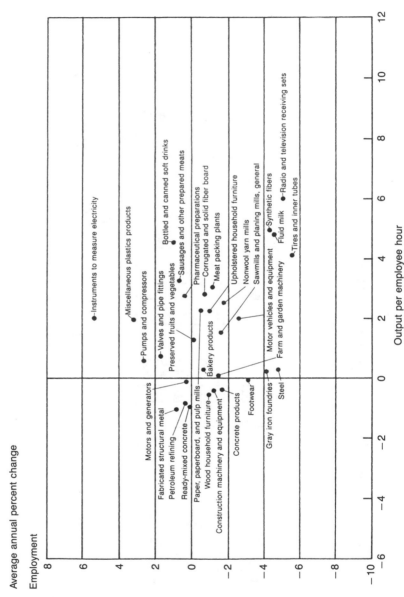

Average annual percent change

Source: Bureau of Labor Statistics, U.S. Department of Labor, *Trends in Manufacturing: A Chartbook*, April 1985, p. 41.

decline, they don't exert a pressure for higher prices to maintain profit rates; in fact, if costs decline, prices can decline and profits still be maintained.

Of key interest in considering production costs is the relation between wages and productivity, which is referred to as unit labor costs (ULC).[38] ULC also may be expressed as compensation per unit of output because, in the identity below, labor hours is the common term in both compensation and productivity, and thus cancels out in the numerator and denominator. As in the case of productivity, the term ULC refers to the business sector—that is, it excludes output of governments, nonprofit organizations, and households.

$$\text{Unit labor costs} = \frac{\text{Compensation per hour}}{\text{Productivity}} = \frac{\frac{\text{Compensation*}}{\text{Labor hours}}}{\frac{\text{Output}}{\text{Labor Hours}}} = \frac{\text{Compensation}}{\text{Output}}$$

*Wages and fringe benefits.

If wages rise faster than productivity, ULC increase and there is an upward pressures on prices; if wages increase slower than productivity, ULC decline and there is a downward pressure on prices. Figure 39 shows the five-year changes from 1950–85 (Panel A) and annual changes from 1975–85 (Panel B) of ULC and the business sector implicit price deflator (from the GNP estimates). These indicate parallel movements in both indicators. In addition, the differential movements tend to even out from one five-year period to the next, as a faster increase in the ULC in one period is followed by a faster increase in prices in the next period. On an annual basis, the relative movements tend to be within 1 to 2 percentage points of each other.

The postwar experience of ULC suggests that these measures of costs are an important but not determining factor affecting prices. *In using the ULC to assess trends in price pressures, the analyst should supplement it with economic growth rates and the conditions in markets having important spillover impacts on other prices, such as the secondary effects of energy and food prices.*

## SUMMARY

### Unemployment Rate

The unemployment rate (UR) moves in accordance with business cycles, declining in expansions and rising in recessions. However, its monthly movements sometimes are contrary to trends in economic growth because of persons newly seeking jobs or unemployed persons giving up in their job search, which makes short-term movements in the UR difficult to interpret. It is thus useful to supplement analyses of the UR with a consideration of flows in and out of the labor force.

Figure 39a. **Unit Labor Costs and Prices: Business Sector**

Percent change

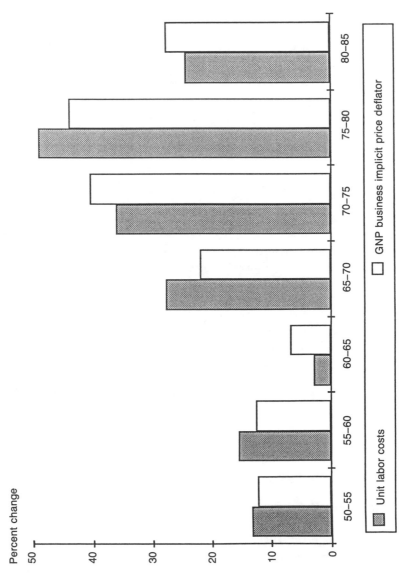

*Note:* Based on Bureau of Labor Statistics and Bureau of Economic Analysis data.

Figure 39b. **Unit Labor Costs and Prices: Business Sector**

Percent change

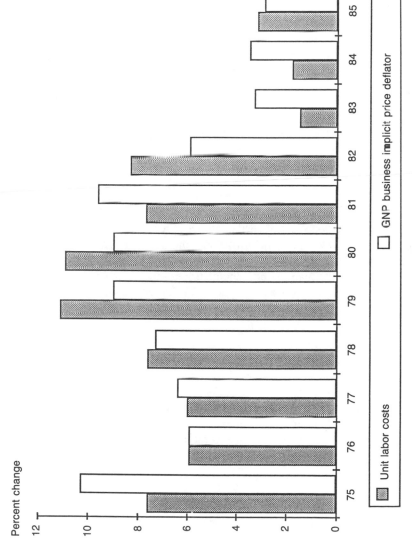

*Note:* Based on Bureau of Labor Statistics data.

The UR has drifted upward over the postwar period, with the low point at the peak of each expansion tending to be higher than the level at the peak of the previous expansion. This upward drift results from the rising proportion of teenagers in the labor force until the mid–1970s and the slowdown in economic growth after the 1960s. Because of lower birthrates in the 1960s and 1970s, the teenage component is a factor that would lower URs in the 1980s and 1990s. The upward drift affected perceptions that minimum unemployment rates associated with low inflation rates rose over the period.

The relationship between economic growth and unemployment is quantified in Okun's Law. Broad measures of these relationships establish break-even points indicating the required growth in real GNP necessary to maintain a steady unemployment rate and indicating the economic growth rates above or below the break-even point that lower or raise the unemployment rate by particular amounts. However, these are long-term averages that can diverge substantially from the theory in particular periods.

## Employment

Employment measures are provided from two surveys, which have differing definitions and data-collection methodologies. One is a survey of employers, and the other is a survey of households (the household survey is also the source of the unemployment rate figures). The employer survey typically has more extreme cyclical movements than the household survey—increasing more in expansions and decreasing more in recessions—and is considered more relevant for assessing cyclical changes in employment.

## Weekly Hours Worked

Changes in weekly hours worked in manufacturing are an early indicator of turning points at cyclical expansion peaks and recession troughs, and are included as a leading indicator of economic activity. However, the erratic monthly movements in the weekly hours figures make it difficult in some periods to establish a trend; they are best treated as a clue to future economic activity that should be compared with indicators on employment and unemployment.

## Wages

Wages represent income to workers and costs to employers. Average weekly earnings in constant dollars declined for most of the 1970s and then stabilized at the lower level. This decline and subsequent leveling out in the material well-being of workers suggest that this will be one factor in future union-management wage negotiations—unions tend to bargain for higher wages to make up for declines in purchasing power.

There has also been strong resistance to large wage increases in the first half of the 1980s in an environment of slower economic growth, increasing import competition, the shift to nonunion labor, and a generally more aggressive stance by management. Wage bargaining in the second half of the decade will hinge on the perception by both unions and management of the linkage between wage increases and job security.

As costs to employers, wages affect profits depending on the extent that wage changes are reflected in price movements. However, wages, prices and profits have not moved in consistent patterns over the years, indicating that other factors such as sales volume and nonwage costs impact heavily on profits. Two measures of wage costs show somewhat different movements: the hourly earnings index (provided monthly) and the employment cost index (provided quarterly). The latter is superior technically (although less timely) because it measures wages for the same occupations over time; it has shown higher wage increases than the hourly-earnings index. When using the hourly earnings index to monitor wage costs on the more timely monthly basis, an allowance should be made for its tendency to understate wage increases.

## *Productivity*

Productivity refers to the efficiency of production operations. Basic factors affecting productivity are the skills of workers, use of capital equipment, level of technology, and managerial know-how. These factors change gradually and are reflected in productivity movements over several years. By contrast, shorter-term quarterly and annual movements in productivity mainly reflect cyclical changes in economic growth. The causes of the decline in productivity in 1973–81 are not well understood, and the rebound during 1981–85 appears to be driven by the cyclical expansion beginning at the end of 1982.

Productivity also affects inflation through its relationship to unit labor costs. Unit labor costs are an important but not determining factor affecting prices; in assessing price trends, data on unit labor costs should be supplemented with measures of economic growth and developments in markets that impact heavily on prices, such as food and energy.

## NOTES

1. For a detailed description of the methodology, see Bureau of Labor Statistics, U.S. Department of Labor, *BLS Handbook of Methods*, Volume 1, December 1982, Chapter 1. For the evolution of unemployment measurements, see John E. Bregger, "The Current Population Survey: A Historical Perspective and BLS' Role," *Monthly Labor Review*, June 1984.

2. Bureau of Labor Statistics, U.S. Department of Labor, Employment and Earnings, June 1986, Table C, p. 151.

3. Richard J. McDonald, "The 'underground economy' and BLS statistical data," *Monthly Labor Review*, January 1984, pp. 11–13.

4. National Commission on Employment and Unemployment Statistics, *Counting the Labor Force* (U.S. Government Printing Office: Labor Day, 1979), p. 34. The rates of the alternative URs have continued to move in similar patterns since this report was published.

5. These figures are based on or calculated from data in the *Economic Report of the President*, February 1986, Tables B-31 and B-39, pp. 288 and 297.

6. Gary Burtless, "Why is Insured Unemployment So Low?," *Brookings Papers on Economic Activity*, 1:1983.

7. These rates are calculated from data in the *Economic Report of the President*, February 1986, Table B-31, p. 288.

8. *Ibid.*, Table B-34, p. 292.

9. Carol Boyd Leon, "The employment-population ratio: its value in labor force analysis," Bureau of Labor Statistics, *Monthly Labor Review*, February 1981, pp. 37–38.

10. *Economic Report of the President*, January 1962, pp. 46–48.

11. Sherman J. Maisel, *Macroeconomics: Theories and Policies* (W. W. Norton & Company: 1982), pp. 555–557.

12. Milton Friedman, "The Role of Monetary Policy," *American Economic Review*, March 1968, pp. 7–11.

13. Paul O. Flaim, "The effect of demographic changes on the nation's unemployment rate," *Monthly Labor Review*, March 1979. Since the study was completed, the actual 1977 civilian UR was revised minimally, from 7.0 to 7.1 percent. The year 1956 typically is used as the base for comparisons of demographic change because it had the lowest peacetime unemployment since the Korean War (total UR of 4.0 percent). The year 1957 was used in the referenced study because it was the first year that statistical data were available on unemployment by five-year age groups for use in the calculations. Since 1957 also was a relatively low unemployment year (4.2 percent), it did not affect the estimates. These findings on the demographic shifts were corroborated in a subsequent study; this latter study also pointed to the slowdown in economic growth as a contributing factor to the upward drift of the UR (see Michael Podgursky, "Sources of secular increases in the unemployment rate, 1969–82," *Monthly Labor Review*, July 1984).

14. Douglas M. Woodham, "Potential Output Growth and the Long-Term Inflation Outlook," *Quarterly Review* (Federal Reserve Bank of New York), Summer 1984.

15. "Counting the Labor Force," *op. cit.*, pp. 119–120.

16. John F. Stinson, Jr., "Comparison of Nonagricultural Employment Estimates From Two Surveys," *Employment and Earnings*, March 1984. For more detail on the factors contributing to these differences, see Gloria P. Green, "Comparing employment estimates from household and payroll surveys," *Monthly Labor Review*, December 1969. These annual reconciliations have not been published since 1984, but they are available for later years from the Bureau of Labor Statistics. Dual jobholders are not included in the BLS annual reconciliations because the data are not collected on them every year—for example, dual-jobholder figures in the 1980s are available only for 1980 and 1985. However, dual jobholders are included by the author in the reconciliation noted in the text because of the availability of dual-jobholder data for 1985; in May 1985, 3.9 million persons are estimated to have had nonagricultural wage and salary jobs (these exclude self-employment) as a second job that would be counted in the employer survey.

17. *Employment and Earnings*, June 1986, pp. 150–151 (particularly Table B).

18. For a detailed description of the methodology, see *BLS Handbook of Methods*, *op. cit.*, Chapter 2.

19. "Counting the Labor Force," *op. cit.*, pp. 153–165.

20. Harvey R. Hamel and John T. Tucker, "Implementing the Levitan Commission's recommendations to improve labor data, *Monthly Labor Review*, February 1985, pp. 20–22.

21. Green, *op. cit.*, p. 19. This 1969 assessment tends to be repeated in current newspaper reports on monthly employment trends.

22. "Comparison of Nonagricultural Employment Estimates from Two Surveys," *op. cit.*, p. 9.

23. John F. Stinson, Jr., "Comparison of Nonagricultural Employment Estimates From Two Surveys," *Employment and Earnings*, March 1983, pp. 8–9.

24. Eugene H. Becker, "Self-employed workers: an update to 1983," *Monthly Labor Review*, July 1984, pp. 15–16.

25. In manufacturing, mining and construction for employees up through the level of working supervisors, "production" designates workers who engage directly in the work. The analogous designation in other industries—transportation, utilities, trade, finance, and other services—is "nonsupervisory" workers.

26. The union share of all wage and salary workers declined over the postwar period from 35.5 percent in 1945 to 23 percent in 1980 to 18 percent in 1985. Actual membership increased until 1978, although at a slower rate than employment; however, from 1978 to 1984 the number of union members also declined, which accelerated the falling share in the later period. The above percentages refer to farm and nonfarm labor organizations involved in collective bargaining. For 1945, they are limited to organizations designated officially as unions, while in 1980 and 1985 they include employee associations of professional groups that subsequently began to act as unions although not called unions, such as the National Education Association and the Fraternal Orders of Police. See Larry T. Adams, "Changing employment patterns of organized workers," *Monthly Labor Review*, February 1985, p. 26, and *Employment and Earnings*, January 1986, Table 57, p. 213. For the effect of the accelerated decline in union membership in the first half of the 1980s, see Daniel J. B. Mitchell, "Shifting Norms in Wage Determination," *Brookings Papers on Economic Activity*, 2.1985, pp. 586–587.

27. Because of changes in the availability of data on wage rates in the 1970s and 1980s, there are breaks in the continuity of the figures between 1976 and 1977 and between 1980 and 1981. Data from 1970 to 1976 are for scheduled wage adjustments (excluding fringe benefits) in manufacturing; from 1977 to 1980 they cover wages (excluding fringe benefits) in all private nonagricultural industries; and from 1981 to 1985 they cover wages and fringe benefits in all private nonagricultural industries. However, the union/nonunion differentials are consistent in each year, as the same definition for union and nonunion wages is used in each year. This Bureau of Labor Statistics information is based on the survey of wage developments in manufacturing for 1970–76 and the employment cost index for 1977–85.

28. These union/nonunion differentials are calculated from household survey information published in Paul O. Flaim, "New Data on Union Members and Their Earnings," *Employment and Earnings*, January 1985, pp. 13 and 211 (Table 55). Because they combine all occupations in each industry, such as executives (relatively low union membership and high wages), and machine operators (relatively high union membership and low wages) into one industry total, the patterns give a broad notion of the wage differentials but are not definitive and sometimes are misleading. For example, an obvious distortion caused by this "occupational" problem occurs for communications and public utilities, which shows union workers earning much less than nonunion workers. Such distortions probably wouldn't occur if the data were refined to compare the same occupations within each industry. Analogously, union/nonunion differentials for specific occupations but combined for all industries into one occupational total (also provided in the above noted article) have the similar problem of not distinguishing between high- and low-wage industries.

29. See Wayne Vroman, *Wage Inflation: Prospects for Deceleration* (The Urban Institute Press: 1983), Chapter 5; Robert J. Flanagan, "Wage Concessions and Long-

Term Union Wage Flexibility," *Brookings Papers on Economic Activity*, 1:1984, pp. 215–216; Robert S. Gay, "Union Settlements and Aggregate Wage Behavior in the 1980s," *Federal Reserve Bulletin*, December 1984, pp. 854–857; and Daniel J. B. Mitchell, "Shifting Norms in Wage Determination," *Brookings Papers on Economic Activity*, 2:1985, pp. 597–599.

30. For a detailed description of the methodology, see *BLS Handbook of Methods*, *op. cit.*, Chapter 11.

31. However, because of the high inflation in the 1970s and the sharp increase in oil prices (in 1973 and 1979), the changes in employment distributions may have a greater than usual effect.

32. For a detailed description of the methodology, see *BLS Handbook of Methods*, *op. cit.*, Chapter 13.

33. Lawrence J. Fulco, "Strong post-recession gain in productivity contributes to slow growth in labor costs," *Monthly Labor Review*, December 1984.

34. Jerome A. Mark, William H. Waldorf, et al, Bureau of Labor Statistics, *Trends in Multifactor Productivity*, Bulletin 2178, September 1983, Chapters III and IV. "Multifactor productivity," which is annual as distinct from the conventional quarterly measure, analyzes the contributions to productivity of three broad components: (a) output per hour of employed persons (b) output per unit of capital services (derived from plant, equipment, inventories and land), and (c) the joint influences of all other factors affecting efficiency (referred to as multifactor productivity). Multifactor productivity includes the combined effects of the skills and effort of workers; technology used in production; managerial know-how; level of output; utilization of capacity, energy and materials; organization of production; and the interaction of these and all other underlying causes of productivity. The conventional measure used in this chapter, output per worker hour, encompasses the total effect of all labor, capital and multifactor elements. For an analysis of the factors contributing to the productivity slowdown, see Edward F. Denison, *Trends in Economic Growth, 1929–1982* (The Brookings Institution: 1985).

35. Charles S. Morris, "The Productivity 'Slowdown': A Sectoral Analysis," *Economic Review* (Federal Reserve Bank of Kansas City), April 1984; and Michael R. Darby, "The U.S. Productivity Slowdown: A Case of Statistical Myopia," *American Economic Review*, June 1984.

36. Paul O. Flaim and Ellen Sehgal, "Displaced workers of 1979-83: how well have they fared?," Bureau of Labor Statistics, Bulletin 2240, July 1985, p. 5.

37. *Ibid.*, pp. 8–10, and Jerome A. Mark, "Technological change and employment: some results from BLS research," *Monthly Labor Review*, April 1987.

38. For a detailed description of the methodology, see *BLS Handbook of Methods*, *op. cit.*, Chapter 13.

# 6 • Consumer Price Index

The consumer price index (CPI) measures changes in the prices of goods and services bought by households. It is the most widely recognized gauge of inflation, a key measure of consumer purchasing power and economic well-being. There are three broad uses of the CPI: (a) it is central to macroeconomic analysis and policy decisions about balancing unemployment and inflation; (b) it is the basis of cost-escalation estimates used to compensate for inflation in wage contracts, pensions, income-maintenance programs, business contracts, and indexing of federal individual income taxes; and (c) it is used to deflate economic measures of real gross national product, real wage earnings, and real interest rates. Additionally, CPI futures contracts are traded on the Coffee, Sugar, and Cocoa Exchange as a hedge against future price increases or declines. In cost escalation alone (excluding indexing of federal income taxes), the CPI directly affected the income of over 140 million persons in the early 1980s.[1]

The CPI is provided monthly by the Bureau of Labor Statistics. It covers spending by households for everyday living expenses such as food and beverages, housing, apparel, transportation, medical care, education, entertainment, tobacco products, and other personal goods and services. In addition to the national CPI, there are CPIs for certain metropolitan areas and regions of the country.

Two CPI indexes are provided at both the national and local levels. One is based on the spending patterns for goods and services of all urban *consumers* (CPI-U); the other is based on the spending patterns of urban *wage and clerical workers* (CPI-W). The CPI-U includes all urban employed, unemployed and retired persons (81 percent of the noninstitutional population in 1981).[2] It is assumed that price changes for the remaining 19 percent of the population (17 percent rural and 2 percent military) are similar to those for urban consumers.

The CPI-W represents urban household units in which one of the members worked at least 37 weeks during the year in jobs usually paid on an hourly or commission basis in the craft, operative, clerical, sales, service, and laborer occupations. These workers accounted for 30 percent of the noninstitutionalized population in 1981.[2]

Both indexes are provided monthly. Although the CPI-W coverage of the population is less than half the coverage of CPI-U, many cost escalations under labor and business contracts are based on the CPI-W. It has been in existence longer—it was begun in 1921, while the CPI-U was begun in 1978—and is thus more familiar. The CPI-W was initially started for use in wage negotiations, and because its uses broadened, the CPI-U was introduced to provide a more representative measure of price change.[3] Different spending patterns for particular goods and services in the two indexes have resulted in the CPI-U increasing slightly faster than the CPI-W—for example, from 1980 to 1985 the CPI-U increased by 30.6 percent and the CPI-W by 28.9 percent. The spending patterns represent the proportions of consumer budgets spent for various items (for example, the CPI-U includes less spending for food and more spending for housing than the CPI-W), and are discussed below in Part A under "Index-Number Weights." The general properties of index numbers were discussed in Chapter 2.

The CPI is sometimes referred to as the cost of living, although it doesn't conform to a theoretical cost of living in two respects. First, it measures the relative change in prices as the percent movement between two periods to maintain a fixed standard of living, rather than the dollar amounts of the costs. For example, the CPIs for the New York and Cleveland metropolitan areas may show prices rising faster in Cleveland than in New York, but in dollars it still may cost more to live in New York.

Second, specifying the appropriate living standard for measuring price change is elusive, and the CPI concept of using living standards that are constant for periods of about 10 years is only one way of doing it. Measures of consumer price movements based on alternative methodologies are available from the gross national product measures (see Chapter 3), and are compared to the CPI in this chapter.

# PART A.  ESTIMATING METHODOLOGY

By definition, the CPI measures the actual price charged for items. This includes sales taxes and premiums and discounts from list prices. In practice, there probably are a minority of cases in which actual prices net of premiums and discounts from list prices are not obtained.

## QUALITY

As a measure of price change, the CPI includes the effect of quality change in the goods and services priced. The CPI's measure of quality change includes improvements or reductions in the performance of an item, but not changes in its aesthetic qualities. For example, if a loaf of bread is increased (decreased) in size or nutrients, the changes are quality improvements (declines), which will be included in the CPI. Similarly, if a car's design is changed to increase (decrease) its braking power, maneuverability, pollution controls or comfort, the changes are quality improvements (declines), which the CPI will take into account as cost changes. By contrast, a change in styling such as sculptured lines or chrome is not a quality change.

The idea behind the CPI is that the measured price movements from one period to the next should reflect only those price changes that occur independent of quality changes. Thus, in the monthly pricing of the CPI items, prices are compared to the specifications of the item to determine if changes in specifications have occurred as well as to obtain an estimate of the value of the specification changes. Changes in quality and selling price affect the price used in the CPI as shown below. The implementation of quality changes in CPI is governed by the availability of data on the extent of the change—the CPI reflects the change only if the dollar value of the quality change can be quantified.

| *Quality change* | *Selling price* | *CPI price* |
| --- | --- | --- |
| Improvement | Increase by amount of improvement | No change |
| Improvement | Increase less than improvement | Decrease |
| Improvement | No change | Decrease |
| Improvement | Increase more than improvement | Increase |
| Decline | Decrease by amount of decline | No change |
| Decline | Decrease less than decline | Increase |
| Decline | No change | Increase |
| Decline | Decrease more than decline | Decrease |

## INDEX NUMBER WEIGHTS

The CPI is an index number that combines the prices for a wide range of goods and services into a single figure.[4] The goods and service items are combined by using the percentage shares of total dollar spending by housholds for each item in the base period as weights. Data for the spending patterns are obtained from surveys of representative samples of households in geographic areas around the country conducted for the Bureau of Labor Statistics by the Census Bureau. These spending patterns are updated about every 10 years—for example, the weights from 1978 to 1986 are based on spending patterns in 1972–73, which were modified to the 1978 base period using relative price changes between 1973 and December 1977 to partially update the survey estimates of the proportions spent on each item.[5] In 1983, a new method of pricing owner-occupied housing was introduced that further modified the weights; the index beginning in 1983 is calculted from these modified weights which represent December 1982. Starting in 1987, the weights reflect spending patterns in 1982–84[6]; these will be used until more current spending patterns are introduced in the late 1990s.

As a fixed-weight index for the approximate 10-year periods between the updating of the spending patterns, the CPI measures the effect of price changes assuming constant living standards—that is, a constant quantity and quality of goods and services—over the period. Because of the fixed weights, the effect of changing consumer preferences for spending among different goods and services (say, between food, housing and recreation) or for substituting products due to changes in taste or relative prices (for example, beef vs. chicken) are not fully included in the estimation of the CPI. Because the 1972–73 weights used in the 1978 revision predated the sharp inflation of the 1970s including the considerable increase in oil prices, the 1987 revision is the first time that shifts in consumer preferences resulting from this inflation are fully accounted for in the index.

Changing consumer preferences are, however, partially reflected to the extent that changing demand for particular items affects their prices. Current monthly price data are obtained mainly by surveyors visiting the same retail stores and service businesses and pricing the same items (or close substitutes) every collection period, monthly or bimonthly depending on the city and item in the survey samples. The businesses included in the sample from which the price data are obtained are selected proportional to their sales volume as reported in a household survey of where consumers buy, thus giving greater importance to price changes in the larger outlets. Only prices obtained for identical items in two successive months are used in the CPI measures.

Price data for electricity are obtained from mail surveys of utilities conducted by the Department of Energy. Rents are obtained from a sampling procedure in which six groups of single-family homes and apartment buildings are each visited every six months to obtain rental charges for the current and previous months; this technique, which is used to hold down the size and cost of the rental survey, provides the change in monthly rent by weighting the one-month and six-month changes for comparable housing units.

Although highly simplified, Table 13 shows the basic procedure for calculating the monthly CPI-U seasonally unadjusted level using December 1985 as the example. The table is calculated for the unadjusted CPI level because the seasonally adjusted level is not published; the unadjusted level and the month-to-month changes for both the seasonally adjusted and unadjusted measures are published.[7] The weights of the major components are from the spending patterns introduced in 1978, as modified in 1983 by the new procedure for pricing owner-occupied housing noted above. These are multiplied by the relative price change between 1983 and December 1985 to obtain the proportions of each component in December 1985, and the proportions are summed to obtain the total CPI for 1985 on a base of 1978 = 100. To convert this level to the base of 1967 = 100 which is in use through 1987, the summed total is multiplied by the ratio of the CPI price change between 1967 and December 1982 (to reflect the modified weights introduced in 1983); this results in a December 1985 CPI level of 327.4. (The CPI base period

Table 13

**Estimating the CPI-U for December 1985\***
**(1967 = 100)**

| (1)<br>Item | (2)<br>Base-period<br>Weights,<br>Dec. 1982 | (3)<br>Ratio change,<br>Dec.1982 to<br>Dec. 1985 | (4)<br>December 1985<br>Proportions<br>(2) x (3) |
|---|---|---|---|
| Food & beverages | 20.069 | 1.095 | 21.976 |
| Housing | 37.721 | 1.125 | 42.436 |
| Apparel & upkeep | 5.205 | 1.079 | 5.616 |
| Transportation | 21.791 | 1.099 | 23.948 |
| Medical care | 5.995 | 1.204 | 7.218 |
| Entertainment | 4.206 | 1.117 | 4.698 |
| Other | 5.014 | 1.216 | 6.097 |
| Total | 100.000 | | 111.989 |

Adjustment to 1967=100:
CPI for December 1982 based on 1967 = 100 is 292.4
CPI for December 1985 based on 1967 = 100 is 327.4
(111.989 x 2.924 = 327.4)

\*Not seasonally adjusted.

*Note*: Detail does not equal totals due to rounding.

will be changed to 1982–84 = 100 beginning in January 1988.) Thus, the CPI increased by 227.4 percent between 1967 and December 1985. In practice, the computations are made at a much greater level of detailed items within each major component—food prices, for example, are calculated for a wide range of bakery, meat, dairy, produce items, beverages, and the like—and distinctions are made between food consumed in homes and restaurants. The percent change in the CPI between any two periods is calculated as the relative movement in the CPI levels between the periods. For example, from June to December 1985, the CPI, seasonally unadjusted, increased by 1.6 percent as follows:

| | |
|---|---|
| December CPI | 327.4 |
| less: June CPI | 322.3 |
| equals: Index point change | 5.1 |
| Ratio of index point change<br>(5.1/322.3) | .016 |
| Percent change (0.016 x 100) | 1.6% |

## PRICE EFFECT OF UPDATING WEIGHTS

The effect of updating the CPI weights to reflect more recent spending patterns can be analyzed by comparing the official CPI based on new weights to hypothetical figures based on continued use of old weights. For example, using the 1964 updating, the official CPI during 1967–77 rose by 0.7 of a percentage point less than it would using the old 1952 weights; using the 1978 updating, for 1978–85 the official CPI increased 3 percentage points more than it would have using the old 1964 weights. Although these differences occur in different directions (in one case the official CPI is higher, and in the other it is lower than the hypothetical CPI), their total effect is relatively small, amounting to 1 percent of the official change between 1967 and 1977 and 5 percent of the official change from 1978 to 1985. *Thus, the 10-year spans in which the weights remain constant do not appear to result in exceptional discontinuities in the measure of price change.*

## RELIABILITY OF THE CPI

Because the monthly price data are collected from a sample of retail and other businesses selling to households, the CPI is subject to errors associated with sampling rather than surveying an entire group. The sampling errors vary with the level of inflation, increasing as an absolute measure but becoming proportionately smaller with higher rates of inflation.[8] For example, in 19 chances out of 20 if the CPI increases by 0.3 percent from one month to the next (an annual rate of 4 percent), the sampling error is plus or minus 0.24 percent and thus the "true" movement is within a range of 0.06 to 0.54 percent; and if the monthly inflation rate is 0.8 percent (an annual rate of 10 percent), the sampling error is plus or minus 0.52 percent for a range of 0.28 to 1.32 percent.

## DIGRESSION ON POVERTY MEASURES

Changes over time in the CPI weights resulting from more current information on consumer spending patterns are also of interest because of what they suggest about the official estimates of the number of persons in poverty. The poverty measure is based on establishing an annual cash-income line as a threshold minimum standard of living—households with annual incomes below the line are included in the poverty figures. The income standard hasn't been changed since it was developed in the early 1960s, other than to adjust it for the effect of rising prices according to movements in the CPI. Therefore, the minimum living standards in the 1980s are the same as those in the 1960s.

The poverty income line was developed using data on the cost of a nutritious diet and the average proportion of income spent on food. The data were obtained from two U.S. Department of Agriculture studies: a 1961 assessment of the least costly nutritionally adequate diet, and a 1955 measure of the proportion of after-tax income that the average family spent on food. No direct standards were established for nonfood items such as housing, transportation, and medical care. To substitute for direct measures of nonfood components, the 1961 diet was used to determine the total minimum income figure according to the 1955 proportion of income spent on food, with adjustments to account for spending variations between families of different size. For example, families with three or more persons spent about one-third of their income on food; thus, the least costly diet was multiplied by three to obtain the poverty income line for those families.

If this procedure were updated to reflect more recent spending-pattern weights for food in the CPI, the line would have been progressively raised and therefore more persons would be counted in poverty than presently are included in the official figures. The 1964 CPI updating showed a 25 percent weight for food; the 1978 updating, a 19 percent weight. Thus, if the original methodology were updated, starting in 1964 the least costly food budget would be multiplied by four, and starting in 1978 it would be multiplied by five to obtain the poverty threshold income. On the other hand, since the early 1960s the government has introduced or augmented many in-kind (noncash) income maintenance supports for the needy that also are not included in the official cash-income poverty threshold, such as food stamps, school lunches, rent supplements, Medicare, and Medicaid. If these in-kind programs were included as income, the poverty figures in the mid-1980s would be overstated.

The sensitivity of the poverty measures to the methodology used is considerable. For example, based on a slight reduction in the food proportion of the budget from 0.33 to 0.29 and a more nutritious diet than that used in the official poverty measure, the number of persons in poverty in 1977 was estimated to increase by 52 percent.[9] Analogously, the inclusion of in-kind income in the poverty measure was estimated to result in a poverty population in 1984 ranging from 22.6 million to 30.9 million persons depending on the methodology used, compared to the official poverty figure of 33.7 million persons, which is based on cash income only.[10]

The official measure of poverty remains based on cash income only and reflects the living standards and methodology used in the early 1960s. The hypothetical measures discussed here indicate how certain underlying data in the CPI may be used in the debate on the extent of poverty in the nation. From a policy standpoint, a good case could be made that the poverty measures should be updated. Such an updating may lead to more persons classified as living in poverty and therefore more government spending on income maintenance programs. Because of this possibility, an updating hasn't had much political support, since increased spending would conflict with the drive to reduce the federal deficit.

## PART B. ANALYSIS OF TRENDS

Many terms are used to characterize various rates of price change. *Inflation* is the rate at which prices increase; *deflation* is the rate of price declines; *disinflation* is a slowdown in the rate of inflation such as occurred in the first half of the 1980s; *creeping inflation* is a low increase in inflation as from 1950–65; and *accelerating inflation* is a speedup in the rate of price increase as from 1973–81. A steady price level may be referred to as *zero inflation*. Because the CPI represents the weighted average price level for all household goods and services, of which some components are increasing and others are decreasing in price, zero inflation is said to occur when the CPI remains unchanged—that is, when increases and decreases in prices of the components are offsetting in the aggregate.

## LONG-TERM SHIFTS
## IN THE RATE OF INFLATION

Figure 40 shows inflation rates in the CPI for 1950–85, highlighting periods during which the inflation rate changed noticeably. The CPI increased at an average annual rate of 4.3 percent over the entire period. Because prices as a whole almost always rise—they increased in all but one year (in 1955 prices decreased by 0.4 percent)—the rate of increase is what concerns the analyst. Even during periods of general inflation, however, certain components of the CPI show declines—gasoline and oil in the first half of the 1980s, for example.

From 1950–85, the periods that are of interest for the changing rate of inflation are the low and declining creeping inflation of 1950–65; the acceleration during 1966–81 (this period included an inflation slowdown in 1971–72 while mandatory price controls were in effect); and the disinflation in 1982–85. While the average inflation rate in 1982–85 of 4.3 percent is the same as the long-term 1950–85 rate, it is twice the rate of the 1950–65 period.

The inflation acceleration in the late 1960s resulted from the Vietnam War buildup. In the 1970s, several factors converged to cause the sharp acceleration in inflation: energy prices increased substantially when the Organization of Petroleum Exporting Countries (OPEC) became an effective cartel in 1973; the value of the dollar declined following the shift to floating exchange rates; unit labor costs rose because of a productivity slowdown and higher wage increases; and the wage-price spiral fed an inflationary psychology of expected continued higher inflation.

These factors generally turned around in the first half of the 1980s, which together with the slowdown in economic growth weakened the inflationary pressures. The result was the disinflation of 1982–85, but the stability of these factors is uncertain and bears watching. Various analyses have differed noticeably regarding the importance of each of the factors in the disinflation, although the slowdown in economic growth is generally given the largest single weight.[11]

Figure 40. **Annual Average Changes in the Consumer Price Index**

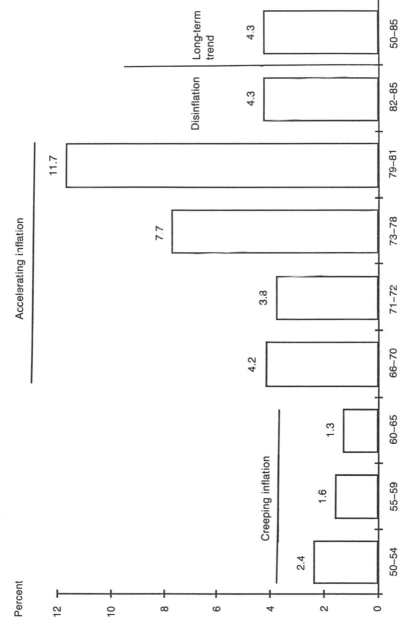

*Note*: Based on Bureau of Labor Statistics data. Annual changes are at compounded rates

In the case of oil prices, direct energy components of the CPI understate the full impact of higher oil and gas prices on the overall CPI. Thus, the sharp increases in energy prices resulting from the OPEC oil-price hikes in 1973–74 (associated with the Arab oil embargo) and in 1979–80 (associated with the Iranian revolution) may appear in the CPI to be less important than they actually were. For example, from 1975–80 when energy prices increased by 15.4 percent annually, there was little difference in the movements of the total CPI (8.9 percent) and the CPI excluding the use of fuels for cars and home heating (8.4 percent). However, both the total CPI and the nonenergy CPI increased much faster than in the past, part of which was due to the fact that many of the items in the CPI (such as apparel, appliances, furniture, cars, food, and pharmaceuticals) use petroleum derivatives as intermediate materials in their production. Following the peak of crude oil prices of $35 to $40 per barrel in 1981, prices declined slowly in 1982–84 and then dropped sharply in 1985–86 to $10 to $15 per barrel in the summer of 1986, as supply shortages turned to gluts and the OPEC cartel's price discipline was overwhelmed by market forces. This price decline resulted from the combination of conservation, additional worldwide sources of oil, and slower economic growth in the industrial nations. Should these factors again be reversed, as through lax conservation or sustained rapid economic growth, oil prices could again rise sharply.

The value of the dollar in relation to currencies of other nations declined by 20 percent from 1972 to 1980, making imported goods more expensive and thereby raising the CPI. By contrast, from 1980 to 1985 the dollar rose by 64 percent, thereby lowering the inflation rate. As noted in Chapter 3 under "Exports and Imports," in 1985 the dollar was estimated by various analysts to be "overvalued" by 30 to 60 percent. While the dollar dropped by 30 percent from the first quarter of 1985 to the second quarter of 1986, some overvaluation remains, suggesting a further decline in the future. However, further declines in the dollar will hinge on underlying factors such as relative movements in U.S. and foreign economic growth, interest rates, and inflation; the dollar's movements will also be affected by whether the United States is perceived as a desirable place for investment or for protecting money as a political haven.

Recent research on the inverse relationship between the value of the dollar and the CPI suggests that a 10 percent increase in the dollar will result in a drop in the inflation rate of about 1.5 to 3.0 percentage points over the ensuing three to four years (analogously, a 10 percent decrease in the dollar will result in a similar rise in the inflation rate).[12] As in all such "parameters," this represents an order-of-magnitude response rather than a precise relationship. One reason for a departure from the expected average response, for example, is that if the dollar declines, foreign producers may drop their export prices to compensate at least partially for the dollar decline in order to maintain their competitive positions and thus their sales volume in the U.S. market.

Prices are also affected by wage costs. The patterns of price movements are similar to those of unit labor costs (ULCs), as noted in Chapter 5 under "Productivity." Since these costs increase if wages rise faster than productivity, and decrease when wages rise more slowly than productivity, changes in either wages or productivity can affect the ULC trend. Following a marked slowdown in productivity growth from 1973–82, productivity rebounded partially in 1983–84 and then slowed again in 1985, raising a question about the future extent of the upturn. It is also uncertain whether the slowdown in wage-rate increases in the first half of the 1980s will continue (see Chapter 5).

Expectations of price changes are an important intangible to monitor since they affect the behavior of lenders, business, and labor in the setting of interest rates, prices, and wages. An expectation of high inflation tends to be a self-fulfilling forecast: the various groups act to insulate themselves by raising interest rates, prices, and wage demands in order to maintain the purchasing power of their future incomes. Similarly, an expectation of low inflation tends to result in smaller price increases. Inflationary expectations fueled the large price increases in the 1970s; while it lessened substantially in the first half of the 1980s, uncertainties regarding oil prices, the value of the dollar, unit labor costs, or other developments could again generate inflationary behavior.

A structural tendency toward inflation is resulting from the continuing shift in the American economy from the consumption of commodities to the consumption of services. Over 1950–85, prices of services increased at an annual rate of 5.4 percent, compared with 3.4 percent for commodities; this pattern of higher price increases for services occurred in all four decades of the period. The higher prices for services are partially due to the higher labor content in the production of services in contrast to commodities, which use proportionately more machinery in their production; services don't benefit as much as commodities from cost-saving productivity improvements in machinery. Another part of the difference may be statistical inadequacies resulting from the difficulty of quantifying quality changes in services such as housing, transportation, medical care, education, and entertainment. If quality improvements are understated in services, the price increases would be overstated (see Part A of this chapter).

## CYCLICAL INFLATION MOVEMENTS

Table 14 shows the pattern of CPI movements at the peak of expansions and trough of recessions in the post-World War II business cycles. As would be expected, prices tend to rise faster in expansions and slower in subsequent recessions. There were, however, two exceptions: in the 1949 recession overall prices declined faster at the expansion peak than at the recession trough, and in the 1957–58 recession, prices increased faster at the recession trough than at the expansion peak. In both of these cases, food prices played a partial role. Because food prices are often driven by supply shortages or surpluses caused by weather conditions and harvests, they are not directly related to cyclical price fluctuations. Two additional factors in 1949 were the still-unsatisfied demand after

Table 14

### CPI Movements at Cyclical Turning Points
### (Three-month annual rates at expansion peak and recession trough)

| Expansion peak | | Recession trough | |
|---|---|---|---|
| Nov 48 | −4.3 | Oct 49 | −0.6 |
| Jul 53 | 1.5 | May 54 | −0.8 |
| Aug 57 | 4.1 | Apr 58 | 4.3 |
| Apr 60 | 2.3 | Feb 61 | 0.8 |
| Dec 69 | 6.3 | Nov 70 | 5.9 |
| Nov 73 | 8.2 | Mar 75 | 6.6 |
| Jan 80 | 15.8 | Jul 80 | 8.3 |
| Jul 81 | 11.7 | Nov 82 | 1.7 |

*Source*: John F. Early, Mary Lynn Schmidt, and Thomas J. Mosimann, "Inflation and the business cycle during the postwar period," *Monthly Labor Review*, November 1984, Table 1, p. 4.

World War II for automobiles and the rapidly growing market for television sets that propped up prices in 1949. While overall prices typically don't decline in recessions (slight declines occurred only in the first two of the eight postwar recessions), the slower rate of increase in recessions indicates they are responsive to declining sales volume. Prices for the broad groups of both commodities and services (not shown in the table) have the same pattern of faster increases in expansions.

The tendency in recessions for the rate of price increases to slow down rather than for prices to decline reflects the perception of business that price declines would not generate enough additional sales to raise profits. This reluctance to lower prices is referred to as the "stickiness" of prices.

## CPI AND GNP PRICE MEASURES

In addition to the CPI, three alternative measures of changes in consumer prices are available from the GNP figures: the implicit price deflator, the fixed-weighted price index, and the chain price index for personal consumption expenditures. They differ from each other in their treatment of expenditure weights: the implicit price deflator has continually changing weights to reflect current spending patterns; the fixed-weighted index maintains constant weights (based on 1982 spending patterns); and the chain price index utilizes both current and constant weights by maintaining constant spending patterns only between two consecutive quarters (annually for two consecutive years), and then updating the weights to the current spending patterns (see Chapter 3, Part A, under "Real GNP and Inflation").

The net effect of these differences in weighting is that the implicit price deflator tends to show the least amount of inflation while the fixed-weighted price

Table 15

## Alternative Measures of Price Change
### (annual percent change)

|      | Consumer price Index | Implicit price deflator[a] | Chain price index[a] | Fixed-weighted price index[a] |
|------|---------------------|----------------------------|----------------------|-------------------------------|
| 1983 | 3.2 | 4.1 | 4.2 | 4.2 |
| 1984 | 4.3 | 3.8 | 4.0 | 4.0 |
| 1985 | 3.6 | 3.5 | 3.6 | 3.7 |

[a]Based on the gross national product price measures for personal consumption expenditures.

index shows the most; the chain price index's inflation rate lies between the extremes. Since the implicit price deflator reflects households' spending substitutions among different goods and services due to changes in prices or consumer preferences, it tends to give greater weight to lower-priced items. In contrast, the fixed-weight price index doesn't reflect these shifts from higher-to lower-priced items; the chain price index reflects them, but with a time lag.

Since the CPI retains fixed weights for about 10 years, conceptually it is closest to the fixed-weighted price index. There are differences, however. In 1986, the CPI uses 1972–73 base expenditure weights with modifications as noted in Part A, and the fixed-price index uses 1982 weights; the CPI updating in 1987 shifts to 1982–84 expenditure weights. There also are differences in the coverage and measurement of several items between the CPI and GNP price measures. For example, life insurance is excluded from the CPI and included in the GNP price measures, while school tuition is included in the CPI but excluded from the GNP figures. The change in the CPI method of pricing owner-occupied housing made the CPI and GNP measures much more comparable beginning in 1983.

Table 15 compares the CPI with the GNP consumer price measures for 1983 to 1985 (as noted above, the comparability was enhanced in 1983). In this three-year period, the major difference was that the CPI rate of inflation increased from 1983 to 1985 although with a tapering off in 1985, while the GNP-measured inflation rates all declined over the period. The implicit price deflator also showed the lowest rate of inflation, which is consistent with the continually shifting weights noted above. Although these differences are relatively small, overall they indicate that the CPI had different and more volatile year-to-year movements than the GNP price measures.

No single concept of constructing index numbers is necessarily best for capturing actual economic trends (see Chapter 2). For example, if the analyst wants to assess the effect of price movements under constant living standards, the CPI and fixed-weight index are the most appropriate; if the interest is in price trends of items actually bought, the implicit price deflator and chain price index are the most appropriate; and if the interest is in the "true" rate of inflation, the range between the lowest and highest rates of the various measures may be considered as bracketing the actual amount. In general, the advantage of alternative measures is that they emphasize the inherent ambiguity in measuring price movements by providing a range rather than a single figure of price movements.

# RELATION OF INFLATION TO UNEMPLOYMENT

Inflation and unemployment are the most obvious indicators of the economy's performance. Clearly, the economic well-being of individuals is enhanced by low inflation and low unemployment. However, the compatibility of the two for the economy as a whole is the focus of much of the debate on economic policies. To the extent that low inflation and low unemployment are incompatible, debate focuses on whether emphasis should be placed on reducing unemployment or reducing inflation. Much of the public policy discussion is influenced by the Phillips curve, which depicts a direct trade-off between unemployment (see Chapter 5) and inflation. As discussed below, the trade-off is apparent primarily in periods when both unemployment and inflation are relatively low. This limits the application of the Phillips curve considerably. It is discussed here because of its importance in the economic debate.

While the trade-off between unemployment and inflation concerns policy analysts and government officials, the population is concerned with the effects of both factors in daily life. Everyone experiences inflation continuously in the cost of household items. Fewer persons are directly affected by unemployment, but for those out of work the impact can be severe. Since the 1960s, the combined effect of unemployment and inflation, termed the misery index, has had noticeable effects on voter behavior. Its impact on presidential elections over the postwar period is discussed below.

## *Phillips Curve*

The most direct measure of the relationship between inflation and unemployment is the Phillips curve. It is named for A. W. Phillips, who in the late 1950s assessed the relationship between wage rates and unemployment in England over a 100-year period.[13] In recent analyses, the wage-rate component is replaced by prices; it is this adaptation, termed the augmented Phillips curve, that is used here.[14]

The Phillips curve depicts graphically the idea of an inverse relationship between unemployment and inflation: as unemployment decreases, prices increase, and vice versa. The underlying principle is that declining unemployment results in higher production costs as more outmoded and inefficient machinery is used and less-productive workers are employed; in addition, when unemployment is low or declining, unions tend to get higher wage increases because they are in a stronger bargaining position. Conversely, when unemployment is high or rising, production and wage increases are lower.

Figures 41a, b, c, and d show annual Phillips curve trends in four periods from the 1950s to the mid–1980s. The unemployment rate is shown one year behind the change in the CPI, on the premise that changes in the unemployment level don't immediately affect prices—for example, unemployment in 1984 affects prices in 1985.[15]

The figures conform to the concept of an inverse trade-off between unemployment and inflation when the plotted line connecting one year to the next slopes downward to the right. The average relationship for all years is represented by the dashed line. The figures indicate that the theoretical inverse relationship was most in evidence in the 1960s when both unemployment and inflation were relatively low. Experience was contrary to the theory in the 1950s, when there was a slight direct relationship (upward-sloping dashed line), and the relationship was tenuous in the 1970s (slightly downward-sloping dashed line). In the first half of the 1980s, the average experience was consistent with the theory, but 1984 and 1985 did not show any correspondence. In general (other than the 1960s), there were wide variations in the year-to-year movements, making them highly unpredictable, as evidenced by the wide dispersion of the individual years from the average long-term relationship (dashed line).

This divergence between the theory and experience indicates that, for the most part, the economy is too complex for simple Phillips curve relationships. The relationship breaks down in two very different economic environments. In the 1970s both inflation and unemployment were relatively high, and in some years both were rising; in part this reflected the substantial increase in inflationary expectations, which became self-fulfilling when they led to rapid price and wage increases as business and labor tried to make up for declines in real income and insulate their incomes against further price increases. In the expansion from 1983 to 1985, which followed periods of high unemployment during the recessions of 1980 and 1981–82, both inflation and unemployment declined. Fuller utilization of resources during this period raised productivity by lowering fixed overhead costs, which was also an incentive to business to hold down the rate of price increases even though the economy was expanding. (As noted previously, inflation also slowed in this period because oil prices fell following the weakening of the OPEC cartel, the value of the dollar increased, and inflationary expectations slowed.)

Another problem of Phillips curve analysis is that the threshold level of unemployment below which inflation tends to accelerate and above which inflation tends to slow down is hard to pinpoint. This threshold is referred to as the nonaccelerating inflation rate of unemployment. As noted in Chapter 5, it is perceived by some to have risen from about 4.5 percent in the 1960s to as high as 7 percent in the 1970s. The higher rate is ascribed mainly to the influx of

Figure 41a. **Phillips Curve: 1948–59**

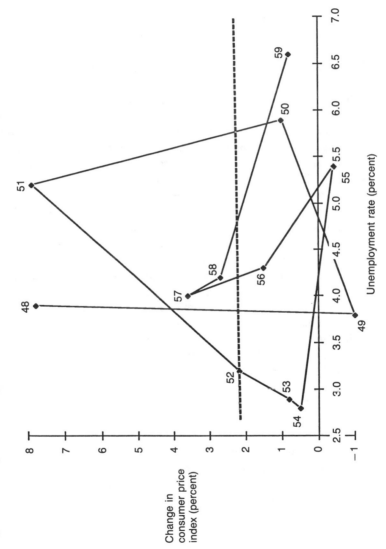

━━━━━ Average relationship over entire period.

*Note:* Unemployment rate of previous year corresponds to CPI change of current year (e.g. UR 1958 and CPI 1959).

199

Figure 41b. **Phillips Curve: 1960–69**

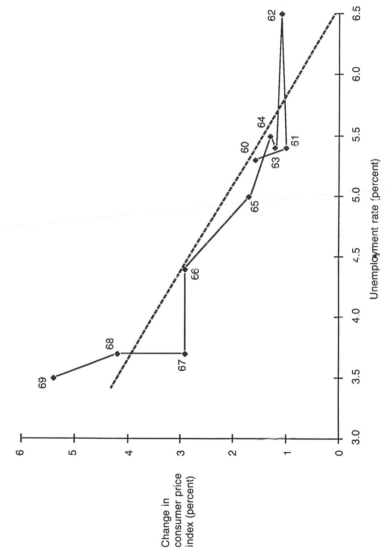

▬▬▬▬▬ Average relationship over entire period.

*Note:* Unemployment rate of previous year corresponds to CPI change of current year (e.g. UR 1968 and CPI 1969).

Figure 41c. **Phillips Curve: 1970–79**

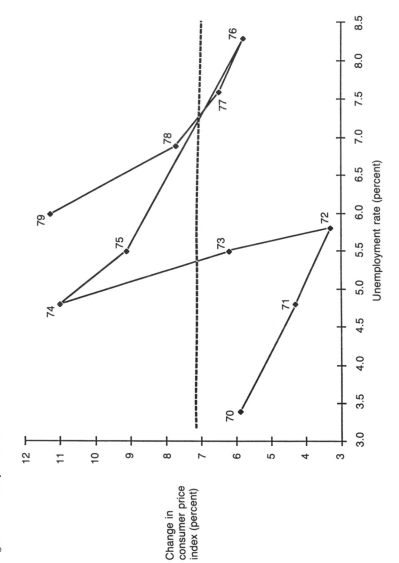

▬▬▬ Average relationship over entire period.

*Note:* Unemployment rate of previous year corresponds to CPI change of current year (e.g. UR 1978 and CPI 1979).

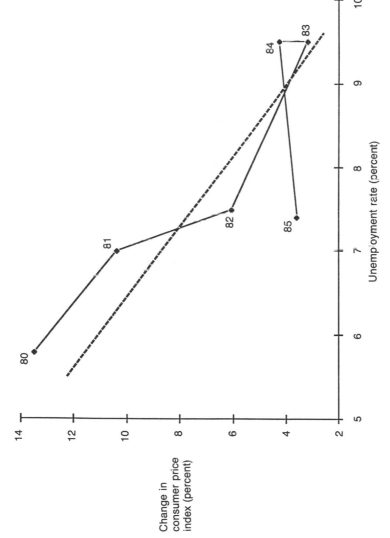

Figure 41d. **Phillips Curve: 1980–85**

Change in consumer price index (percent)

Unemployment rate (percent)

▬▬▬▬ Average relationship over entire period.

*Note:* Unemployment rate of previous year corresponds to CPI change of current year (e.g. UR 1984 and CPI 1985).

teenagers (who have high unemployment rates) into the labor force and to a small extent to the increase in working women (whose unemployment rates had been slightly higher than those for men). In the mid–1980s the threshold is considered to have declined to the 6 percent range because of the fall-off in the teenage population and the greater experience of women workers.[16] Other long-term factors affecting the nonaccelerating inflation rate of unemployment are productivity increases, tariffs and other import restrictions, farm subsidy price supports, minimum wages, monopolistic pricing, deregulation of industry pricing, and social compacts between business and labor to hold down price and wage increases. The threshold unemployment rate falls when these factors change in the direction of causing lower prices, and it rises when changes in these factors tend to increase prices. These changes in the threshold unemployment rate are referred to as improving or worsening the Phillips curve trade-off.

The Phillips curve trade-off between inflation and unemployment is most apparent when inflation and unemployment are in relatively low ranges. During other periods, experience reveals considerable divergence from the theory. For example, high inflation and low unemployment may not be compatible over sustained periods, as spending by households and business is moderated or lowered because the higher prices reduce the purchasing power of their incomes, leading to lower economic growth and higher unemployment. By contrast, low unemployment and low inflation may be compatible if business and labor pursue a concerted anti-inflation policy by deliberately holding down the rate of wage and price increases and thus maintain the purchasing power of incomes, leading to faster economic growth and lower unemployment.[17] *The analyst should consider Phillips curve projections of inflation rates at various unemployment levels most relevant during periods when both unemployment and inflation are relatively low.*

## Misery Index

In recent national elections, the CPI has become part of the debate between candidates by its inclusion in a figure called the misery index. The misery index is the sum of the CPI inflation rate and the unemployment rate, and has been used in election campaigns since 1976 as a summary measure of the pocketbook issue. Because high rates of inflation and unemployment are undesirable, economic well-being and the misery index are inversely related. Thus, the nation is better off when the misery index is declining than when it is rising, and the incumbent party will gain from a declining index and be at a disadvantage from an increasing one.

The misery index is only a rough guide to how voters perceive their economic well-being, however. Its limitations are that it gives equal weight to unemployment and inflation, which may be an accurate reflection of the public's perceptions only when the two components are at certain levels; it excludes employment, which may be rising while unemployment also is rising, as discussed in Chapter 5; and it doesn't distinguish whether the index level is particularly high or low except in relation to past periods. However, because of its use in recent campaigns, it is interesting to review the experience of the index with the outcome of presidential elections.

Figure 42 shows the misery index in the 10 postwar presidential election years from 1948 to 1984 and in each of the years preceding the election year. The adjacent years are included as an indication of the recent economic record of the incumbent party, which may be best remembered by the voters. In seven of the ten elections, the party won when the recent movement in the misery index favored it—for example, the incumbent party benefited if the index declined between the pre-election year and the election year. This pattern didn't occur in the first three postwar elections, when in two cases (1952 and 1956) the misery index didn't favor the winner; however, in six of the seven elections from 1960 to 1984 (1976 was the exception), the party that won was favored by the recent movement of the misery index.

Since 1960, then, the change in the misery index in the election year has generally corresponded to the outcome of the presidential election. However, it should be remembered that the misery index is a highly simplified view of pocketbook issues. It reflects neither the impact of other important domestic and international election issues nor the personalities of the candidates. Elections are won on a combination of factors, of which the pocketbook issue is important but not necessarily decisive. *Thus, while the misery index may suggest which candidate has an advantage because of the economic environment, it doesn't necessarily presage the outcome of the election.*

## SUMMARY

The CPI has moved consistently upward over the postwar period but at varying rates. Even in recessions, the CPI tends to show a slower rate of increase rather than an absolute decline. Thus, although prices for particular items sometimes decline, assessments of overall price movements focus on changes in the rate of increase.

The relationship between inflation and unemployment is most directly expressed in Phillips curve analysis. Experience with the Phillips curve indicates that the assumed inverse relationship, in which a change in the unemployment rate leads to a change in the inflation rate in the opposite direction, holds up best during periods of low unemployment and low inflation; by contrast, the relationship has been quite limited during periods of high unemployment, high inflation, or both.

The combined effect of inflation and unemployment, referred to as the misery index, has been used as an indication of the pocketbook issue in presidential elections since 1976. The index is a broad measure of how the economic environ-

204

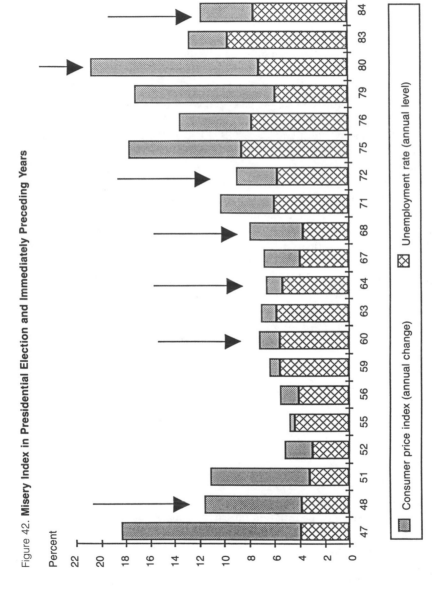

Figure 42. **Misery Index in Presidential Election and Immediately Preceding Years**

Consumer price index (annual change)   Unemployment rate (annual level)

*Note:* Arrow indicates that the winning presidential candidate had advantage of the misery index movement.

ment affects voters' perceptions of their economic well-being. Movements in the misery index in the year preceding the election and in the election year tend to be consistent with the result of the election. However, they are more useful as a guide to which candidate has the advantage because of economic conditions, and not as a prediction of the winner.

## NOTES

1. Bureau of Labor Statistics, *BLS Handbook of Methods: The Consumer Price Index*, Volume II, April 1984, p. 6.
2. The noninstitutional population excludes persons in prisons, long-term care hospitals, and old-age and other protected homes, a group that makes up 1 percent of the population.
3. *BLS Handbook of Methods*, Volume II, *op. cit.*, p. 3.
4. For the detailed methodology of constructing the CPI, see *Ibid.*, pp. 4–5 and Part II.
5. Because the Consumer Expenditures Survey data refer to 1972–73 but were introduced in the CPI in 1978, they were modified to be more representative of 1978. This was done by allowing for the effect of price changes between 1973 and December 1977 on the dollar expenditures of each item. This adjustment assumed that the relative price changes did not affect the quantities of each item bought—in other words, that no substitution occurred because of price changes.
6. Charles Mason and Clifford Butler, "New basket of goods and services being priced in revised CPI," *Monthly Labor Review*, January 1987.
7. Seasonally adjusted total CPI levels are not published because cost-escalation contracts are typically calculated using unadjusted levels, and the publication of two levels could confuse the parties to the contracts regarding the appropriate index to use. However, seasonally adjusted levels for the components are published.
8. This information on sampling errors is based on conversations with the Bureau of Labor Statistics. The sampling errors are not published in statistical reports.
9. Timothy M. Smeeding, *Alternative Methods for Valuing Selected In-Kind Transfer Benefits and Measuring Their Effect on Poverty*, Technical Paper 50, U.S. Bureau of the Census, March 1982, p. 12. This is based on study by Fendler and Orshansky which is summarized in Smeeding.
10. U.S. Bureau of the Census, *Estimates of Poverty Including the Value of Noncash Benefits: 1984*, Technical Paper 55, August 1985, Table C, p. 6. The methodology for the in-kind estimates was developed by Smeeding (Footnote 9 above).
11. Albert A. Hirsch, "An Analysis of Disinflation: 1980–83," *Business Economics*, January 1985.
12. For a discussion of various studies giving the range of impacts, see Jeffrey D. Sachs, "The Dollar and the Policy Mix: 1985," *Brookings Papers on Economic Activity*, 1:1985.
13. A. W. Phillips, "The Relation between Unemployment and the Rate of Change of Money Wage Rates in the United Kingdom, 1861–1957," *Economica*, November 1958.
14. For a good discussion of the conceptual aspects of the Phillips curve, see Sherman J. Maisel, *Macroeconomics: Theories and Policies* (W. W. Norton & Company: 1982), pp. 443–460.
15. Detailed studies using monthly or quarterly data have shorter lags of about six months between unemployment and prices. Lagging the effect of unemployment on infla-

tion one year improves the observed relationship in terms of the Phillips-curve theory in the 1970s and 1980s, has no appreciable effect in the 1960s, and worsens the relationship in the 1950s.

16. A. Steven Englander and Cornelis A. Los, "The Stability of the Phillips Curve and Its Implications for the 1980s," Federal Reserve Bank of New York, Research Paper 8303, January 1983, pp. 20–23, and "Recovery Without Accelerating Inflation?", *Quarterly Review*, Federal Reserve Bank of New York, Summer 1983, pp. 24–26.

17. Robert Kuttner, *The Economic Illusion: False Choices between Prosperity and Social Justice* (Houghton Mifflin Company: 1984), p. 22 and Chapter 4.

# 7 • Money Supply

The money supply is a measure of certain financial assets held by households, business, nonprofit organizations, and state and local governments that are available for consumer, investment, and government spending. It is used, along with other economic indicators, by the Federal Reserve Board (FRB) to determine monetary policies. The FRB influences the money supply by affecting the levels of bank reserves available for loans, and thus affecting interest rates on loans to households and business. Monetary policies aim at moderating extreme cyclical fluctuations of high inflation during expansions and high unemployment during recessions, with the goal of achieving steadier economic growth, high employment, and low inflation over the long run.

In developing the money supply measures, the FRB provides four alternative definitions—M-1, M-2, M-3 and L—which range in coverage of financial assets from M-1 as the most limited to L as the broadest. For example, M-1 includes only currency, demand (checking) deposits, interest-bearing negotiable order of withdrawal (NOW) accounts (which are also used by households for writing checks), and nonbank traveler's checks, while L includes all of these plus savings accounts, short-term Treasury securities, commercial paper, and more. All of the money supply measures are available monthly, while M-1 is also provided weekly.

The various assets included in the four measures also differ in terms of liquidity (the ease with which they can be used immediately as money without the risk of losing value) and in the amount of control the FRB has over their rate of expansion (through regulation of reserve requirements for commercial banks and other depository institutions). M-1 is the most liquid and subject to the most FRB control; M-2, M-3, and L are increasingly less liquid and subject to less FRB control.

The money supply differs from other economic indicators in this book in a basic way: it is the only indicator on which a governmental authority acts solely and directly to affect its performance. The federal budget deficit is acted on directly, but as noted below, the federal budget is not solely associated with managing the economy. The other indicators reflect economic activity but are not active instruments in economic policy. Even when incomes policies of voluntary price and wage guidelines or mandatory controls are in effect, the consumer price index and wage rate indicators, while they record the impact of those policies, are not used as instruments to achieve the price and wage goals.

Monetary policy and fiscal policy are the federal government's main tools for managing the overall economy. As noted in Chapter 2 under "Economic Policies," monetary policy is more focused than fiscal policy because it is geared solely to managing the economy, while fiscal policy is derived secondarily as the outcome of spending programs and tax laws to meet the nation's civilian and defense needs in the most efficient and equitable manner. Monetary policy is also more flexible because it can be and is modified throughout the year to stimulate or restrain economic activity; fiscal policy responds more slowly to changing economic conditions, because of the lengthy legislative process involved in changing spending programs and tax laws. (Fiscal policy is discussed in Chapter 3 under "Government Spending and Finances.")

## MONEY SUPPLY AND ECONOMIC ACTIVITY

The money supply in part reflects the decisions of households, business, nonprofit organizations, and state and local governments to hold their assets in certain financial forms—currency, checking accounts, saving accounts, money market mutual funds, money market deposit accounts, large time deposits, Eurodollars, short-term Treasury securities, commercial paper, etc. The money supply is also influenced by FRB monetary policies.

In economic theory, the amount of money is related to spending and the resultant economic growth, employment and inflation. A larger money supply means more spending, and a smaller money supply means less spending. The FRB manages the supply of money through its policies to expand or restrain the amount of commercial bank reserves available for loans, amount of bank reserves affects the interest rates charged for loans (the techniques for managing the money supply are discussed in the next section).

There is an assumed short-run inverse relationship between bank reserves and interest rates—more bank reserves result in lower interest rates, and less bank reserves result in higher interest rates. Abstracting from longer-run changes in the rate of economic growth and inflation and the resulting demand for money, as more reserves become available there is increasing competition among banks, finance companies, and other lending institutions to extend credit, tending to result in lower interest rates. In turn, lower interest rates are an inducement to households to borrow money for consumer items and housing mortages and for businesses to borrow money for plant and equipment investment. As these loans become checking accounts for borrowers, the money supply increases. The opposite occurs when less reserves are available, which tends to raise interest rates and lower borrowing, and consequently lowers the money supply.

Schematically, these relationships appear as:

Reserves > Interest rates > Spending > Growth, employment, inflation

There tends to be a direct relationship between money supply growth rates on the one hand and economic growth, employment and inflation on the other, although with time lags from when changes in the money supply occur to when they impact on economic activity. The time lags are difficult to quantify with precision; estimates range from less than one year to about two years, because other factors affecting the economy (unemployment levels and economic growth, the federal deficit, the value of the dollar, oil prices, inflationary expectations, etc.) vary over time.

These nonmonetary conditions also sometimes override the money supply movements assumed in the theoretical schemata. During periods of high inflation or expected increases in inflation, rapid growth in the money supply may be perceived by lenders as overstimulating the economy and causing further price increases; therefore, interest rates may continue to increase (contrary to the expected theoretical decrease), as lenders act to keep the purchasing power of their incomes from deteriorating due to inflation when the loan is repaid. When lenders raise interest rates above what they would be in periods of less inflation, the higher rate is referred to as an "inflation premium." This occurred in the late 1970s and first half of the 1980s. A similar pattern of nonmonetary factors weighing heavily may occur during recessions and periods of high unemployment when, despite lower interest rates, households and businesses don't increase their borrowing and spending because of declining incomes.

## FRB MONEY SUPPLY TARGETS AND THEIR IMPLEMENTATION

As discussed previously, the Full Employment and Balanced Growth Act of 1978 (the Humphrey-Hawkins Act) established goals for reducing unemployment and inflation (see Chapter 5 under "Unemployment"). The Act also requires the FRB to report to Congress twice a year, in February and July, on its objectives and plans for growth rates of the money supply during the calendar year.[1] In these reports to Congress, the FRB provides target ranges for the growth of M-1, M-2, and M-3; targets are not included for L because several of the financial assets included in L are too far removed from FRB control. Occasionally the FRB doesn't provide targets for all of the money supply measures, as when no 1987 target was given for M-1 in the February 1987 report to Congress because of problems in managing M-1 growth (see Part B below under "Money Supply and Velocity").

These target ranges are set to provide the amount of money necessary to accommodate what the FRB considers to be an achievable path for balancing economic growth, employment, and inflation. However, they do not represent preconceptions of how fast the economy should grow over particular periods.[2] Because the money supply figures are in current dollars, in gauging their effect on spending they should be considered in relation to the gross national product in current dollars. Because current-dollar GNP reflects both the quantity of production (real GNP) and price inflation, assessments of the economic impact of money supply movements inherently allow for the combined effect of economic growth and inflation rather than distinguishing the two components separately. This combined impact provides an overall consistency check on other analyses that identify the economic growth and inflation components separately, as discussed in Part B.

The target ranges typically allow the FRB considerable discretion in modifying growth rates in the money supply as economic trends and the demand for money evolve through the year. For example, in the February 1986 report, the ranges for 1986 were 3 to 8 percent for M-1, 6 to 9 percent for M-2, and 6 to 9 percent for M-3. The Humphrey-Hawkins Act treats these targets as guides rather than requiring that they be met, so long as the reasons for not achieving them are reported to Congress.

The FRB uses three methods to manage the money supply: open market operations, the discount rate, and reserve requirements.[3] All three methods initially affect commercial bank reserves, which in turn affect the volume of bank loans and the money supply, as discussed above. *Open market operations* refer to the purchase and sale of federal government securities by the FRB. Bank reserves are increased when the FRB buys and decreased when it sells. These operations can be carried out daily, if needed, and are the FRB's primary means of controlling bank reserves.

The *discount rate* is the interest rate that the FRB charges commercial banks for loans. Banks typically obtain such loans (a) when they need to supplement their reserves to meet seasonal demands for money, or (b) to meet short-term liquidity needs when their reserves are close to or below the legally required minimums, due to economic conditions affecting their customers that are expected to be reversed in the near future. Banks may also need longer-term loans (referred to as extended credit) when they have more serious liquidity or management difficulties that can be resolved only over protracted periods. The FRB changes the discount rate when it considers it necessary to bring it in line with other short-term interest rates, or to signal a change in FRB policy on the rate of growth in the money supply; the discount rate is changed more frequently when market interest rates are rising or falling, and less frequently when market interest rates are relatively stable.

*Reserve requirements* are the legally required reserves that banks must maintain with the FRB in proportion to their deposits, and are used solely to implement monetary policies in conjunction with open market operations. If there were no reserve requirements, open market operations would be ineffective because there would be no specific limit on the volume of loans a bank could make. The FRB changes reserve requirements within certain prescribed ranges, but because such changes can drastically affect banks' liquidity, the requirements are changed infrequently and then typically with offsetting open market operations to blunt any immediate sharp effect. Reserve requirements may be changed to counteract developments in particular financial markets—such as varying international interest rates that cause money to flow between the United States and other nations in a way that hinders the implementation of monetary policies—or as a signal that the FRB is changing its policies toward expansion (lower reserves) or restraint (higher reserves). (Reserve requirements are not used to maintain the financial soundness of banks. This is done by the banking regulatory agencies—FRB, Comptroller of the Currency (Treasury), and Federal Deposit Insurance Corporation—in their oversight of bank operations.)

Over the long run, independent of changes in the demand for money during cyclical expansions and recessions, an increase in the money supply is needed to accommodate the increasing population. This continuing increment is put into the economy by the FRB's purchase of Treasury securities in open market operations.

## MONETARY POLICIES

Economists differ over the appropriateness of monetary policies adopted by the FRB. The differences center on two points: (a) whether monetary policies should emphasize the level of interest rates or growth in the money supply, and (b) whether money supply targets should continue to be developed as a range, giving the FRB discretion in adjusting to changing economic conditions, or if a single figure should be adhered to as the target. In the evolution of this debate, economists who emphasize the use of the money supply rather than interest rates and who opt for a single figure for the money supply targets are referred to as monetarists; Milton Friedman and the Federal Reserve Bank of St. Louis are among those who are identified with the monetarist approach.[4] By contrast, the FRB approach is eclectic in that it modifies the emphasis placed on money supply or interest rate targets based on its assessment of current and future economic conditions. For example, from October 1979 to August 1982, in order to slow down inflation the FRB followed a restrictive money supply policy, resulting in substantial increases in interest rates; in August 1982, the policy was modified in order to lower interest rates because of the deep recession and high unemployment.

Monetarists believe economic history shows that, in the long run, the money supply is the ultimate determinant of economic activity as measured in current dollars. While some monetarists may reassess this view in light of the weak relationship the money supply and current dollar GNP in the mid–1980s, their basic argument has been as follows: because little is known about forecasting economic activity, frequent changes in monetary policies cause undue uncertainty in the business community and volatile interest rates and economic activity, while a steady and predictable growth in the money supply would be conducive to a more certain economic environment encouraging more business investment and less cyclical fluctuation. Monetarists recommend a steady annual growth in M-1 that would reflect what they consider to be the maximum potential growth in the real gross national product based on long-run employment and productivity trends; it tends to be about 4 percent, but the precise number is less important than that it be steady. This approach emphasizes holding down inflation—for example, a 4 percent annual increase in the money supply would be consistent with a zero rate of inflation, in which the overall price level is steady. Eclectics, on the other hand, believe that emphasizing the money supply over all other factors would cause excessively high unemployment by not allowing for some price inflation. To them, monetarism is based on a simplistic view of the economy and would hamstring the FRB in its job of balancing the goals of reducing unemployment and inflation (see Chapters 5 and 6).

Opinions also differ within the eclectic approach on the desirable degree of expansion or restraint and on whether the focus should be on achieving certain rates of economic growth (as measured by the real gross national product) or of inflation. This divergence of opinion is apparent in the public record of the meetings of the FRB's Federal Open Market Committee, which determines the FRB money supply targets. The committee—which is composed of the seven Federal Reserve governors, the president of the Federal Reserve Bank of New York, and a rotating panel of the presidents of four of the 11 other regional Federal Reserve Banks—typically has majority rather than unanimous opinions in setting money supply targets. *In assessing the future course of FRB monetary targets, the analyst should consider the underlying assumptions of those policies and their consistency with trends in economic growth, employment and inflation.*

## NOTE ON FRB INDEPENDENCE

The Federal Reserve system is composed of the seven-member Board of Governors in Washington, D.C., which determines FRB policies, and 12 regional Federal Reserve banks located around the country. The seven FRB governors are appointed by the president subject to the confirmation of the Senate; the presidents of the regional Federal Reserve Banks who are the other members of the Federal Open Market Committee are appointed by the regional bank directors subject to the approval of the FRB governors. Thus the Board of Governors and the presidents of the regional Federal Reserve banks are appointed to their positions rather than elected by the general public.

Institutionally, the FRB reports to Congress; it is independent of the President. Since the executive branch doesn't participate in formulating monetary policies and the FRB doesn't participate in formulating fiscal policies, there is a problem of coordination. The FRB and the President are in fact sometimes at odds, a situation that has been criticized for leading to unbalanced monetary and fiscal policies.

This leaves Congress as the only branch with direct links to all parties engaged in developing fiscal and monetary policies. While congressional review of the FRB's semiannual reports could provide a vehicle for partial coordination, in practice this doesn't occur. Congress has the authority to redirect FRB policies if it is dissatisfied with them, but because it treats the reports as information, it does not take an active role in devising monetary policies; nor is it even clear when Congress agrees or disagrees with FRB policies.

Proposals have been made over the years to bring the FRB under the direction of the President, to lodge the responsibility for monetary policies *directly* with elected officials.[5] Any such change will require new legislation. This would have to resolve the benefits of better coordination between fiscal and monetary policies against the concerns that it would unduly politicize the FRB in its management of the economy, gearing it to help the party in power win elections.

## PART A. ESTIMATING METHODOLOGY

Table 16 shows the components of the M–1, M–2, M–3, and L measures of the money supply. The measures encompass increasingly broader definitions of money and "near money" (assets that can readily be converted to cash) in progressing from M–1 toward L; each successive measure takes the previous one as a base and adds new elements. The differences in the dollar levels of the alternative measures are substantial, most notably between M–1 and M–2; as of December 1985, M–2 was four times larger than M–1, M–3 exceeded M–2 by 25 percent, and L exceeded M–3 by 20 percent.

More significant for economic analysis are the differential growth rates in the money supply measures over time. M–1 typically has grown more slowly than the other measures, as certain elements not in M–1 have increased substantially, such as the new money market instruments and the large increase in Treasury securities due to the growing federal debt. There have been exceptions to this tendency recently: in 1982 there was a substantial increase in NOW accounts, which resulted in M–1 increasing at almost the same rate as M–2; and in 1985, when interest rates declined by two percentage points, M–1 increased faster than all of the other money supply measures. The relationships of these differential rates to economic growth and inflation are discussed in Part B.

From an analytic perspective, the various money supply measures are distinguished by two factors: FRB control and liquidity. M–1 is subject to the greatest FRB control because it has the highest proportion of assets subject to FRB reserve requirements. Analogously, L is subject to the least FRB control because

Table 16

## Money Supply Measures
### (Billions of dollars, December 1985)

| | |
|---|---:|
| **M–1** | **$639.9** |
| Currency (excludes bank-owned cash in bank vaults) | 173.1 |
| Demand (checking) deposits | 281.3 |
| NOW accounts (used for checking and saving) | 180.1 |
| Travelers checks, nonbank (e.g. American Express) | 5.5 |
| **M–2** | **2,574.7** |
| M–1 | 639.9 |
| Small time deposits (less than $100,000) | 882.5 |
| including open accounts and certificates of deposit | |
| Savings deposits | 301.8 |
| Money market deposit accounts | 512.0 |
| Money market mutual funds (households, business, | 176.5 |
| broker-dealers) | |
| Overnight repurchase agreements (used in open | 53.3 |
| market operations) | |
| Overnight Eurodollars held by U.S. residents at 17.0 | |
| overseas branches of U.S. banks | |
| **M–3** | **3,213.8** |
| M–2 | 2,574.7 |
| Large time deposits ($100,000 and more) | 438.7 |
| Term Eurodollars (maturities longer than 1 day) | 76.7 |
| Money market mutual funds (institutions only) | 64.6 |
| Term repurchase agreements (longer than 1 day) | 66.0 |
| **L** | **3,844.4** |
| M–3 | 3,213.8 |
| Short-term Treasury securities (maturities | 307.1 |
| less than 1 year, excluding savings bonds) | |
| Commercial paper (unsecured promissory notes | 2209.5 |
| of well-known businesses) | |
| Savings bonds (Treasury securities) | 79.5 |
| Bankers' acceptances ( bankers agreements to pay | 41.1 |
| bills of customers) | |

*Note*: The M-1, M-2, M-3 and L totals and certain components are seasonally adjusted. Other components are not seasonally adjusted. The sum of the components do not equal the totals because certain adjustments are made at the total level to avoid double-counting—e.g., money fund holdings of repurchase agreements and Eurodollars are excluded from the M–2, M–3, and L totals.

it has the lowest proportion of assets with reserve requirements—reserve requirements are imposed only on demand (checking) deposits and NOW accounts (included in all money supply measures), and on nonpersonal time deposits and Eurodollar borrowing by U.S. residents (included in M–2, M–3 and L).

Distinctions in terms of liquidity—based on assessments of the risks of particular assets losing value if converted to cash—are not are not as easily quantified as the variations in the degree of FRB control. For example, nonbank traveler's checks function as currency; demand deposits often require minimum balances below which penalty fees are paid; saving deposits may forfeit some interest payments if withdrawn before certain dates; and money market and Treasury securities are subject to current market interest rates, which impose a greater risk regarding the future value of these assets. M-1, then, is the most liquid of the money supply measures, while M-2, M-3, and L are increasingly less liquid, because they include progressively greater proportions of assets that are based on current market rates.

As noted earlier, the M-1 measure is provided weekly and monthly, while M-2, M-3, and L are provided monthly only. The monthly data for all measures are based on reports from samples of large and small commercial banks, saving and loan associations, mutual savings banks, credit unions, and brokers and dealers. Because the weekly M-1 data are bassed on fewer reports, they should be used with caution: they fluctuate considerably from week to week, and are sometimes substantially revised based on the more complete information underlying the monthly measures.

## PART B. ANALYSIS OF TRENDS

The introductory section to this chapter discussed the theoretical relationships between movements in the money supply, GNP, and interest rates (see "Money Supply and Economic Activity"). Because comparable data for the four money supply measures are available only since the fourth quarter of 1959, comparisons of money supply trends with economic growth, inflation, and interest rates are made for the 1960–85 period.

### MONEY SUPPLY AND GNP

Relationships between growth in the money supply and the gross national product are theoretically most consistent for the GNP in current dollars, because money supply measures are in current dollars and thus relate to actual price levels. As for which of the four money supply measure is most closely related to GNP movements, theoretical arguments could probably be made in support of any one of them.

In the comparisons shown here, the change in the money supply in one year is assumed to affect the GNP growth rates in the same year and the year following, showing in effect a two-year impact on the GNP. The money supply's impact on the GNP for (a) the same year as the money supply change, and (b) the same year and the two years following the money supply change did not result in as close a correspondence; therefore, these other relationships are not shown here.

Figure 43 shows M–1 in relation to the GNP in current dollars, and Figures 44 and 45 compare M–1 movements to real GNP and inflation (measured by the GNP implicit price deflator). The points representing each year shows the money supply growth rate in the initial year and the GNP measure used in the particular chart for that year and the following year. For example, 1961, which is the first year shown in the figures, represents the change in the money supply in 1960 and the change in the GNP in 1960 and 1961. Over the long run, the closest relationship would appear as an upward-sloping line to the right when the yearly points are connected in chronological sequence—thus, an increase or slowdown in the the rate of money supply growth would be associated with similar movements in GNP and inflation. The closest comparison is with GNP in current dollars (Figure 43); this typically (although not always) occurs in the expected direction, but it is not particularly stable or predictable from year to year, as indicated by the changing slopes of the lines connecting each year to the next. The dashed upward-sloping line to the right represents an average relationship over the years; because of the wide dispersion of the years around the line, there would be a large margin of error in using it to predict GNP in any particular year.

The M–1 relationships with real GNP and inflation (Figures 44 and 45) are both less consistent than that with GNP in current dollars, although there is a stronger correspondence for inflation than for real GNP. In fact, there is little linkage between the money supply and real GNP. The correlation coefficients are: GNP in current dollars (0.65); inflation (0.48); and real GNP (0.04)—the closer the correlation coefficient is to 1 or –1, the more similar are the movements of the variables, while the closer they are to zero, the less similar are the movements.[6]

However, the money supply in constant dollars, which is calculated by the Department of Commerce, has much closer movements to real GNP—the correlation coefficients are 0.6 for M–1 and 0.7 for M–2 in constant dollars.[7] (The measure of M–2 in constant dollars is one of the leading indicators discussed in Chapter 8.) These constant-dollar measures of the money supply still have a wide year-to-year dispersion around the average trend and aren't shown here. It is also difficult to relate them to the Federal Reserve money supply targets, because the targets are projected in current dollars to be consistent with the actual price levels at which open market operations are conducted in buying and selling Treasury securities.

These contrasts of the impact of the money supply in current and constant dollars indicate the difficulty of using the money supply to determine the distribution of the current dollar GNP into the inflation and real GNP components, as distinct from using the money supply to assess future movements of the GNP in current-dollar GNP as a whole. The separation of the GNP into the real (output) and inflation components is essential for determining the rate of economic growth implied in the current-dollar GNP measure. Other factors discussed in previous chapters are needed to determine this distribution into the real GNP and inflation

Figure 43. **Money Supply (M-1) vs. GNP, 1959(4) to 1935(4): Money Supply Impact for Two Years**

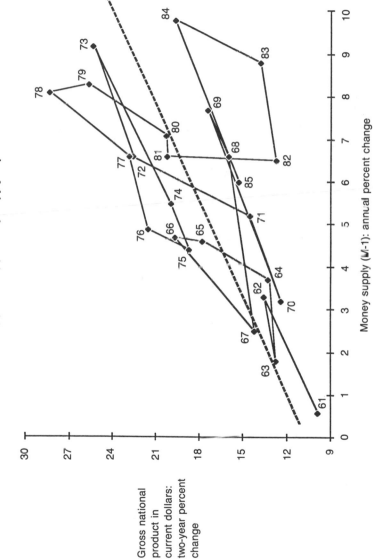

**━━━━** Average relationship over entire period.

*Note:* Money supply annual change, and GNP same-year and next-year change (e.g., MS 83 to 84 = GNP 83 to 85).

Figure 44. **Money Supply (M-1) vs. Real GNP, 1959(4) to 1985(4): Money Supply Impact for Two years**

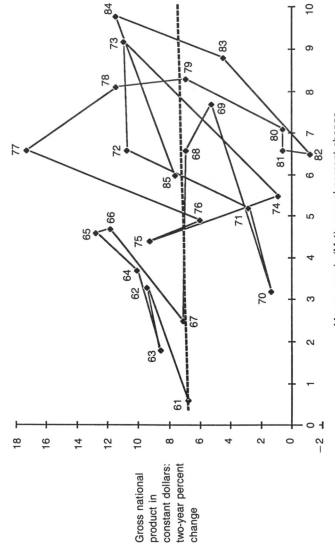

Money supply (M-1): annual percent change

▬▬▬▬ Average relationship over entire period.

*Note:* Money supply annual change, and GNP same-year and next-year change (e.g., MS 83 to 84 = GNP 83 to 85).

Figure 45. **Money Supply (M-1) vs. GNP Implicit Price Deflator, 1959(4) to 1985(4): Money Supply Impact for Two Years**

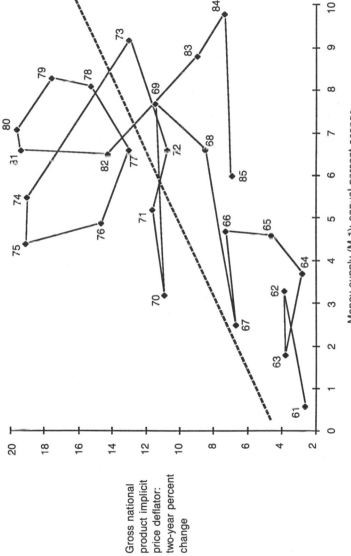

Gross national
product implicit
price deflator:
two-year percent
change

Money supply (M-1): annual percent change

▬▬▬▬ Average relationship over entire period.

*Note:* Money supply annual change, and IPD same-year and next-year change (e.g., MS 83 to 84 = IPD 83 to 85).

components—for example, personal income, business profits, capacity utilization, federal budget deficits, the value of the dollar, employment, unit labor costs, oil prices, and inflationary expectations.

Similar comparisons between M-2, M-3, and L with GNP in current dollars showed little difference from the above M-1 relationship.

*In assessing movements of the money supply measures as a gauge of future economic activity, the analyst should consider the money supply as a broad guide for GNP in current dollars. This is useful as a consistency check on the combined effects of expected real GNP and inflation which are projected separately from other economic indicators. M-1 typically shows similar relationships to GNP as the other money supply measures. This suggests that unless special circumstances, such as the development of new financial instruments, indicate the use of a particular money supply measure, in most cases it is appropriate to use M-1, which also is the most widely cited figure. M-1 is also the measure most directly subject to FRB control, which gives it the greatest policy relevance for achieving the money supply targets.*

## MONEY SUPPLY TARGETS AND VELOCITY

The money supply targets used by the FRB in conducting monetary policy are based on an expectation of the demand for money in relation to economic activity. One simple measure of this relationship is the ratio of the GNP to the M-1 money supply. This ratio is called velocity of money, and indicates the extent to which households, business, nonprofit organizations, and state and local governments hold financial assets in the most liquid form (it also may be thought of as the turnover of money). If the GNP grows faster than the money supply, velocity increases; if the money supply increases faster than the GNP, velocity decreases. Velocity is a behavioral relationship of the tendency for the public to hold money in the most liquid forms, such as low-interest or non-interest-bearing assets, because it perceives a need for the money in the near future and wants it readily available, or because it does not want to risk a loss in capital value. The future need may be for consumer and business spending, investments in anticipation of higher interest rates, etc.

Velocity increased for most of the postwar period (until 1982–85), as progressively smaller amounts of M-1 were held in relation to GNP. For example, from a level of under 4 in the early 1960s, velocity rose persistently to 7 in 1980–81; however, velocity declined slightly from 1982–85, to an average of 6.7. The upward trend through 1981 probably was caused by the rising inflation and interest rates of the period, which encouraged putting funds where they could earn more interest than the relatively low interest paid on NOW accounts. The subsequent slight decline during 1982–85 appears to be in response to declining interest rates and financial deregulation, which allowed interest payments on NOW checking accounts for individuals, nonprofit organizations, and state and local governments. These factors reduced the spread that had existed between interest on the highly liquid M–1 elements and the financial assets in the other money supply measures. The availability of NOW accounts also reduced incentives for further financial innovations, such as money market funds, which had increased M–1 velocity in previous years (by encouraging a shift from M–1 assets to M–2); the NOW accounts also appeared to increase the sensitivity of the holding of M–1 assets to interest-rate movements.[8]

Shorter-term movements in velocity are difficult to predict. Consequently, money supply targets are subject to the uncertainty of the movement of velocity. For example, when the GNP growth rate turns out to be close to the rate assumed when the money supply targets were projected, the money supply will exceed the target if velocity is much lower than anticipated; the money supply will be lower than the target if velocity is much higher than expected. This occurs even with the wide upper and lower limits set by the Federal Reserve for its money supply targets.

An instance of the money supply exceeding the upper range of the target occurred in 1985. Apparently because of the declining interest rates in that year, households, business, nonprofits, and governments tended to keep more of their financial assets in interest-bearing M–1 NOW accounts. Another possible reason noted by the Federal Reserve for the 1985 decline in velocity was that companies and banks adopted more cautious cash-management policies in light of financial problems in certain markets (such as risky bank loans, bank failures, and investment companies' abuses in handling securities funds).[9] The further decline in velocity in 1986 caused M–1 to grow much faster than the target for the year. As a result, the FRB didn't provide a M–1 target for 1987 in its February 1987 report to Congress because of the increasing uncertainties regarding the M–1 relationships to GNP and interest rates.[10]

These long-term trends and short-term volatility in velocity movements point up the difficulty of projecting money supply targets in relation to the GNP. *In assessing the likely outcome of money supply targets, the analyst should keep in mind that while the Federal Reserve can influence the quantity of money, underlying economic factors such as economic growth, unemployment, capacity utilization, the federal deficit, the value of the dollar, oil prices, and inflationary expectations dominate movements in the money supply.*

## MONEY SUPPLY AND INTEREST RATES

While influencing the money supply is an important intermediate tool for conducting monetary policy, decisions to borrow and spend are directly affected by interest rates. Households, businesses, and other borrowers think in terms of interest rates because they represent the cost of credit, while money supply movements as such are removed from borrowing decisions. Theoretically, in the short run a speedup in the money supply's growth rate would lower interest rates, and a slowdown in the money supply's growth would raise interest rates, as indicated at the beginning of the chapter.

Figure 46 shows the relationships for 1960–85 of changes in M–1 and interest rates. The interest rates are yields on Treasury securities with a 10-year remaining maturity.[11] The 10-year rate is used to reflect long-term borrowing for plant and equipment investments. The comparison is based on money supply and interest rate changes in the same year—the percent change in the money supply from 1984 to 1985, for example, is related to the percent change in interest rates from 1984 to 1985. Comparisons using a two-year impact of the money supply on interest rates as well as using M–2, M–3 and L did not have as close a correspondence and are not shown here.

The figure shows an inverse relationship between the money supply and interest rates; however, although consistent with economic theory, the relationship is rough. The inverse relationship is represented by the downward-sloping line to the right, which is the average for all years. This indicates a wide dispersion of the individual yearly points around the average line, and thus a wide margin of error for using it to predict interest rates in a particular year. Statistically, the correlation coefficient is -0.32, which indicates a very limited relationship, as –1 would show indentical inverse movements and zero would show no similarity in their movements.[6]

One of the factors affecting the general inverse relationship between the money supply and interest rates is the effect of inflation. When inflationary expectations are high, lenders raise interest rates above what they would be when lower inflation is expected; as noted at the beginning of the chapter, this "inflation premium" is intended to protect the purchasing power of the loan when it is repaid. Inflationary psychology thus reverses the expected relationship between money supply and interest rate. In this situation, an acceleration of money supply growth is associated with fueling inflation by making money more readily available for borrowing and spending; the resulting rate of economic growth, higher than the economy can sustain without causing further inflation, leads to higher interest rates as lenders act to compensate for expected higher inflation.

*Real interest rates*, defined as the market rate minus inflation, represent the cost of borrowing that is associated with lenders' expectations of future inflation. Higher real interest tends to retard borrowing and economic growth, while lower real interest tends to stimulate borrowing and growth.

Figure 47 shows trends in real interest and real GNP over 1955–85. Real interest is calculated as the yields on Treasury securities with 10-year remaining maturities less the rate of inflation represented by the GNP implicit price deflator. Real interest over the 30-year period averaged 2 percent. However, it was much higher in the first half of the 1980s than it was in the earlier years. Until 1981, it was always below 3 percent; it rose sharply during 1981–85, reaching a peak of 8.3 percent in 1984 and averaging 6.7 percent for the period. This sharp increase occurred when both market interest rates and inflation were declining, but real

Figure 46. **Money Supply (M-1) vs. Interest Rates, 1959(4) to 1985(4): Money Supply Impact for One Year**

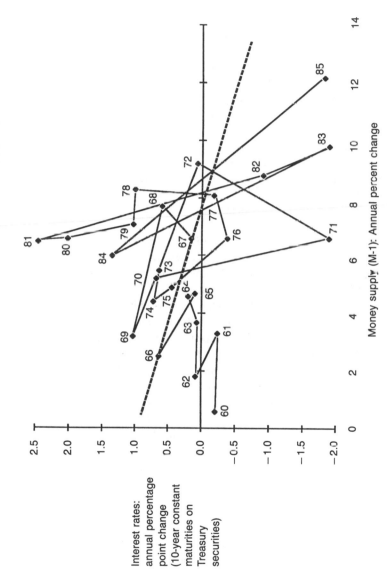

Money supply (M-1): Annual percent change

■■■■■■ Average relationship over entire period.

*Note:* Money supply annual change, and interest rate annual change for the same year (e.g., MS 84 to 85 = IR 84 to 85).

interest rose because inflation declined more than interest rates. While real interest dropped in 1985 by 1 percentage point, to 7.3 percent, it was still considerably above the long-term 2 percent average.

During 1973–78, real interest was exceptionally low and averaged zero (1974 and 1975 had negative real interest—the only other time it was negative was in 1955 and 1956). The low real interest rates during 1973–78 coincided with the 1973–74 and 1979 oil price shocks; thus, they may have reflected the recycling of OPEC oil income into American money markets, which increased the supply of loan funds and consequently tended to moderate interest rate increases that lenders ordinarily would have sought to compensate for the higher inflation. Whatever the causes of the low real interest rates, they ended in 1979 when the Federal Reserve sharply slowed money supply growth in order to dampen inflation. Subsequently, real interest rates remained high for several years, despite the fact that starting in 1982 the Federal Reserve accelerated money supply growth in order to lower interest rates and counteract the 1981–82 recession. Lenders evidently were still concerned that inflation would start increasing again, even though it had slowed down; this is an example of the importance of inflationary expectations on interest rates.

The rate of economic growth (real GNP) during 1955–85 was faster until the late 1970s than from 1979–85. This is consistent with the theoretical expectation that low real interest rates are a stimulus to growth. Although there is no existing hypothesis of a threshold level of real interest in relation to economic growth— what real interest rate is the break-even level above which economic growth slows and below which economic growth accelerates—the high real interest rates of the late 1970s and first half of the 1980s appear to have retarded economic growth.

*In assessing the impact of changes in the money supply on interest rates, the analyst should review both the changing demand for money and inflationary expectations. The changing demand for money arises from the needs of borrowers for consumer, investment and government spending. Inflationary expectations reflect lenders' perceptions of future price movements. Thus, while the money supply affects interest rates, it isn't sufficient to explain interest rate movements. Moreover, unless inflationary expectations and the demand for money are considered, a mechanical interpretation of money supply movements can often lead to an incorrect assessment of future trends in interest rates.*

## SUMMARY

The money supply is the main measure used by the Federal Reserve Board to formulate monetary policies. It is the only indicator discussed in this book that is acted on directly to affect its performance. The FRB influences the money supply in its use of targets by the role it takes in affecting the level of commercial bank reserves through open market operations, the discount rate, and reserve requirements.

Figure 47. **Real Interest Rate vs. Real Gross National Product**

Percent

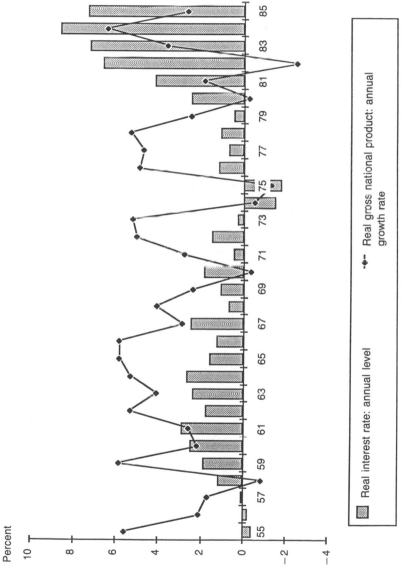

*Note*: Real interest is Treasury securities 10-year yields minus the GNP implicit price deflator annual change.

Money supply movements affect the economy through their impact on economic growth, inflation, and interest rates. The relationship of the money supply to the gross national product in current dollars provides an overall perspective of the combined effect of money supply movements on economic growth and inflation, but other analyses are needed to separate this total impact into the growth and inflation components. Of the four money supply measures (M-1, M-2, M-3 and L), M-1 is the appropriate one to use in most cases.

A key consideration in assessing the appropriateness of money supply targets in relation to projections of the GNP is the uncertainty of the movements of velocity. Velocity, the ratio of GNP to M-1, indicates the tendency of households and business to hold money in the most liquid form. Because of substantial fluctuations in velocity, it is evident that while the Federal Reserve monetary policies influence movements in the money supply, other factors dominate the rate of growth in the money supply.

The immediate impact of changes in the money supply is on the level of interest rates. Theoretically, a rapid growth in the money supply would tend to lower interest rates, and a slower growth would tend to raise interest rates. This tendency exists in practice, but the relationship is limited, because inflationary expectations and the demand for money by household, business and government borrowers strongly affect interest rates. In addition, real interest rates—the market rate minus inflation—appear to have an important impact on economic growth. Thus, while the money supply influences interest rates, a mechanical use of money supply movements to assess future trends in interest rates can often be misleading.

## NOTES

1. Full Employment and Balanced Growth Act of 1978, Section 108. This is also discussed in Board of Governors of the Federal Reserve System, *Federal Reserve System: Purposes and Functions*, 1984, p. 20.

2. Paul A. Volcker, chairman of the Board of Governors of the Federal Reserve System, Statement to the Committee on Banking, Housing and Urban Affairs, U.S. Senate, February 20, 1985, Attachment III ("Targeting Real Growth").

3. For a detailed discussion of these methods, see *Federal Reserve System: Purposes and Functions*, *op. cit.*, chapters 3 and 4.

4. For example, Milton Friedman, "The Role of Monetary Policy," *American Economic Review*, March 1968; and Dallas S. Batten and Courtenay C. Stone, "Are Monetarists an Endangered Species," *Review* (The Federal Reserve Bank of St. Louis), May 1983. For a statement of the monetarist position within the executive branch, see the discussion by the Council of Economic Advisers in the *Economic Report of the President*, February 1986, pp. 58–70; this CEA view is not necessarily the President's position.

5. For a proposal in the mid-1980s to bring the FRB under the President, see Lester C. Thurow, *The Zero-Sum Solution: Building a World-Class American Economy* (Simon and Schuster: 1985), pp. 325–327.

6. A correlation coefficient of 1 occurs when the variables move in identical patterns in a direct relationship (both increase or decrease in tandem), and a coefficient of $-1$ occurs when the variables move in identical patterns in an inverse relationship (one increases and the other decreases).

7. The constant-dollar money supply figures are estimated by adjusting the official money supply measures to eliminate the effects of inflation according to movements in the consumer price index. See Bureau of Economic Analysis, U.S. Department of Commerce, *Handbook of Cyclical Indicators: A Supplement to the Business Conditions Digest*, 1984, pp. 29–30.

8. Board of Governors of the Federal Reserve System, *Monetary Policy Report to Congress Pursuant to the Full Employment and Balanced Growth Act of 1978*, February 19, 1986, Appendix A, p. A–2.

9. *Ibid.*, p. 26. The Federal Reserve statement on this topic is worded generally, with no specific examples of the financial problems leading to the more cautious cash-management policies. Examples of the problems cited here are based on discussions with the Federal Reserve.

10. Board of Governors of the Federal Reserve System, *Monetary Policy Report to Congress Pursuant to the Full Employment and Balanced Growth Act of 1978*, February 19, 1987, pp. 6–8.

11. These estimates are based on constructing yield curves (interest rates and years to maturity) for the most actively traded Treasury securities, and reading the 10-year interest rate from the curve. See Joint Economic Committee of Congress, *1980 Supplement to Economic Indicators*, p. 108.

# 8 • Leading, Coincident, and Lagging Indexes

The leading, coincident and lagging (LCLg) indexes of economic activity are based on the concept that each phase of the business cycle contains the seeds of the following phase. By focusing on the factors operating in each phase, the LCLg system provides a basis for monitoring the tendency to move from one phase to the next. The LCLg system assesses the strengths and weaknesses in the economy as clues to future rates of economic growth as well as to cyclical turning points in moving from the upward expansion to the downward recession and vice versa.

The LCLg indexes are provided monthly by the Bureau of Economic Analysis of the U.S. Department of Commerce and are published in *Business Conditions Digest*. They are based on business cycle concepts and measuring techniques developed by Wesley Mitchell in the first half of the 20th century, and represent the most systematic quantification of how various aspects of the economy behave in cyclical expansions and recessions.

The three classifications of leading, coincident, and lagging refer to the timing in the turning points of the business cycle: the leading index turns down before a general recession begins and turns up before the recovery from the recession begins; the coincident index moves in tandem with the cyclical movements of the overall economy, tending to coincide with the designations of expansions and recessions (discussed in Chapter 2); and the lagging index turns down after the beginning of a recession and turns up after the beginning of a recovery.

The LCLg system is based on the theory that expectations of future profits are the motivating force in the economy. When business executives believe their sales and profits will rise, companies expand production of goods and services and of investment in new plant and equipment, but when they believe profits will decline, they reduce production and investment. These actions generate the expansion and recession phases of the business cycle. As discussed below, the LCLg indexes suggest the future course of profits by indicating business expectations of future rising sales (leading index), and by the differential movements in current business activity (coincident index) and production costs (lagging index).

## THE PROCESS OF CYCLICAL CHANGE

As background for the role of the three indexes, it is useful to summarize the cyclical phenomena considered to be the major elements underlying the LCLg system. To illustrate, assume as the cyclical starting point the beginning of the expansion from the previous recession (sometimes referred to as the recovery). In this initial stage, an impetus for increasing production starts an upward movement. Sales increase as consumers begin purchasing durable goods they had deferred during the recession; unit costs of production decline, because the increasing volume of sales is spread over the fixed depreciation and maintenance costs of exisiting plant and equipment, as well as over the lowered work force and other services resulting from the cutbacks of nonessential costs in the preceding recession. Thus, profits (sales minus costs) increase. As this momentum spreads and employment and consumer spending increase, business executives become more optimistic about future sales and order more goods for inventories and invest in new plant and equipment to increase and modernize productive capacity; as increasing numbers of new businesses come into existence in anticipation of continued growing markets and higher profits, they in turn stimulate more production, hiring, and spending, all of which encourage continued growth.

However, at some point the upward momentum will slow. Sales of some items are no longer as brisk because consumers' needs have changed, and higher prices cause consumers to defer purchases. Unsold inventories of goods accumulate, resulting in reduced prices to sell them, reduced orders for new goods to replace them and thus lower future production. When capacity utilization rates rise to high levels, production costs rise because of increasing use of outmoded and less-efficient equipment, hiring of less efficient workers when unemployment rates fall to low levels, and obtaining loans at high interest rates when the overall demand for money is strong. The higher production costs lead businesses to maintain prices in order to limit reductions in profit margins, but the higher prices in turn lead to lower sales; the combination of lower sales and higher production costs reduces profits enough to dampen the incentive for investing in new plant and equipment capacity. This slowdown in demand leads to lower production, and thus less employment and income for consumers, resulting in lower spending. The slowdown has a snowballing effect (analogous to the upward spiral in the earlier stages of the expansion) as consumers and business retrench in their spending. There is less incentive to take out additional loans (which would bolster spending), because, thanks to lower incomes, existing loans have become a greater burden to repay. Thus, production and employment are further reduced, bringing on a recession.

Increasing numbers of businesses close down during the recession, and businesses cut costs by maintaining lower inventories and reducing employment. This depressed level of economic activity ultimately runs its course as consumers who have deferred spending because of the economic uncertainty begin to replace their older goods and buy new housing at the lower recession-induced interest rates. With this turnaround in sales, businesses are encouraged to order more goods for inventories, thus stimulating production, and the stage is set for the recovery phase, which completes the cycle.

While this is a highly simplified version of cyclical economic movements, it depicts the basic rationale of the LCLg system. Each business cycle will have its unique characteristics because of other factors that vary over time, such as the intensity of inflation, level of unemployment, population growth, development of new products, soundness of the banking system, competition from abroad, etc.

## CONCEPTS OF THE LCLG SYSTEM

The LCLg system is based on the idea that profits are the driving force in the private enterprise economy. Business decisions on production, prices, employment, and investment are understood in relation to profits—both past trends in profits and the perception of future profits.[1]

The LCLg system combines several data series into a composite leading index, a composite coincident index, and a composite lagging index. The following discussion capsulizes the three composite indexes and the rationale for each of the components.[2] The component data series that have been discussed in previous chapters are noted in parentheses.

The *leading* index indicates business perceptions of future profits. It represents business' anticipations of future economic developments and the response in actions and plans to those expectations. The twelve components of the leading index, including one which was discontinued in 1987 (No. 5 below), are:

1. *Average weekly hours of manufacturing production workers* (see Chapter 5). Because of uncertainty in the economic outlook in the early stages of recovery from the previous recession and in the early stages of a downturn from the previous expansion, employers are more likely to adjust the hours of existing workers before hiring new workers during recovery or laying off workers during recession.

2. *Average weekly initial claims for unemployment insurance.* Increases or decreases in unemployment indicate business expectations of the demand for labor.

3. *Manufacturers' new orders for consumer goods and materials, in constant dollars.* Business commitments to buy items indicate future levels of production.

4. *Vendor performance (percent of companies receiving slower deliveries).* Delivery time reflects the strength of demand—brisk when the time from the placement of the order to delivery is long (because of the large backlog of orders),

and weak when the delivery time is short.

5. *Net business formation*. Because new businesses hire workers and buy equipment, changes in the rate of business formation indicate the pace of future employment and investment growth. (This component was eliminated from the index beginning with the February 1987 figures because the quality of the source data underlying the business formation measure had deteriorated. Business formation remained at a constant level during the 1984-86 period—rather than showing the expected upward trend—with only random, up-and-down monthly movements. Therefore, its elimination doesn't affect the overall patterns of the leading index except to reduce erratic month-to-month movements.)

6. *Contracts and orders for plant and equipment, in constant dollars* (see Chapter 3). These business commitments indicate future production and employment.

7. *New private housing building permits* (see Chapter 3). Permits provide advance indication of housing construction, which is cyclically sensitive to changes in employment and interest rates.

8. *Manufacturing and trade inventories on hand and on order, monthly change* (see Chapter 3). The rate of accumulation of inventories is associated with expectations of future sales.

9. *Prices of crude and intermediate materials, monthly change*. Prices of certain farm, mineral, and scrap products in which supplies cannot be changed quickly (because of production lead times and delays in obtaining used goods for scrap) are sensitive to sharp changes in demand.

10. *Prices of 500 common stocks*. Stock prices reflect investor expectations of economic growth and profits, and both investment and consumer spending. High stock prices make it easier for business to raise funds for plant and equipment investment and other ventures by selling new stock to the public (equity financing), which entails no required payback to the buyer of the value of the stock or the payment of dividends. By contrast, low stock prices make it more likely that business will obtain funds from the public by selling bonds (debt financing, in which the principal is repaid and there are specified interest payments). Generally, business would prefer to obtain outside funds by selling stock rather than bonds. Stock prices also affect household wealth, which affects future consumer and investment spending. Stockholders perceive they have more money to spend and invest when stock prices (and thus their wealth) are rising than when they are falling.

11. *Money supply (M–2) in constant dollars* (see Chapter 7). The amount of financial liquid assets reflects the purchasing power available for business and household transactions such as buying materials, hiring labor, investing in plant and equipment, and buying consumer goods. M–2 is used rather than M–1 because M–2 includes money market instruments that are quite liquid; it thus provides a broader measure of funds available for economic transactions.

12. *Business and consumer credit outstanding, monthly change*. Changes in

the level of loans and credit indicate the willingness of business and households to spend with borrowed funds that will have to be repaid.

The *coincident* index measures various aspects of production which reflect the current level of economic activity. The four components of the coincident index are:

1. *Employees on nonagricultural payrolls* (see Chapter 5). This measures the labor component in the current production of goods and services.

2. *Personal income less transfer payments, in constant dollars* (see Chapter 3). Real income earned by labor and investors reflects the resources used in producing the nation's output.

3. *Industrial production index* (see Chapter 4). Because manufacturing, mining, and gas and electric utilities tend to be the more cyclically volatile industries, current production levels in these industries are a good indicator of the cyclical elements in the economy.

4. *Manufacturing and trade sales, in constant dollars*. Movement of goods within the economy between manufacturing plants, from manufacturers to wholesalers, from wholesalers to retailers, and from retailers to consumers indicates the flows of goods in production and from production to distribution.

The *lagging* index reflects production costs and inventory and debt burdens that may encourage or retard economic growth. A slow increase or a decline in the lagging index is conducive to economic growth, while rapid increase in the lagging index is conducive to a recession. The six components of the lagging index are:

1. *Average duration of unemployment*. Persons unemployed for long periods are assumed to have less marketable skills than those unemployed for short periods. Recruiting and training costs are therefore higher if there are large numbers of long-term unemployed persons.

2. *Inventory-to-sales ratio for manufacturing and trade, in constant dollars* (see Chapter 3). Inventories are a major cost factor for business, and the higher they are relative to sales, the more expensive to hold—either because they represent borrowed money which results in interest costs, or because they tie up company funds.

3. *Labor cost per unit of output in manufacturing* (see Chapter 5). Labor costs in relation to production affect profits, which in turn affect decisions to expand or contract production and employment.

4. *Commercial and industrial loans outstanding, in constant dollars*. Interest burden on existing loans is higher and the availability of money for new loans is lessened the greater the level of outstanding loans, which tends to rise in expansions and fall in recessions.

5. *Ratio of consumer installment credit outstanding to personal income*. The debt burden of consumers suggests they are likely to take on more loans for

further spending when the ratio is low, and pay off existing loans when the ratio is high, thus contracting spending.

6. *Average prime rate charged by banks*. Interest rates charged for business loans indicate the cost of borrowing, which affects profits and the willingness to borrow.

## PART A. ESTIMATING METHODOLOGY

The LCLg composite indexes are developed by combining the component indexes according to an established weighted distribution. The weights represent the relative importance of the component items of each composite index in the base period. They are revised based on comprehensive evaluations approximately every 10 to 15 years; the weights remain unchanged between these revisions. The index for each new month is calculated based on the monthly movements of each of the components.[3] The general concept is similar to that used for the index numbers on industrial production (see Chapter 4) and consumer prices (Chapter 6), although there are some differences in the procedures.

In developing the weights, many economic indicators are evaluated to determine their appropriateness for inclusion in the composite indexes. The overall considerations in selecting them are: (a) their theoretical role in the leading, coincident and lagging process, and (b) how they perform empirically in terms of leading and lagging general business cycles over the post-World War II period. The specific criteria used are economic significance (theoretical importance); statistical adequacy (quality of the underlying survey and other statistical data from which they are calculated); timing (consistency in leading, coinciding, or lagging general business cycles); conformity to business cycle directional movements (upward in expansions and downward in recessions); smoothness (extent of erratic increases and decreases that obscure cyclical movements); and currency (promptness of the availability of current data; they must be monthly, not quarterly, series—in time for preparing the montly indexes). Numerical scores for each of these categories determine whether they qualify for inclusion in the composite indexes.

The component items selected for use are then combined into the three composite indexes with the items weighted according to how well they performed in the above criteria; indicators with the higher scores have greater weights. Other statistical adjustments are made so that the long-run trends of the indexes (over several cycles abstracting from the cyclical movements) will be similar; this insures that the monthly percent charges in the three indexes are comparable for cyclical comparisons because they are not affected by differential long-run trends. Additional modifications are made to insure that components with large upward and downward cyclical movements do not dominate the index.

In the monthly calculation of the indexes, the monthly movements of each of

Table 17

## Weights for the Composite Indexes

**Leading Index:**

| | |
|---|---|
| 1. Average weekly hours of manufacturing production workers | 1.014 |
| 2. Average weekly claims for unemployment insurance | 1.041 |
| 3. Manufacturers' new orders for consumer goods and materials, in constant dollars | 0.973 |
| 4. Vendor performance (percent of companies receiving slower deliveries | 1.081 |
| 5. Net business formation (see text for elimination in 1987) | 0.973 |
| 6. Contracts and orders for plant and equipment, in constant dollars | 0.946 |
| 7. New private-housing building permits | 1.054 |
| 8. Manufacturing and trade inventories on hand and on order, monthly change | 0.986 |
| 9. Prices of crude and intermediate materials, monthly change | 0.892 |
| 10. Stock prices of 500 common stocks | 1.149 |
| 11. Money supply (M–2), in constant dollars | 0.932 |
| 12. Business and consumer credit outstanding, monthly change | 0.959 |

**Coincident Index:**

| | |
|---|---|
| 1. Employees on nonagricultural payrolls | 1.064 |
| 2. Personal income less transfer payments, in constant dollars | 1.003 |
| 3. Industrial production index | 1.028 |
| 4. Manufacturing and trade sales, in constant dollars | 0.905 |

**Lagging Index:**

| | |
|---|---|
| 1. Average duration of unemployment | 1.098 |
| 2. Inventory-to-sales ratio for manufacturing and trade, in constant dollars | 0.894 |
| 3. Labor cost per unit of output in manufacturing | 0.868 |
| 4. Commercial and industrial loans outstanding, in constant dollars | 1.009 |
| 5. Ratio of consumer installment credit outstanding to personal income | 1.009 |
| 6. Average prime rate charged by banks | 1.123 |

the components are multiplied by the corresponding weights and the products are summed to a total single figure, which is the index.

Table 17 shows the weights for the three composite indexes. The average weight for each component is 1.000. The weights cover the following ranges:

Leading index: 0.892 for sensitive materials prices to 1.149 for common stock prices.

Coincident index: 0.905 for manufacturing and trade sales to 1.064 for employees on nonagricultural payrolls.

Lagging index: 0.868 for labor cost per unit of output to 1.123 for the prime rate.[4]

Thus, movements of the composite indexes are determined to some extent by the differential movements of the components. For example, in the month-to-month movement of the leading index, if stock prices increase by 5 percent, sensitive materials prices decrease by 5 percent, and all other components are unchanged, the leading composite index increases because of the greater weight of stock prices. The differences in weights among component items are moderate, but from time to time they may impact on the monthly index.

*In assessing monthly changes in the composite indexes, the analyst should consider whether the movements represent a broad-based pattern of most of the indicators or if it results mostly from the movements of the indicators with the largest weights. The movement is more likely to be sustained in the coming months if it is widespread among the components.*

## REVISION OF WEIGHTS

The LCLg system is comprehensively reassessed and revised approximately every 10 to 15 years, although there is no set schedule for such revisions. The most recent major revision was made in 1975. The next major revision will probably be made in 1988. Modifications between these major revisions have been limited to occasionally updating the use of particular indicators—substituting a new indicator because it was found to perform better than the one originally selected, or because the original indicator was no longer provided by the source agency or had deteriorated in quality.

There is a concern that the LCLg system doesn't adequately represent the structure of the economy in the mid-1980s. Thus, the Center for International Business Cycle Research at the Columbia University Business School began a study in 1986 of the contribution that services and foreign trade (both large and growing sectors of the economy) would make if they were included in the composite indexes.[5] These aren't typical LCLg cyclical indicators. For example, services don't exhibit the cyclical volatility of goods (see Chapters 3 and 6) and foreign trade, which is driven by foreign exchange values and economic activity at home and abroad (Chapter 3), doesn't have the self-generating cyclical characteristics discussed earlier in this chapter—that is, foreign trade is not part of the business cycle in which one phase propagates the next. The results of this study will be an interesting area to follow in the development of the LCLg system.

## INVERSION OF UNEMPLOYMENT
## INDICATORS

Statistical data that are plotted on charts typically are depicted as rising when the line moves upward and as declining when the line moves downward. These upward and downward movements conform to the directional movements of the upward (expansion) and downward (recession) phases of the business cycle. However, in two indicators of the LCLg system—initial claims for unemployment insurance (leading index) and average duration of unemployment (lagging index)—this movement is reversed. For these two, for example, a decline indicates a rise in or stimulus to economic activity. They thus conform to the business cycle phases in the reverse direction. For these two indicators, the scales on the charts' vertical axes are inverted so that, graphically, an increase is shown as declining and a decrease is shown as rising. This makes their directional movements visually consistent with general business cycle movements. These two unemployment components are also inverted when used to calculate the monthly movements of the leading and lagging composite indexes, so that the unemployment figures don't distort the indexes' movements; if they were not inverted, they would offset part of the cyclical movement of the other components.

# PART B. ANALYSIS OF TRENDS

The behavior of the three composite indexes over the general business cycle in the nine expansions and eight recessions since World War II are summarized below. Their behavior is consistent with their theoretical role discussed earlier—the leading index turns down in a recession and up in a recovery before these movements occur in the general business cycle; the direction and timing of the coincident index are similar to those of the general economy; and cyclical turns in the lagging index occur after those in the general economy.

---

### Difference from the General Business Cycle in Months:
### Average for the postwar business cycles

|  | (− lead; + lag) | |
|---|---|---|
|  | Peaks | Troughs |
| Leading Index | − 10 | − 3 |
| Coincident Index | − 2 | + 1 |
| Lagging Index | + 5 | + 10 |

---

Because the lagging index is last in the sequence of cyclical movements, it plays a role (in addition to its conceptual one of costs) in confirming that a cyclical turn has occurred. Generally, the lagging index turns down two quarters after a general recession begins and turns up three quarters after a general recovery from the previous recession, although these time lags have not been systematically quantified. The actual designation of the turning points of the general business cycle is made by the National Bureau of Economic Research, and is based on the movements of several indicators as discussed in Chapter 2.

Figure 48 shows that leads and lags for individual cycles don't always parallel the long-term average patterns above. Using differences of more than one quarter (four months or more) from these averages as a guideline for determining relatively high variations, the most noticeable deviations from the long-term averages occurred as follows: in the leading index, at the business cycle peaks before the recessions of 1953–54, 1957–58 and 1981–82; and in the lagging index, at the troughs after the upturn from the recessions of 1957–58 and 1969–70 and at the peak before the 1973–75 recession. The coincident index did not vary by more than one quarter from the long-term average.

Variations of more than one quarter do not dominate the LCLg system. However, they occur often enough to make it difficult to portray the current phase of any cycle as having average lead and lag characteristics. *The analyst should keep this limitation in mind when using the system as a clue to future economic trends.*

## COINCIDENT/LAGGING RATIO

The coincident index divided by the lagging index is considered by some as an additional leading indicator.[6] Theoretically, this ratio is significant because it relates costs to production, providing in effect a view of profits—the underlying concept of the LCLg system. For example, if the coincident index (production) increases or decreases at the same rate as the lagging index (costs), there is no change in the profit picture, thus signifying continued economic growth at the current rate. However, differential movements in the two indexes suggest other tendencies in the economy. If the coincident index increases at a faster rate or decreases at a slower rate than the lagging index, this indicates an increase in profits (since revenues are exceeding costs) and higher economic growth in the future; but if the coincident index increases at a slower rate or decreases at a faster rate, a decline in profits and lower future economic growth are indicated.

Over the postwar business cycles, on average the coincident/lagging ratio led the general recessions at the expansion peaks by 15 months and led the general recoveries at the recession troughs by two months. As indicated below, these leads exceed those of the leading index by four months at peaks, and are almost the same as the leading index at the troughs. Thus, during expansions the coincident/lagging ratio tends to give an earlier signal than the leading index of an

Figure 48. **Leading, Coincident, and Lagging Composite Indexes**

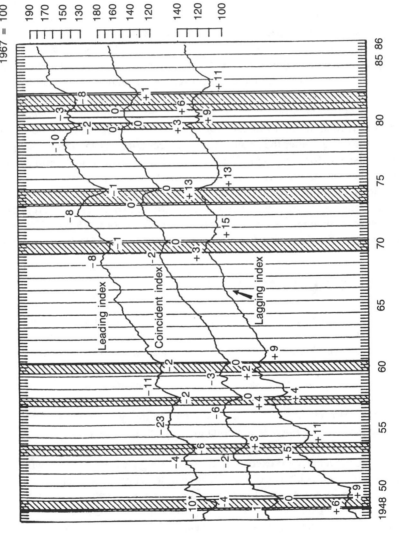

*Note:* Based on Bureau of Economic Analysis data. Lined bars are recession periods. Numbers are monthly leads (−) and lags (+) from cyclical turning points.

*Not necessarily the peak but is the high for the available data.

**Difference from the General Business Cycle in Months:
Average for the postwar business cycles**

| | (− lead; + lag) | |
| --- | --- | --- |
| | Peaks | Troughs |
| Coincident/Lagging Ratio | − 15 | − 2 |
| Leading Index | − 11 | − 3 |
| Difference | − 4 | + 1 |

impending recession, while there is little difference during recessions between the two indicators in signaling the subsequent recovery. In the latter stages of expansions, the lagging index typically increases rapidly while the increase in the coincident index slows down, causing the coincident/lagging ratio to decline. This indicates a squeeze on profits (costs rising faster than revenues) and signals lower economic growth in the future. By contrast, during recessions the lagging index declines proportionately more than the coincident index, indicating that costs have been reduced relative to revenues and thus suggesting a future upturn in profits.

Figure 49 shows that the timing of the coincident/lagging ratio also varies over the long run and from cycle to cycle. While the leading index over the long run has a rising trend, the coincident/lagging ratio is generally level because the upward trend in both components cancels out in dividing through to obtain the ratio:

$$\frac{\text{Coincident (upward trend)}}{\text{Lagging (upward trend)}} = \text{Coincident/Lagging ratio}$$

This partially accounts for the longer lead before expansion peaks of the coincident/lagging ratio compared with the leading index. Experimental data have indicated that if a long-term upward trend were added to the coincident/lagging ratio, its lead time would be closer to that of the leading index. However, more work is necessary with this technique before it cna be used in the official methodology. The coincident/lagging ratio shows significantly different patterns from decade to decade—it declined in the 1950s, was steady in the 1960s, and rose in the 1970s and 1980s back to the 1950s level. These differential movements in the coincident/lagging ratio over the long run may reflect structural changes in the economy, but they are difficult to explain.

As in the case of the leading index, the coincident/lagging ratio shows noticeable variations in the pattern of lead times for individual cycles compared with the average lead time for all cycles; this limits applying average relationships to the current phase in any cycle. Using the criterion of variations of more than one quarter from the long-term average noted above, relatively large variations occurred at the peaks before the 1957–58, 1973–75, 1980, and 1981–82 recessions and at the trough before the recovery from the 1981–82 recession. In addition, there was a tendency in the late 1970s and mid–1980s for the coincident/lagging ratio to turn down substantially earlier than the leading index—preceding the 1980 recession, the ratio turned down 21 months before the cyclical peak while the leading index turned down 10 months before the cyclical peak, and in the 1982–86 expansion, the ratio started turning down early in 1984, while the leading index rose modestly during 1984–86. In both periods, these patterns were accompanied by slow economic growth in expansionary periods.

An advantage of using the coincident/lagging ratio to predict economic movements is that it is based on different data and a different concept from those in the leading index. The independent data base provides a consistency check on the leading index. In addition, the coincident/lagging ratio suggests a concept of equilibrium between sales and costs in which the economy is considered to be relatively well balanced with no significant excesses or deficiencies in production, incomes, costs and prices. Yet, this state may never be reached in practice, as adjustments are made continually to production, prices, wages, and interest— all aimed at increasing profits.[7] Despite these continually changing relationships, one tendency that may be observed from historical behavior of the leading/lagging ratio is that the economy is more balanced when the ratio is unchanged at a relatively high level during the expansion period, suggesting that further expansion is likely.[8]

Because cyclical patterns of the coincident/lagging ratio vary sharply from the long-term average and from the timing of the leading index, it is unrealistic to use the ratio as a simple consistency check on current trends in the leading index. *In periods when such divergences are marked, the analyst should consider other economic tendencies as being dominant—for example, a downturn in the coincident/lagging ratio that is accompanied by a rising leading index suggests a slowdown in economic growth rather than an impending recession.*

## FALSE SIGNALS

The economy moves unevenly in both expansions and recessions, slowing down and speeding up as well as declining for short spells in expansions and rising for short spells in recessions. Because of these variations, it is often difficult in the current period to determine if a changing rate of growth or a reversal of direction signifies a fundamental change or a temporary counter-movement from which the previous trend will reappear. Temporary reversals of direction in the LCLg

Figure 49. **Ratio of Coincident Index to Lagging Index**

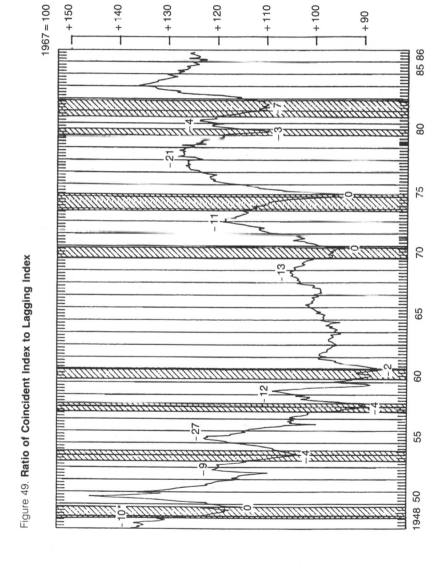

1967 = 100

*Note:* Based on Bureau of Economic Analysis data. Lined bars are recession periods. Numbers are monthly leads (−) and lags (+) from cyclical turning points.

*Not necessarily the peak but is the high for the available data.

system—reversals, that is, suggesting a cyclical change that didn't follow—occurred during the expansions of 1949–53, 1961–69, and 1982–86: the leading index declined temporarily in 1951–52, 1966, and 1984. Those downturns could have suggested pending recessions, but the movements were subsequently reversed. Slowdowns in economic growth as measured by the coincident index did follow these downturns, but the changes were limited and didn't turn into a recession. Such situations are referred to as false signals.

False signals highlight the limitations of the LCLg system as a forecasting tool. The system suggests changes in economic activity that will occur. It also gives additional information for analyzing the strengths and weaknesses of the economy in terms of past changes, current developments, and future tendencies to move in different directions.[9] But it doesn't provide specific forecasts of growth rates or cyclical turning points. *In using the LCLg system, the analyst should regard it as giving additional insights to the analysis of consumer and investment demand, fiscal and monetary policies, and productivity, costs and inflation, rather than as forecasting cyclical turning points and economic growth rates.*

## SUMMARY

The leading, coincident, and lagging indexes provide clues to business cycle turning points and the future course of economic growth. The indexes are based on the theories that profits are the primary force driving the economy and that each phase of the business cycle contains the seeds of the next phase.

The leading index reflects business' expectations, plans, and actions for economic developments. During the expansion phase of the business cycle, the leading index turns down before the general economy declines into a recession, and during the recession phase it turns up before the general economy moves into a recovery. The coincident index measures current economic activity and moves in tandem with the cyclical turning points of the general economy. The lagging index represents business costs; it turns down after the general economy moves from expansion into recession, and it turns up after a general recovery from a recession begins.

A fourth measure, the ratio of the coincident index to the lagging index, relates trends in production (coincident index) to costs (lagging index). As a general indicator of profits, which determine business decisions to expand or contract production, employment and investment, the movements of this ratio also lead the general business cycle at cyclical turning points.

The LCLg system suggests future changes in economic activity. It provides information for assessing the strengths and weaknesses of the economy. But it doesn't provide specific forecasts of economic growth rates and cyclical turning points. When applying the long-term average relationships of the system to the analysis of a particular time period, it is important to recognize that each business cycle has unique characteristics. The special factors in the period under analysis that may cause its movements to diverge from the long-term averages must be taken into account.

## NOTES

1. For the role of profits, see Wesley C. Mitchell, *Business Cycles: The Problem and Its Setting* (National Bureau of Economic Research, Inc.: 1927), pp. 105–107. For a history of the formal development of the system of leading, coincident, and lagging indicators, see Geoffrey H. Moore, *Business Cycles, Inflation, and Forecasting* (Ballinger Publishing Company, a subsidiary of Harper & Row, Publishers, Inc.), Second Edition, 1983, Chapter 24.

2. This itemization draws heavily on Feliks Tamm, "An Introduction to the System of Coincident, Leading and Lagging Indexes," Bureau of Economic Analysis, U.S. Department of Commerce, October 1984 (unpublished), pp. 2–11.

3. These are detailed in two articles by Victor Zarnowitz and Charlotte Boschan: "Cyclical Indicators: An Evaluation and New Leading Indexes," *Business Conditions Digest*, May 1975, and "New Composite Indexes of Coincident and Lagging Indicators," *Business Conditions Digest*, November 1975. An elaboration of how the monthly indexes are calculated is in Bureau of Economic Analysis, *Handbook of Cyclical Indicators: A Supplement to the Business Conditions Digest*, 1984, pp. 65–70.

4. *Handbook of Cyclical Indicators, op. cit.*, p. 67.

5. Geoffrey H. Moore, "Those Misleading Economic Indicators," *The New York Times*, March 16, 1986, p. D3.

6. See Geoffrey H. Moore, "Generating Leading Indicators from Lagging Indicators," *Western Economic Journal*, June 1969, for the initial formulation of the coincident-/lagging ratio. It also is discussed in "New Composite Indexes of Coincident and Lagging Indicators," *op. cit.*, and "An Introduction to the System of Coincident, Leading and Lagging Indexes," *op. cit.*

7. *Business Cycles: The Problem and Its Setting, op. cit.*, pp. 186–188.

8. "An Introduction to the System of Coincident, Leading and Lagging Indexes," *op. cit.*, p. 12.

9. Discussion by Julius Shiskin on the paper by Saul H. Hymans, "On the Use of Leading Indicators to Predict Cyclical Turning Points," *Brookings Papers on Economic Activity*, 2:1973, pp. 378–379.

# • *Index*